AUSTRIA, CROATIA, AND SLOVENIA

AUSTRIA, CROATIA, AND SLOVENIA

EDITED BY LORRAINE MURRAY, EDITOR, GEOGRAPHY

Britannica®
Educational Publishing

IN ASSOCIATION WITH

ROSEN
EDUCATIONAL SERVICES

Published in 2014 by Britannica Educational Publishing
(a trademark of Encyclopædia Britannica, Inc.)
in association with Rosen Educational Services, LLC
29 East 21st Street, New York, NY 10010.

First Edition

Britannica Educational Publishing
J.E. Luebering: Director, Core Reference Group
Adam Augustyn: Assistant Manager, Core Reference Group
Marilyn L. Barton: Senior Coordinator, Production Control
Steven Bosco: Director, Editorial Technologies
Lisa S. Braucher: Senior Producer and Data Editor
Yvette Charboneau: Senior Copy Editor
Kathy Nakamura: Manager, Media Acquisition
Lorraine Murray, Editor, Geography

Rosen Educational Services
Shalini Saxena: Editor
Nelson Sá: Art Director
Cindy Reiman: Photo Manager
Brian Garvey: Designer, Cover Design
Introduction by Lorraine Murray

Library of Congress Cataloging-in-Publication Data

Austria, Croatia, and Slovenia/edited by Lorraine Murray.—First Edition.
    pages cm—(The Britannica guide to countries of the European Union)
"In association with Britannica Educational Publishing, Rosen Educational Services."
Includes bibliographical references and index.
ISBN 978-1-61530-970-2 (library binding)
1. Austria—Juvenile literature. 2. Croatia–Juvenile literature. 3. Slovenia–Juvenile literature.
4. European Union—Austria—Juvenile literature. 5. European Union—Croatia—Juvenile
literature. 6. European Union—Slovenia—Juvenile literature. I. Murray, Lorraine.
DB17.A825 2014
943.6—dc23

2013011010

Manufactured in the United States of America

On the cover: The flag of the EU (right) flies next to the Slovenian flag in front of the
Slovenian Parliament Building in Ljubljana, Slovenia. © *iStockphoto.com/Helena Lovincic*

Cover, p. iii (map contour and stars), back cover, multiple interior pages (stars) ©iStock-
photo.com/pop_jop; cover, multiple interior pages (background graphic) Mina De La O/
Digital Vision/Getty Images

CONTENTS

8/17

26

27

52

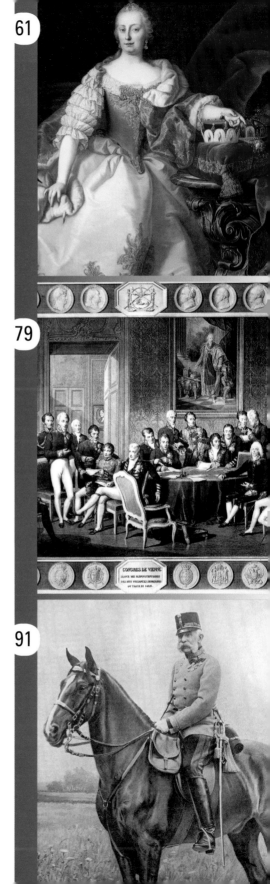

University of Texas Libraries

A ustria, Croatia, and Slovenia, in innumerable ways so disparate, together form the very heart of Central Europe. Historically, Austria was profoundly more significant as a continental power than Slovenia and Croatia. As the House of Habsburg rose to great prominence in Europe, Austria became a leading political force and a seat of high culture. Although the country's dominance was finally reduced, in the late 19th century, to its role as part of the Dual Monarchy of Austria-Hungary, it had for centuries been far more thoroughly intertwined with the other major powers of Europe than were the two smaller countries. They, however, are notable for having sustained a sense of nationhood through centuries during which they were contained within larger empires or political aggregations. Most recently, Croatia and Slovenia were integral republics of the country of Yugoslavia, which existed in several iterations throughout the 20th century and from which they became independent in 1991. Austria became a full member of the European Union (EU) in 1995. Slovenia joined the EU in 2004 and Croatia in 2013. This book introduces readers to the land, people, politics, economy, culture, traditions, and events that define the three countries.

Geographically, a look at a map of Austria, Croatia, and Slovenia reveals the countries' meandering borders and irregular sprawl that—in the way of most political divisions—speaks to the presence of natural boundaries such as mountains and rivers. One also sees that they stretch to encompass the age-old culture areas of their inhabitants, peoples who both withstood and initiated invasions and alliances among themselves almost from time immemorial. These cultural areas represent both the "Eastern" and "Western" elements of Europe. The long westward-reaching tendril of Austria extends to follow much of the southern border of Germany and half the northern border of Italy, touching Liechtenstein and Switzerland at its farthest point. Here we are well into the territory of Western Europe, where history and cultures have been shaped primarily by Roman and Germanic influences. Austria's eastern portion, on the other hand, borders the Eastern and Southern European countries of the Czech Republic, Slovakia, Hungary, and, to the south, Slovenia. These lands may be considered as having also been shaped by cultures other than those of Western Europe: the Byzantine Empire and, in some places, the Ottoman Empire.

Austria needs almost no introduction. With a mention of its name alone, there immediately spring to mind its predominantly Alpine landscape, the flowing Danube, and its peerless intellectual and musical traditions. Austria has, of course, loomed very large in European and world history and culture, though in the late 20th and early 21st centuries it was relatively quiescent and mostly known to foreigners as a pleasant and educational tourist destination. Vienna is an undisputed world capital. That city alone claims countless past inhabitants of artistic and intellectual stature. Salzburg, too, is storied as a centre of musical achievement. The country's cultural history is one with many high points, owing greatly to the patronage of the Viennese court. A list even of just the highlights would be lengthy: those who flourished in Austria include composers Wolfgang Amadeus Mozart, Ludwig van Beethoven, Johannes Brahms, Josef Haydn, Franz Schubert, Johann Strauss, and Gustav Mahler; and artists Gustav Klimt, Oskar Kokoschka, and Egon Schiele. A number of highly influential artistic movements have flourished in the country as well—some native and some a part of wider trends in the German-speaking world, including Rococo, the Baroque, and the Vienna Secession, allied with the Art Nouveau movement.

Austria's initial burgeoning may be traced to the tenure of the Babenberg margraves (976–1246). During those centuries Austria's territory was greatly extended from the initial seed of the

Bavarian Ostmark (later to be called Austria). With the election of Rudolf IV of Habsburg to the throne of Germany in 1273 and his granting of the rule of Austria and Styria to his sons in 1282, the long rule of the House of Habsburg (1278–1918) began in Austria.

Austria increased and sustained its political position through its royal alliances and imperial conquests. Through subsequent centuries its territory included, at various times, lands that dotted westward across northern and central Europe (the Low Countries, parts of France, the Tirol) and southwest to large swaths of Italy; northeast to Moravia and Bohemia and Russia; and south and southeast to Hungary, the Ottoman Empire (in part), and what are now Croatia and Slovenia. Much reduced in strength by the mid-19th century, the Austrian empire—though still large, by then restricted to lands in Central Europe—acceded to the nationalistic demands from its constituent region Hungary in 1867 and divided its power to create the dually governed empire of Austria-Hungary. Thus for centuries were Austria's rulers also the leaders of a varied aggregation of territories and peoples, and the heart of the empire attracted leading minds and talents from all over Austria-Hungary as well as elsewhere in Europe and Russia.

Whereas Austria was a power that extended its might to dominate the region, the inverse was the case in the other two countries, Slovenia and Croatia, whose land was usually on the receiving end of expansionist desires. Slovenia is situated immediately south of Austria, and Croatia is located south of Slovenia. Together they span from Italy to the west to Hungary to the east. Croatia also shares borders with Serbia to the east and Bosnia and Herzegovina to the south. Although it was controlled by Austria for much of its history, coastal Slovenia was also greatly affected by its proximity to Italy. So was Croatia, whose Dalmatian coast was ruled by the republic of Venice beginning in 1420.

By the 15th century, in fact, the peoples of the region had been ruled by more than two dozen powers. The Greeks established colonies on the Adriatic coast in the 7th century BCE. The Romans came in 229 BCE, and the people became Romanized. After the end of the Roman Empire in 395 CE, the whole region became part of the Byzantine Empire. Slavic invasions in the 6th and 7th centuries resulted in the interior becoming Slavicized, changing the language and culture. The influence was somewhat mutual, however, as the Slavs became assimilated and adopted the Roman Catholic religion, a legacy of Rome's former dominance. The Ottoman Empire attached most of Croatia and Slovenia in the 15th and 16th centuries; when the Turks were eventually expelled (with Hungary coming to the aid of Croatia), they left behind their own legacy, including a minority Muslim population. Both Slovenia and Croatia were within the spheres of Austria, Hungary, or

Austria-Hungary for centuries. For some 800 years beginning in 1102, Croatia was intimately associated with (or subordinated to) Hungary, whose monarchs held the country's crown, though Croatia retained more than just a notional identity as a nation, maintaining its own institutions of governance.

As inhabitants of transitional lands between a number of powers on almost every side, Slovenians and Croatians were thus subject to the attempted (and often successful) dominance of multiple and varied cultures and rulers and different religions, languages, and traditions. Some who passed through—and some who stayed—had benign or neutral intent: immigrants, refugees, traders, artisans, missionaries seeking to bring their own brand of enlightenment. Borders changed frequently and populations shifted. Yet through the centuries, the people of both Croatia and Slovenia maintained distinct ethnic and national identities. Their fellow South Slavs, the Serbs, did the same. And in the 19th century, when these peoples experienced nationalist resurgences amid the decline of Austria-Hungary, they began agitating for autonomy. After World War I and the final fall of the Habsburgs, they united and together declared themselves a separate kingdom: the Kingdom of Serbs, Croats, and Slovenes (later, Yugoslavia; Yugoslav meaning "South Slav").

This alliance of separate peoples, each with a very long—centuries-long —memory, was to last for the better part of the 20th century in one form or another,

though never entirely comfortably. The country's post–World War II identity was that of a socialist federal republic, made up of individual republics such as Croatia, Slovenia, and Serbia (together with Macedonia, Montenegro, and Bosnia and Herzegovina) under central control. The national government was at pains to balance its mission of unifying the country economically and politically under the Communist Party with some degree of the autonomy expected by the republics, which sometimes chafed at their union. The attempted pan-Yugoslav nation did not outlast the republics' individual national identities, nor did it outlast the century. As Yugoslavia dissolved, it broke up into independent republics; Slovenia's transition was largely peaceful, but in other republics, old inter-ethnic tensions came to a boiling point. By the early 21st century, however, relative calm had settled upon the independent countries of the former Yugoslavia.

In the early years of the 21st century, Austria and Slovenia, as full EU members and part of the euro zone (countries that use the euro as their official currency), found themselves dealing with the upheaval created by the global financial downturn of 2008-09 and the public-debt crisis in some euro-zone countries. Austria after World War II has been one of the most politically and financially stable countries of Europe. Holding to its postwar formal declaration of political neutrality, Austria is also well established as a prime global tourist destination and one of the leading economies of Europe. Led for much of the post-war period by a "grand coalition"—in which power was shared by a centre-left party (SPOe) and the conservative People's Party—Austria surprised the EU in 2000 when the far-right Freedom Party made electoral gains and entered government for the first time as part of the coalition. The party was in and out of government over the next decade, but the far right continued to play a part in the country's national politics.

Slovenia, which in May 2004 notably became the first former Communist state to join the EU, initially enjoyed financial stability as a new member of the union. It had also experienced some 20 years of relative political stability since achieving its independence, but in 2012 citizens began protesting the continued entrenchment of the post-communist leadership and their alleged corruption. Danilo Turk, the incumbent president, was perceived as a member of that set, and he was defeated by a large margin by former Prime Minister Borut Pahor in the December 2012 election. Slovenia also tended to have strained relations with Croatia. At first opposed to Croatia's membership in the group of nations because of border disputes with that country that dated to the breakup of Yugoslavia, Slovenia eventually dropped its objections in 2009 after the two countries reached partial agreement on the issues.

Croatia, on its long road to EU membership, had survived a war of independence from Yugoslavia and bloody inter-ethnic conflict in its post-Yugoslav period. It also experienced nearly a decade of autocratic rule by Franjo Tudjman (1990-99). Tudjman's leadership—because of his hostility toward Croatia's ethnic Bosnians and Serbs and his alleged human rights abuses—isolated the country internationally and was a major sticking point in the process of EU approval. In the early 21st century the country was affected by the global economic downturn and continued to sort out the aftermath of the 1990s war. Several military generals were tried and convicted at the UN war-crimes tribunal at The Hague. Croatia was finally able to sign the EU accession treaty in December 2011; its citizens approved accession by a two-to-one margin in a referendum held in January 2012, and the country joined on July 1, 2013.

This book gives a thorough introduction to Austria, Croatia, and Slovenia. Readers will learn about the physical and human geography of the three countries and come to understand their complex, fascinating, and often intersecting histories. The book traces their journeys from small settlements and polities in the post–Roman Empire world, through the rise and fall of empires and federations. It illustrates how Austria, Croatia, and Slovenia have progressed through the centuries, sometimes at odds with one another and sometimes allied, and now join together through their membership in the European Union as coequals facing the future together.

CHAPTER 1

AUSTRIA: THE LAND AND ITS PEOPLE

Austria is a largely mountainous, landlocked country of south-central Europe. Together with Switzerland, it forms what has been characterized as the neutral core of Europe, notwithstanding Austria's full membership since 1995 in the supranational European Union (EU).

Physical features of Austria.

A great part of Austria's prominence can be attributed to its geographic position. It is at the centre of European traffic between east and west along the great Danubian trade route and between north and south through the magnificent Alpine passes, thus embedding the country within a variety of political and economic systems. Austria is bordered to the north by the Czech Republic, to the northeast by Slovakia, to the east by Hungary, to the south by Slovenia, to the southwest by Italy, to the west by Switzerland and Liechtenstein, and to the northwest by Germany. It extends roughly 360 miles (580 km) from east to west.

RELIEF

Mountains and forests give the Austrian landscape its character, although in the northeastern part of the country the Danube River winds between the eastern edge of the Alps and the hills of Bohemia and Moravia in its journey toward the Alföld, or Hungarian Plain. Vienna, the capital, lies in the area where the Danube emerges from between the mountains into the drier plains.

The Austrian Alps form the physical backbone of the country. They may be subdivided into a northern and a southern limestone range, each of which is composed of rugged mountains. These two ranges are separated by a central range that is softer in form and outline and composed of crystalline rocks. The Alpine landscape offers a complex geologic and topographical pattern, with the highest elevation—the Grossglockner (12,460 feet [3,798 metres])—rising toward the west. The western Austrian *Länder* (states) of Vorarlberg, Tirol, and Salzburg are characterized by the majestic mountains and magnificent scenery of the high Alps. This high Alpine character also extends to the western part of the state of Kärnten (Carinthia), to the Salzkammergut region of central Austria, and to the Alpine blocks of the state of Steiermark (Styria).

North of the massive Alpine spur lies a hilly subalpine region, stretching between the northern Alps and the Danube and encompassing the northern portion of the state of Oberösterreich (Upper Austria). To the north of the river is a richly wooded foothill area that includes a portion of the Bohemian Massif, which extends across the Czech border into the state of Niederösterreich (Lower Austria). This part of Austria is furrowed by many valleys that for centuries served as passageways leading to the east and southeast of Europe and even—in the case of medieval pilgrims and Crusaders—to the Holy Land. The lowland area east of Vienna, together with the northern part of the state of Burgenland, may be regarded as a western extension of the Little Alföld (Little Hungarian Plain).

TIROL

The western Austrian *Bundesland* (federal state) of Tirol (also spelled Tyrol) consists of North Tirol (Nordtirol) and East Tirol (Osttirol). It is bounded by Germany on the north, by *Bundesländer* Salzburg and Kärnten (Carinthia) on the east, by Vorarlberg on the west, and by Italy on the south. Tirol, which has an area of 4,883 square miles (12,647 square km), is wholly Alpine in character. North Tirol is traversed from southwest to northeast by the Inn River, and East Tirol is drained by the Drava (Drau) River. The Lechtaler Alps lie between the Lech and the Inn rivers in the northwest, while the rugged and barren Karwendel and Kaiser ranges of the Limestone Alps extend across the north and northeast. Several ranges of the Central Alps extend across the southern part of the state. Although they contain the loftiest peak in the Austrian Tirol, the Wildspitze (12,382 feet [3,774 metres]), the Central Alps generally are less rugged than the Limestone Alps, and much of their original wood cover has been cleared for pasture. Their terrain is ideal for skiing. In the eastern part of North Tirol are slate mountains, and the Lienz Dolomites rise in East Tirol. The mountain groups are separated by the Inn Valley and by lower stretches and passes, the most important of which are the Arlberg Pass in the west and the Brenner in the south.

The western Austrian Tirolean Alps, Austria. © Digital Vision/Getty Images

Tirol originated as a family name, derived from a castle near Meran (now Merano, Italy). By 1150 CE scions of the family were counts and bailiwicks (land agents) for the bishops of Trent. In 1248 the counts of Tirol acquired extensive lands from the bishop of Brixen (Bressanone, Italy) and by 1271 had practically replaced the ecclesiastical power in the area. Upon the death of Margaret Maultasch (Margaret of Carinthia), heiress to the Tirol, in 1363, the region passed to the Habsburgs, who retained it until 1918. At first the Tirol was held by a junior branch, but it was united with the main Austrian possessions in 1665. Independent-minded Tirolese rose in 1525, when Protestantism was strong there, and again in 1809, when French and Bavarian rule proved irksome. The Counter-Reformation effectively Catholicized the Tirol after the first incident. In 1617 the area's strategic importance in linking Italy and Germany made it a bargaining counter between the Austrian archduke Ferdinand (later Holy Roman emperor as Ferdinand II), who wanted the imperial crown, and his cousin and potential rival Philip III of Spain, who received the Tirol in return for standing down. After World War I, Italy obtained the southern Tirol, with its sizable German-speaking majority, and retained it after World War II, despite objections by Austria.

Population distribution in the Tirol of modern Austria is uneven, with the highest concentrations in the Inn and Drava valleys. The principal towns are Innsbruck (the capital), Kufstein, Lienz, and Solbad Hall. The rural population is engaged primarily in pasture farming, cattle and livestock raising, dairy farming, and forestry. Wheat and rye are grown in the Inn Valley. There is some mining (salt, copper, magnesite), and most of the industries are small and highly specialized enterprises, some of long tradition, such as the textile mills of Innsbruck. Chemical, pharmaceutical, and electrotechnical industries were developed after World War II. Alpine health and winter-sports resorts support a vigorous tourist trade. Most road and rail traffic follows the Inn Valley, the Brenner Pass road, and the Drava Valley.

DRAINAGE

Austria is a land of lakes, many of them a legacy of the Pleistocene Epoch (i.e., about 2,600,000 to about 11,700 years ago), during which glacial erosion scooped out mountain lakes in the central Alpine district, notably around the Salzkammergut. The largest lakes—lying partly in the territory of neighbouring countries —are Lake Constance (Bodensee) in the west and the marshy Neusiedler Lake (Neusiedlersee) in the east.

Nearly all Austrian territory drains into the Danube River system. The main

Vineyards along the Danube River in the Wachau region, Austria. G. Hofmann/SuperStock

watershed between the Black Sea and the North Sea runs across northern Austria, in some places lying only about 22 miles (35 km) from the Danube, while to the west the watershed between the Danube and the river systems emptying into the Atlantic and the Mediterranean coincides with the western political boundary of Austria. In the south the Julian and Carnic (Karnische) Alps and, farther to the west, the main Alpine range mark the watershed of the region draining into the Po River of northern Italy.

CLIMATE

The wooded slopes of the Alps and the small portion of the plains of southeastern Europe are characterized by differing climatic zones. The prevailing wind is from the west, and, therefore, humidity is highest in the west, diminishing toward the east. The wetter western regions of Austria have an Atlantic climate with a yearly rainfall of about 40 inches (1,000 mm); the drier eastern regions, under the influence of the more continental type of climate, have less precipitation.

In the lowlands and the hilly eastern regions, the median temperature ranges from about 30 °F (-1 °C) in January to about 68 °F (20 °C) in July. In those regions above 10,000 feet (3,000 metres), by contrast, the temperature range is between about 12 °F (-11 °C) in January, with a snow cover of approximately 10 feet (3 metres), and about 36 °F (2 °C) in July, with roughly 5 feet (1.5 metres) of snow cover.

PLANT AND ANIMAL LIFE

Two-thirds of the total area of Austria is covered by woods and meadows. Forests occupy some two-fifths of the country, which is one of the most densely forested in central Europe. Spruce dominates the forests, with larch, beech, and oak also making a significant contribution. In the Alpine and foothill regions coniferous trees predominate, while broad-leaved deciduous trees are more frequent in the warmer zones.

Wild animals, many protected by conservation laws, include the brown bear, eagles, buzzards, falcons, owls, cranes, swans, and storks. Game hunting is restricted to certain periods of the year, with deer and rabbits the most frequent quarry. Austrian rivers nurture river and rainbow trout, grayling, pike, perch, and carp.

ETHNIC GROUPS

Ethnic Austrians constitute the vast majority of the population. Small but significant groups of German-speaking Swiss and ethnic Germans also reside in the country. Serbs, Bosniaks (Muslims from Bosnia and Herzegovina; living mainly in the larger cities), Turks (living primarily in Vienna), Hungarians and Croats (living mainly in Burgenland), and Slovenes (living mainly in Kärnten) constitute the major ethnic minorities.

LANGUAGES

Although Croatian, Hungarian, Slovenian, Turkish, and other languages are spoken by the various minority groups, nearly all people in Austria speak German. The dialect of German spoken in Austria, except in the west, is Bavarian, sometimes called Austro-Bavarian. About 7 million people speak Bavarian in Austria. A Middle Bavarian subdialect is spoken chiefly in Ober- and Niederösterreich as well as in Vienna. A Southern Bavarian subdialect is spoken in Tirol (including southern Tirol), in Kärnten, and in parts of Steiermark. The speech of most of the remainder of the country's inhabitants tends to shade into one or the other of those subdialects. In the west, however, an Alemannic (Swiss) dialect prevails: the inhabitants of Vorarlberg and parts of western Tirol are Alemannic in origin, having cultural and dialectal affinities with the German Swiss to the west and Swabians in Germany to the north.

RELIGION

About three-fourths of Austrians are Christian. The overwhelming majority of Christians are adherents to Roman Catholicism; Protestants (mainly Lutherans) and Orthodox Christians form smaller groups. Islam has a small but important following, mainly among the Bosniak and Turk populations. Vienna's Jewish population, which was all but destroyed between 1938 and 1945, has increased steadily since that time but remains tiny. More than

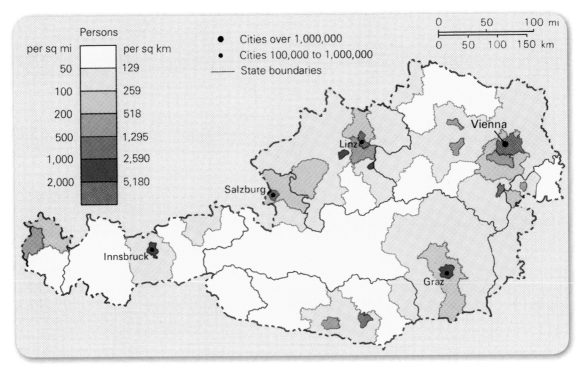

Population density of Austria. © 2002 Encyclopædia Britannica, Inc.

one-tenth of the population is nonreligious.

SETTLEMENT PATTERNS

The pattern of rural settlement in Austria was shaped centuries ago by the exigencies of the Alpine environment, and new rural building is still influenced by these ancient traditions, especially in the west and in the centre of the country. By contrast, rural housing in the eastern parts of the country, especially in the lowlands, is dominated more by agricultural needs than by harsh weather conditions.

While Austria is mountainous, it is also a highly urbanized country. More than half of the population lives in cities and towns of more than 10,000 residents, and about one-fourth of the total population lives in the Vienna urban agglomeration. Graz, Austria's second largest city, is the gateway to the Balkans. Linz is an important industrial centre. Innsbruck, situated just north of Brenner Pass, is the rail centre through which all the mainline rail traffic of western Austria passes, north-south and east-west. Salzburg is a centre of music and Baroque architecture. Klagenfurt lies astride routes that provide access to both Italy and the Balkans.

Innsbruck, Austria. © Digital Vision/Getty Images

VIENNA

Located on the Danube River, Vienna (German: Wien,), the capital of Austria, was founded by the Celts. It became a Roman military station in the 1st century BCE. Ruled by many—including the Franks in the 6th century CE and the Magyars in the 10th century—Vienna was an important trade centre during the Crusades. It was the seat of the Holy Roman Empire (1558–1806), the Austrian (and Habsburg) Empire (1806–67), and the Austro-Hungarian Empire until 1918. In 1814–15 it was the seat of the Congress of Vienna. The administrative centre of German Austria (1938–45), it was frequently bombed during World War II by the Allies, and the city was taken by Soviet troops in 1945. It was under joint Soviet-Western Allied occupation from 1945 to 1955. The Strategic Arms Limitation Talks (SALT) between the United States and Soviet Union took place in Vienna in the 1970s. Vienna is not only the commercial and industrial centre of Austria but also a cultural centre renowned for its architecture and music. It was the birthplace of composers Franz Schubert, Johann Strauss (the Younger), and Arnold Schoenberg and the home of Wolfgang Amadeus Mozart, Ludwig van Beethoven, Johannes Brahms, and Gustav Mahler. It also was the home of Sigmund Freud, Gustav Klimt, Oskar Kokoschka, and Josef Hoffmann. Vienna is the headquarters of many international organizations, including the International Atomic Energy Agency, the UN Industrial Development Organization, and the Organization of Petroleum Exporting Countries (OPEC).

DEMOGRAPHIC TRENDS

Austria's population grew steadily from the mid-20th century to the mid-1990s; it then remained fairly constant into the early 21st century. An increasingly high life expectancy has served to offset the declining birth rate.

Because of its geographic position and historical affinities, Austria in general and Vienna in particular served as a haven for refugees and other emigrants from eastern Europe during the decades of the Cold War, when migration out of the Soviet bloc was severely restricted. Austria supported a generous policy of admitting and maintaining such migrants until places for them abroad could be found. About 170,000–180,000 Hungarians escaped into Austria after the uprising in Hungary in 1956; some remained permanently in Austria, but most were resettled overseas. After the precipitous political upheavals of 1989–91, when the Soviet Union collapsed, Austria became the first station in the West for thousands of emigrants from eastern Europe. Many remained permanently in Austria, particularly in Vienna, Graz, Linz, and other large cities. In the early 21st century, foreign residents accounted for almost one-tenth of the country's total population. Among them were many EU nationals residing permanently in Austria, a large number of them in Vienna.

CHAPTER 2

The Austrian Economy

Austria's government played an important role in the economy from the post–World War II years until the late 20th century. In 1946 and 1947 the Austrian parliament enacted legislation that nationalized more than 70 firms in essential industries and services, including the three largest commercial banks, such heavy industries as petroleum and oil refining, coal, mining, iron and steel, iron and steel products (structural materials, heavy machinery, railway equipment), shipbuilding, and electrical machinery and appliances, as well as river navigation. Later reorganization reduced the number of nationalized firms to 19 and placed the property rights with limited powers of management and supervision into a holding company owned by the Republic of Austria, the Österreichische Industrieverwaltungs-Aktiengesellschaft (ÖIAG; Austrian Industrial Administration Limited-Liability Company). In 1986–89 ÖIAG was restructured to give it powers to function along the lines of a major private industry, and it was renamed Österreichische Industrieholding AG. During the 1990s, particularly after Austria joined the EU in 1995, many companies and enterprises were partially or completely privatized, which reduced the direct role of government in Austria's economy. Indeed, in the late 20th and early 21st centuries, ÖIAG functioned largely as a privatization agency, as it sold off large portions of many of its holdings. However, the government continued to control, at least partially, some companies and utilities. Although Austria's economy may have been somewhat slow to liberalize and privatize, it has made the transition from an industrially and agriculturally based economy to one in which the service sector is increasingly important.

AGRICULTURE AND FORESTRY

Agriculture employs only a small percentage of Austria's workforce and accounts for only a tiny portion of the gross domestic product (GDP). Because of the country's mountainous terrain, only about half of the land can even potentially be cultivated. Agricultural areas are found mainly in the east—particularly in Burgenland, Steiermark, Kärnten, and Niederösterreich—and farms are usually small or of medium size. Crops include sugar beets, wheat, corn (maize), barley, potatoes, apples, and grapes. Pigs and cattle also are raised.

Many farmers need additional income through nonfarm employment, and a significant number of farmers (so-called mountain farmers) receive subsidies from the government and the EU for maintaining the cultural landscape (e.g., preventing the natural reforestation of clearings), which is important for tourism. However, both specialization and concentration on quality rather than quantity allow Austria's small farmers to compete within the EU. For example, the number of organic farms in the country increased from about 100 in the late 1970s to more than 20,000 by the end of the 20th century—more than in any other EU country.

Austria's vast forested areas provide ample timber resources. Some of the timber felled is processed in the country, and most of it is exported, especially to Italy.

RESOURCES AND POWER

The natural resources available within the country for industrial exploitation are of considerable significance. Austria is a leading producer of natural magnesite, a magnesium carbonate used extensively in the chemical industry. Kärnten is the main centre of its production. Other important mineral resources include iron, lignite, anhydrous gypsum, lead and zinc, and antimony. Iron ore from Eisenberg (in Steiermark) is obtained through opencut mining and is processed in such industrial centres as Linz and Leoben.

While oil and natural gas deposits in northeastern Austria are exploited, oil and gas must be imported to meet industrial and consumer needs. The large oil refinery at Schwechat processes crude oil from Austrian sources as well as oil pumped through the Vienna-Adriatic pipeline from the port of Trieste, Italy. Additional natural gas is supplied by pipeline from Ukraine. Coal, mainly bituminous, is found chiefly in Oberösterreich and Steiermark and only in relatively small quantities.

The country's power needs are met by coal, oil, natural gas, and hydroelectric plants. Increases in domestic power production have helped offset the country's import debt in its balance of payments. In fact, with its dense network of rivers and mountainous terrain, Austria is a major exporter of hydroelectric power. In 1978 a plan to build a nuclear power plant on the Danube was roundly opposed, and the Austrian parliament passed legislation prohibiting nuclear power generation.

MANUFACTURING

Austria's manufacturing sector accounts for a significant portion of the GDP; it is also one of the country's main generators of foreign currency through exports, an important factor in the economy of a small country. Austrian manufacturing focuses on specialized high-quality products, mainly in the traditional industries. Although high-technology production was slow to take hold in the country, by the turn of the 21st century a number of firms had begun to find success through advanced technological development.

Iron and steel production has long been a leading industry. An important Austrian innovation in steelmaking was the basic oxygen process, or LD process, originally named for the cities of Linz and Donawitz (the latter now part of Leoben); it is used under license by steelworks throughout the world. A considerable portion of Austria's iron and steel industry is involved with construction abroad. Iron and steel firms furnish plants and installations of all descriptions in every phase of construction and equipping in Europe, North America, and elsewhere. Working alone or in consortia with firms of other countries, Austrian companies typically build hydroelectric or thermal power stations, chemical plants, steelworks, and seamless pipelines. The industrial plants may be largely equipped with such Austrian capital goods as electrical and electronics equipment. Austria is noted for providing plants abroad "completely to measure."

BASIC OXYGEN PROCESS (BOP)

The basic oxygen process is a steelmaking method in which pure oxygen is blown into a bath of molten blast-furnace iron and scrap. The oxygen initiates a series of intensively exothermic (heat-releasing) reactions, including the oxidation of such impurities as carbon, silicon, phosphorus, and manganese.

The advantages of using pure oxygen instead of air in refining pig iron into steel were recognized as early as 1855 by Henry Bessemer, but the process could not be brought to commercial fruition until the 20th century, when large tonnages of cheap, high-purity oxygen became available. Commercial advantages include high production rates,

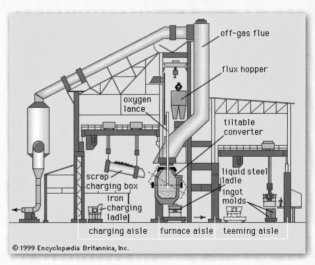

A basic oxygen furnace shop.

less labour, and steel with a low nitrogen content. Development of the BOP was initiated in Switzerland by Robert Durrer in the late 1940s. After experimenting with a 2.5-ton pilot unit, Durrer worked with engineers at the Voest company at Linz, Austria, who set up a commercially operating 35-ton converter in 1952. A second unit began operation within a year at Donawitz, also in Austria. Consequently, the BOP was first known as the LD (Linz-Donawitz) process. Within 40 years, virtually all of the steel in Japan and more than half of the steel worldwide was produced by the BOP.

Other important manufactured products include aluminum, industrial machinery, motor vehicles (especially industrial and rough-terrain vehicles) and parts, chemicals, electronic goods and components, textiles, and such consumer goods as foodstuffs, glass and porcelain, and highly prized handmade products.

In general, Austria's manufacturing sector consists mainly of small- and medium-sized firms, although a small number of large firms do produce such goods as cement, paper, beer, and sugar and sugar products. In the early 21st century the majority of manufacturing companies were Austrian-owned, either held privately or controlled by the government. However, a significant number of German, Dutch, Swiss, and other foreign companies have manufacturing facilities in Austria.

FINANCE

Monetary policy is determined by the European Central Bank and implemented by the Austrian National Bank (Österreichische Nationalbank), founded in 1922. Austria was among the first group of countries to adopt the single currency of the EU, the euro, in 1999; it made the complete switch from schillings to euro notes and coins in 2002.

Financial services are handled by a wide range of institutions, including large nationally owned and foreign banks, the Austrian Post Office Savings Bank (Österreichische Postsparkasse), smaller local savings banks, and commercial credit and agricultural credit cooperatives. The Vienna Stock Exchange (Wiener Börse), founded in 1771 by Empress Maria Theresa, is one of the oldest such institutions in Europe. Shares of both Austrian and foreign companies are traded there.

Since the fall of the Iron Curtain, Austrian private investors and entrepreneurs have found a new arena for foreign investment in Austria's former imperial domains—above all Hungary, but also the Czech Republic, Slovakia, Slovenia, Croatia, and, to a lesser extent, northern Italy. Thousands of Austrian companies, mostly small and medium-sized, have been involved in investment projects in these countries since the mid-1990s. Notable examples of Austrian ventures in eastern European countries have included an extensive network of OMV gas stations and numerous branch offices of Bank Austria.

TRADE

Austria's main trading partners are EU member countries, the United States, and Switzerland. Important exports include machinery, vehicles, chemicals, and iron and steel; among the major imports are machinery, transport equipment, vehicles, chemicals, mineral fuels, and food products.

SERVICES

At the beginning of the 21st century, the service sector employed more than three-fifths of Austria's workforce and generated the large majority of the country's GDP. However, this should not be interpreted as an indication of rapid economic modernization or of the swift development of high-technology service industries. Services, more than any other sector of the Austrian economy, are clearly dominated by the government. Public services were particularly expanded in connection with the so-called "controlled capitalism" concept of the post-World War II years, whereby the social welfare state, through the nationalization of companies, aimed to create more jobs, particularly protected jobs. The public sector also reached out into once privately performed services:

banking and insurance; teaching at all levels; cultural institutions such as theatres, symphony orchestras, and operas; transportation and communication; all levels and kinds of administration; and the general health care system, including hospitals, clinics, and most retirement homes. In all, a minority of service jobs are in the private sector, while the government at all levels (local, state, and federal) still controls the majority.

Despite its leading contribution to the economy, the service sector in Austria creates rather little new money, with the exception of financial services, some services offered abroad (such as banking in eastern European countries), and tourism. Indeed, tourism is Austria's most important invisible asset. With its picturesque landscape, villages, towns, and cities; its highly developed hotel and catering industry; its renowned facilities for skiing and other outdoor sports; its spas and resorts; and its fabled cultural institutions—not to mention its relative ease of access—Austria is to the outsider a tourist destination par excellence.

LABOUR AND TAXATION

Government at various levels remains an important job provider, though to a much lesser degree than it was in the mid-20th century. Public sector jobs are protected, meaning that the government ensures automatic wage raises, certain bonuses, and most often tenure for life —conditions the private sector can hardly match. Public employment agencies are either at the federal, state, or community level or involved in such semipublic entities as social security, mandatory health insurance, public interest groups, unions, and religious administrations. They also may be in the entrepreneurial sector, as communities, states, and the federal government still engage in competitive business (e.g., real estate, housing, and even retail trade). This persistent government involvement has helped to keep unemployment in Austria at a rather low level for many years.

Government, management, and labour follow a wage-price policy that attempts to avoid social cleavages and strikes through cooperative participation in a joint wage-price commission. The representatives of the various segments of the economy—together with the chambers of commerce, agriculture, and labour and the federation of trade unions—have tried, with the active cooperation of the government, to coordinate wage and price movements. It is within this framework that collective bargaining takes place, and agricultural prices are also negotiated by the wage-price commission without infringement of the market economy.

The three important economic groups—labour, management, and farmers—have similar structures. Each has its own independent organization: the trade unions, the management association, and the farmers' federation. At the same time, laws provide for semiofficial "chambers" for each group. This type of guild organization promotes cooperation in the governmental wage-price commission. Despite the divergent interests of the various groups, their cooperation has resulted in relative economic stability, and labour-management relations have remained unmarked by major crises.

Tax revenues are drawn chiefly from an income and wage tax and, in line with the countries of the EU, a value-added tax. Other sources of revenue include expressway usage permits, gasoline taxes, and one-time "environmental assessment" taxes on imported cars.

TRANSPORTATION AND TELECOMMUNICATIONS

Austria has a dense road system inherited from its centuries as the hub of a vast continental empire. The country serves as an important link between western, northern, and central Europe and Italy, eastern Europe, and the Balkans. It has a highly developed transportation infrastructure of highways, passenger and freight trains, waterways, and air services.

Starting with the key link between Salzburg and Vienna, Austria has continued to develop its extensive expressway (autobahn) system. There are routes connecting Bregenz at the Swiss and German borders through Vorarlberg and Tirol, routes connecting Innsbruck with Italy, and routes connecting Salzburg and Vienna to Italy and the Balkans; these are often spectacular feats of highway engineering through unsurpassed Alpine scenery.

The Austrian rail network is controlled by Austrian Federal Railways

DANUBE RIVER

The second longest river of Europe after the Volga is the Danube River. It rises in the Black Forest mountains of western Germany and flows for some 1,770 miles (2,850 km) to its mouth on the Black Sea. Along its course, it passes through nine countries: Germany and Austria (where it is called the Donau); Slovakia (Dunaj); Hungary (Duna); Croatia, Serbia, and Bulgaria (Dunav); Romania (Dunărea), and Ukraine (Dunay).

The Danube played a vital role in the settlement and political evolution of central and southeastern Europe. Its banks, lined with castles and fortresses, formed the boundary between great empires, and its waters served as a vital commercial highway between nations. The river's majesty has long been celebrated in music. The famous waltz *An der schönen, blauen Donau* (1867; *The Blue Danube*), by Johann Strauss the Younger, became the symbol of imperial Vienna. In the 21st century the river has continued its role as an important trade artery. It has been harnessed for hydroelectric power, particularly along the upper courses, and the cities along its banks—including the national capitals of Vienna (Austria), Budapest (Hungary), and Belgrade (Serbia)—have depended upon it for their economic growth.

The Danube River basin and its drainage network.

(Österreichische Bundesbahnen; ÖBB), which is under state ownership but operates as an independent commercial enterprise. More than half of the track is electrified.

The Danube is the most important river connection between Germany and the Black Sea, and both freight and passenger vessels travel along this waterway. Although Austria is landlocked, its shipyards build vessels for Austria and for other countries.

Austrian Airlines, which began operations in March 1958, serves destinations in Europe, the Middle East, Asia, the Americas, and North Africa. Austria's major airport is at Schwechat, near Vienna.

Telecommunications systems, including a fibre-optic network, are well developed, and, as in most neighbouring countries, cellular telephones are commonly used. At the beginning of the 21st century, rates of personal computer ownership and Internet usage, though not as high as in Germany and Switzerland, were higher than those in nearby eastern European countries.

CHAPTER 3

AUSTRIAN GOVERNMENT AND SOCIETY

Under the constitution of 1920—with minor changes made in 1929—Austria is a "democratic republic: its law derives from the people." A federal republic, Austria consists of nine self-governing *Länder* (states): Burgenland, Kärnten (Carinthia),

Austria.

Niederösterreich (Lower Austria), Oberösterreich (Upper Austria), Salzburg, Steiermark (Styria), Tirol, Vorarlberg, and Wien (Vienna). The states have considerable autonomy.

In 1934 the Austrian constitution was replaced by an authoritarian regime under Chancellors Engelbert Dollfuss and Kurt von Schuschnigg. This in turn was eliminated by Adolf Hitler after Nazi Germany annexed Austria in 1938. With the liberation of Austria in 1945, the constitution of 1929 was revived and subsequently became the foundation stone of constitutional and political life in the "Second Republic."

The federal president and the cabinet share executive authority. The president, elected by popular vote for a term of six years, acts as head of state and calls parliament into session. The president can dissolve parliament during the four-year legislative period, unless it dissolves itself by law, and can order new elections. The president also acts as commander in chief of the armed forces.

The head of government is the federal chancellor. The president appoints the chancellor, although the parliamentary majority actually determines the president's choice. The chancellor nominates the other cabinet members, who also are officially appointed by the president. The cabinet cannot remain in office if it and its members do not enjoy the confidence of the majority of the National Council (one of the houses of parliament).

The parliament, known as the Federal Assembly, consists of two houses: the National Council (Nationalrat) and the Federal Council (Bundesrat). The National Council, wielding the primary legislative power, is elected by all citizens who are at least 16 years of age, and every citizen over age 26 is eligible to run for office. The distribution of seats in the National Council is based on a system of proportional representation. The members of the Federal Council represent the states. The assemblies, or diets, of the states elect the members by a proportional system based on the population of the state.

The legislative process originates in the National Council. Each bill—except for the budget, which is the sole prerogative of the National Council—must be approved by the Federal Council. The National Council, however, can override a Federal Council veto by a simple majority vote.

LOCAL GOVERNMENT

Each of the nine states is administered by a government headed by a governor (*Landeshauptmann*); the governor is elected by the legislative diet, which in turn is elected by general ballot. The local municipalities each elect a mayor and a city council. Vienna is a unique case: as it is both a municipality and a state, its mayor functions as the governor.

JUSTICE

The administration of justice is independent of Austrian legislative and administrative authorities. Judges are not subject to any government influence: they are appointed by the cabinet upon nomination by judicial panels and can be neither dismissed nor transferred without the panels' agreement.

Austria has three high courts: one sitting as the highest body of appeal in civil and criminal matters; a top administrative court to which citizens aggrieved by administrative decisions can appeal; and a constitutional court that decides on all constitutional matters, civil rights, and election disputes.

POLITICAL PROCESS

The first popular election of a president, although provided for by a 1929 amendment to the constitution, did not take place until after the death of the first post-World War II president, Karl Renner, who had been unanimously elected by the national assembly after the liberation of 1945.

The system of political parties of Austria, in a close parallel to the party structure of Germany, is characterized by two dominant parties of the centre-right and centre-left, along with two smaller but effective populist parties and the environmentalist Greens. A small communist party and a number of other fringe parties also exist.

The centre-right Austrian People's Party (Österreichische Volkspartei; ÖVP), which describes itself as a "progressive centre party," is the successor of the Christian Social Party founded in the 1890s. A Christian Democratic party, it is a member of the European Union of Christian Democrats and represents a combination of conservative forces and various social and economic groups that form semi-independent federations within the overall party. The divergent economic and social interests of these groups—which include workers and employees, farmers, employers and tradespeople, feminists, young populists, and senior citizens—are not always easy to reconcile.

The centre-left Social Democratic Party of Austria (Sozialdemokratische Partei Österreichs; SPÖ; until 1991 the Socialist Party) was founded in 1945. It is a successor of the original Social Democratic Party (founded in 1889), which was a driving force in the establishment of the First Austrian Republic in 1918. Since 1945 the party has moved from a democratic Marxist doctrine to a more pragmatic and less ideological approach. Party programs have emphasized the correction of social problems, government influence on an expanding and socially oriented economy, full employment, and increase in the standard of living. No longer exclusively the party of the working classes, its appeal has widened to the middle classes.

The populist Freedom Party of Austria (Freiheitliche Partei Österreichs; FPÖ), sometimes referred to as the Liberal Party, was founded in 1955 as a successor to the League of Independents. It is progressive and anticollectivist in character and stands for moderate social reform, participation of workers in management, and European unity. In 2005 disputes between moderates and hard-liners within the party led some members to leave the FPÖ and form a new party under the leadership of the controversial Jörg Haider, the Alliance for the Future of Austria (Bündnis Zukunft Österreich; BZÖ), which entered the legislature in 2006.

The environmentalist parties, including the Green Alternative (Die Grüne Alternative; GA; founded 1986) and the United Greens of Austria (Vereinte Grüne Österreichs; VGÖ; founded 1982), have come to be known collectively as the Greens. The Greens first won seats in the Austrian parliament in 1986.

The Communist Party of Austria (Kommunistische Partei Österreichs; KPÖ; founded 1918) is of only marginal strength and has not been represented in the national parliament since 1959 or in the provincial diets since 1970. An extreme right-wing party, the National Democratic Party (Nationaldemokratische Partei; NDP; founded 1966), has disappeared from the political scene.

In the 13 National Council elections held between 1945 and 1986, the two historically dominant Austrian political parties—the People's Party and the Socialist Party—garnered the largest share of the vote. However, in the November 1990 election the People's Party lost ground to the Freedom Party, which won 17 percent of the vote. In the 1999 national election the Freedom Party narrowly overtook the People's Party and afterward joined the latter in a coalition government. The ascendancy of the Freedom Party—and after 2006 that of its offshoot, the BZÖ—raised concern among some Austrians and other EU member countries because of the apparent far-right-wing tendencies of its leadership. In the early 21st century the declining popularity of both the Social Democrats and the People's Party, as well as antipathy between various party leaders, made the formation of lasting government coalitions difficult.

The Austrian constitution provides for popular initiatives (*Volksbegehren*), by which 200,000 vote-eligible citizens or half the populations of three states can petition parliament for approval of any bill; it also can be initiated by a majority of the National Council. A total revision of the constitution must be approved by plebiscite.

SECURITY

The Austrian military comprises both land and air forces. Conscripts make up a significant portion of the armed forces: all male citizens between ages 18 and 50 are liable for military service, and conscripts are called up for several months of training, followed by an obligation to remain in reserve for a number of years. A national police organization carries out law enforcement.

HEALTH AND WELFARE

Public health in Austria is the responsibility of a federal ministry of health. It supervises a number of subsidiary institutes responsible for the prevention of infectious diseases and inspection of drugs and food. The provincial governments also have public health centres, and each municipality and rural district must employ a public health physician.

National health insurance covers expenses of medical and hospital treatment: blue- and white-collar workers and salaried employees are protected in cases of sickness, disability, unemployment, and maternity and in their old age. There are survivors' pensions as well. Pension systems for self-employed persons and farmers also have been established. Social and medical insurance is funded through payroll deductions and taxes.

EDUCATION

The federal government oversees education in Austria. A major reform of the school administrative structure, providing for a unitary school system with access to higher education and experimentation with various types of schools, was initiated in 1970 and led to an "educational revolution" with free access to many avenues of basic, advanced, and vocational instruction for everyone.

School attendance is obligatory between ages 6 and 15. Intermediate schools include those preparing students for university and other higher studies, for teachers' and commercial colleges, and for other specialized institutions. The academic *Gymnasium* is the secondary school leading to the university.

Austria has a number of universities and fine arts colleges. The University of Vienna was founded in 1365. The University of Graz was founded in 1585, and the universities of Innsbruck and Salzburg were founded during the 17th century. Separate technical universities are located at Vienna and Graz. Reforms were initiated in 1975 to expand and democratize university programs and governing procedures. A wide program of adult education is available throughout the country.

GYMNASIUM

In Austria and Germany, the name *Gymnasium* denotes a state-maintained secondary school that prepares pupils for higher academic education. This type of nine-year school originated in Strassburg (now Strasbourg, France) in 1537. Although the usual leaving age is 19 or 20, pupils may terminate their studies at the age of 16 and enter vocational school. In Germany the *Gymnasium* is differentiated into three main types, according to curriculum: classical, which includes Latin, Greek, and one modern language; modern (*Realgymnasium*), with Latin and two modern languages; and mathematical and scientific (*Oberschule*), with two modern languages and optional Latin. Senior departments of elementary schools, middle schools (*Mittelschulen*), and teachers' training, commercial, and senior girls' colleges also provide general secondary or postprimary education.

CHAPTER 4

AUSTRIAN CULTURAL LIFE

Austria has been a leader and guardian of some of the most sublime achievements in music, theatre, literature, architecture, medicine, and science. Austrian culture is a part of the mainstream of Germanic culture that is shared with Germany and Switzerland. But what has shaped it and dominated it, what has made it essentially Austrian, are the Habsburg empire and the Christian church.

The emperor Maximilian I (reigned 1493–1519) was a poet and a patron of the theatre, and the era that began in the reign of Maria Theresa (1740–80) and ended in that of Francis Joseph (1848–1916) was an age of spectacular flourishing in the arts and sciences. During this time an aggregation of genius and talent in often interlocking circles was gathered in Vienna. Moreover, the Habsburg dynasty's tradition of patronage of the arts has carried over to the modern republic of today.

The church was a powerful influence on Austrian architecture, drama, and music. The great Romanesque monasteries, the Gothic St. Stephen's Cathedral in Vienna, and the splendours of the quintessentially Austrian Baroque—exemplified by the works of Austrian architect Johann Bernhard Fischer von Erlach and the Bohemian architects Christoph Dientzenhofer and Kilian Ignaz Dientzenhofer—and Rococo obviously derive from the church. The Austrian theatre has its origins in late medieval religious drama, and the affinities of the church with Austrian music continue down to modern times.

Despite the fact that Austrian high culture never has been contained by the borders of the country but rather is considered part of the greater cultural realm of the German-speaking world, many Austrians long imagined their country as blissfully isolated and neutral—an "island of the blessed." In fact, for many years after World War II, Austria promoted the idea of having been the first "victim" of Nazi Germany and, some would say, deliberately avoided confronting the guilt surrounding its participation in the Anschluss ("Union") with Germany. But by the end of the 20th century, the forces of globalization and international competition, spurred by the opening of the Iron Curtain in 1989 and Austria's admittance to the EU in 1995, had brought Austria's imagined perfection into question. The increased immigration of foreigners into the country has caused particular concern among many Austrians, who fear that their carefully tailored social welfare system may be overburdened and their own Austrian identity threatened. Such sentiment has appeared particularly strong in Vienna, where large numbers of immigrants reside.

DAILY LIFE AND SOCIAL CUSTOMS

Most ordinary Austrians may be aware of Austria's historical contributions to high culture, but in general only members of the educated middle class and the elite circles of society participate in glamorous cultural events like the Salzburg Festival of theatre and music. Ordinary Austrians, particularly those who live in small towns and in the rural valleys of the countryside, pursue a more common—but in no way less typically Austrian—cultural

life, with its roots in regional traditions, age-old rituals and customs, and a friendly communal spirit. Membership in local organizations called *Vereine* plays a great role in this culture. Informal gatherings are commonplace as well, and going out to meet friends in restaurants or cafés is an integral part of everyday life. A surprisingly large number of Austrians play instruments in bands, sing in choirs, or make music in smaller groups at home or with neighbours. Many wear traditional costumes (*Trachten*), such as full-skirted dirndls or loden coats, every day, and many more wear them on weekends and on festive or special occasions, including weddings and funerals. Although popular music, motion pictures, television, and other elements of popular culture are enjoyed throughout the country, these aspects of traditional Austrian culture remain important, even to the young.

Most Austrians celebrate the major Christian holidays, though many revered Austrian traditions surrounding these holidays are said to have their roots in pre-Christian times. Glöcklerlauf, a festival that takes place the evening before Epiphany (January 6), is celebrated especially in the mountainous regions of Oberösterreich, Steiermark, and Tirol and features activities meant to drive away the evil spirits of winter. During the festival, young men and boys wear loudly clanging bells and carry handmade masks—often extremely large, lighted from within, and decorated with Christian and secular designs—on their heads and shoulders.

THE ARTS

Austria is known for its contributions to music, especially during the Classical and Romantic periods. The major work of outsiders such as Germans Ludwig van Beethoven (from Bonn), Johannes Brahms (from Hamburg), and—in part—Richard Strauss (from Munich) is no less associated with Vienna than that of such natives of Austria and the empire as Joseph Haydn, Wolfgang Amadeus Mozart, Franz Schubert, Anton Bruckner, Gustav Mahler, and Hugo Wolf. Much of the pioneer work in modern music was done by Arnold Schoenberg, Alban Berg, and Anton Webern, who are known collectively as the Second Viennese school. Vienna is also associated with two popular genres of music: the waltz and the operetta. Both forms find a common source in the person of Johann Strauss the Younger, who with his father, Johann the Elder, and his brothers, Josef and Eduard, constituted a virtual musical dynasty in the 19th century. The Viennese operetta, drawing heavily from the Slavic and Hungarian regions of the empire, reached its apogee about 1900, the prototypical composer being Franz Lehár.

The theatre has occupied a central position in the cultural life of Austria. The 19th-century Viennese playwrights Johann Nestroy, Franz Grillparzer, and Ferdinand Raimund developed a drama with distinctly Austrian traits. The stage director Max Reinhardt, the writer Hugo von Hofmannsthal, and the composer Richard Strauss were instrumental in founding the Salzburg Festival in 1920.

Literature in Austria had auspicious beginnings. The great epic of the German Middle Ages, the anonymous *Nibelungenlied*, was written in Austria. The most renowned Middle High German lyric poet, Walther von der Vogelweide, served at the Viennese court in the late 12th century.

In the late 19th century, distinctly Austrian literary styles and mannerisms emerged. The writer Hermann Bahr was associated with an era of literary impressionism, the expressly Austrian characteristics of which—a heightened self-consciousness and feelings of ambivalence and tentativeness—were coupled with forebodings of being at the end of an overripe civilization. Hugo von Hofmannsthal, poet, dramatist, essayist, and librettist of six operas by Richard Strauss, and Arthur Schnitzler, whose dramas are thought to epitomize a hothouse Vienna at the turn of the 20th century, have best conveyed these sensibilities. Karl Kraus, whose literary, political, and social criticism and satire contemplated an entire era in his review *Die Fackel* (1899–1936), focused on the importance of language. Coming from Prague to Vienna, Franz Kafka, with his haunting works of the individual confronted with anonymous, unheeding power, has entered the canon of world literature.

Robert Musil's unfinished novel *Der Mann ohne Eigenschaften* (1930–43; "The Man Without Qualities") is said to be a metaphor for Austria itself. The Expressionist poet Georg Trakl wrote elegiacally of decay and death. Franz

Werfel, another Expressionist, excelled as a poet, playwright, and novelist. Stefan Zweig, poet, dramatist, and story writer of imaginary and historical characters, was influenced by another Viennese, Sigmund Freud. Also writing in the first half of the 20th century were the Vienna-born philosopher Ludwig Wittgenstein and innovative novelist Hermann Broch.

The novelist Heimito von Doderer, who took an earlier Austria as his milieu, is a link between the vanished literary world of the pre-Anschluss years and the later 20th century. Austrian writers completed a number of works that won international attention in the second half of the 20th century; among them are Ilse Aichinger, Ingeborg Bachmann, Thomas Bernhard, and Peter Handke. The Austrian novelist and playwright Elfriede Jelinek won the Nobel Prize for Literature in 2004.

In painting, a distinctly Viennese school developed in the movement known as the Vienna Secession (referring to its breakaway in 1897 from the academic painters of the Künstlerhaus), which was part of the Jugendstil, as Art Nouveau is known in the German regions. Led by Gustav Klimt, the movement tangentially involved a number of innovative architects, including Otto Wagner, Adolf Loos, and Josef Hoffmann, who also helped found a cooperative enterprise for crafts and design called the Wiener Werkstätte ("Vienna Workshop"). Klimt then led a later group that split from the Secession and held an exhibition known as the Kunstschau ("Art Show"); from this group emerged some of the most illustrious modern Austrian painters, including Oskar Kokoschka, Alfred Kubin, and Egon Schiele.

Among later 20th-century artists, the abstract paintings of Friedensreich Hundertwasser recall the Secession. The Vienna School of Fantastic Realism has leaned toward surrealism. Other groups have included Junge Wilde ("Young Wild Ones"), of whom Siegfried Anzinger has won acclaim abroad. In sculpture, which in the interwar years was dominated by Anton Hanak, the preeminent figure after 1945 was Fritz Wotruba.

GUSTAV KLIMT

The Austrian painter Gustav Klimt (born July 14, 1862, Vienna, Austria—died February 6, 1918, Vienna) was among the founders of the school of painting known as the Vienna Sezession. After studying at the Vienna School of Decorative Arts, Klimt in 1883 opened an independent studio specializing in the execution of mural paintings. His early work was typical of late 19th-century academic painting, as can be seen in his murals for the Vienna Burgtheater (1888) and on the staircase of the Kunsthistorisches Museum.

In 1897 Klimt's mature style emerged, and he founded the Vienna Sezession, a group of painters who revolted against academic art in favour of a highly decorative style similar to

The Kiss, *oil on canvas by Gustav Klimt, 1907–08; in the Österreichische Gallery, Vienna. 180 ×180 cm.* Osterreichische Galerie, Vienna —Erwin Meyer/Rudolph Zimpel Breitenfurt

Art Nouveau. Soon thereafter he painted three allegorical murals for the ceiling of the University of Vienna auditorium that were violently criticized; the erotic symbolism and pessimism of these works created such a scandal that the murals were rejected. His later murals, the *Beethoven Frieze* (1902) and the murals (1909–11) in the dining room of the Stoclet House in Brussels, are characterized by precisely linear drawing and the bold and arbitrary use of flat, decorative patterns of colour and gold leaf. Klimt's most successful works include *The Kiss* (1907–08) and a series of portraits of fashionable Viennese matrons, such as *Frau Fritza Riedler* (1906) and *Frau Adele Bloch-Bauer* (1907). In these works he treats the human figure without shadow and heightens the lush sensuality of skin by surrounding it with areas of flat, highly ornamental, and brilliantly composed areas of decoration.

During World War II *Frau Adele Bloch-Bauer* and several other Klimt paintings belonging to the Bloch-Bauer family were confiscated by the Nazis and eventually added to the collection of the Österreichische Gallery in Vienna. These works later became the focus of a lengthy legal battle, and in 2006 they were finally returned to the family. Later that year *Frau Adele Bloch-Bauer* was sold to the Neue Galerie in New York City for a then-record price of $135 million.

Clemens Holzmeister, perhaps the best-known 20th-century Austrian architect, had considerable influence on modern church design and was responsible for the two major festival theatres in Salzburg. The designs of Adolf Loos, Roland Rainer, Erich Boltenstern, and Carl Auböck had an impact on housing and office development. The avant-garde architecture firm Coop Himmelblau and architect Hans Hollein were well known in the late 20th and early 21st centuries.

Moviemaking in Austria has tended to concentrate on highbrow or controversial themes. The German-language motion picture industry has not been able to keep pace with Hollywood imports, and foreign films and television shows outnumber Austrian or German productions. A number of 20th-century Austrian actors began their careers in Austria and later found success in Hollywood, including Paul Henreid, Oscar Homolka, Hedy Lamarr, and Maximilian Schell. Also born in Austria were the directors Erich von Stroheim and Otto Preminger. Arnold Schwarzenegger, the Austrian-born bodybuilder, actor, and politician, is admired for his films and other accomplishments in the United States.

CULTURAL INSTITUTIONS

The Vienna Philharmonic and the Vienna State Opera are Austria's premier musical institutions. Other groups of note have included the ORF (Austrian Radio and Television) Vienna Radio Symphony, the Graz Philharmonic, the Linz Bruckner Orchestra, the Salzburg Mozarteum Orchestra, the Alban Berg Quartet, and the Concertus Musicus. The Vienna Boys' Choir, founded by the emperor Maximilian I in 1498, still sings at Sunday masses in the chapel of the Hofburg, or Imperial Palace.

VIENNA STATE OPERA

One of the world's leading opera houses is the Vienna State Opera (German: Staatsoper) in Vienna. It is known especially for performances of works by Richard Wagner, Wolfgang Amadeus Mozart, and Richard Strauss. The original theatre, located on the Ringstrasse, was built in 1869 to house the expanded operations of the Vienna Court Opera (Hofoper), by which name it was originally known. Particularly famed during the conductorship of Hans Richter (artistic director 1880–96) were productions of Wagner's cycle *Der Ring des Nibelungen*. The directorship of the composer Gustav Mahler (1897–1907) was one of the artistic high points of the opera's history. Among directors from 1908 until the annexation of Austria by Germany in 1938 were Richard Strauss and the conductors Clemens Krauss and Felix Weingartner.

Wartime bombing destroyed the building in 1945. Its reconstruction, completed in 1955, was financed by taxes, contributions, and U.S. Marshall Plan aid. In the interim, performances of the State Opera were held at the Vienna Volksoper (Folk Opera) and the Theater an der Wien. The outstanding musical director of the period after World War II was the conductor Herbert von Karajan. Performances are financed in part by a state subsidy.

Vienna State Opera. © Corbis

The stages of Vienna and Graz are considered among the finest in the German-speaking world and rank with such German-language theatre centres as Berlin, Munich, and Zürich. The high citadel of the Austrian theatre is Vienna's Burgtheater, in which the canon of German classical drama is performed by the leading actors of the German-speaking world. The Theater in der Josefstadt, also in Vienna, performs contemporary drama and German adaptations of foreign plays. All theatres are publicly subsidized.

The great museums of Austria are gathered in Vienna. Its Kunsthistorisches Museum, with holdings extending from antiquity through the great German, Italian, and Dutch masters, contains one of the world's premier collections. The Austrian Gallery in Belvedere Palace exhibits Austrian art from the Middle Ages to the modern era. The Albertina Graphics Collection in Vienna is one of the world's finest collections of prints. In the Hofburg, the Collection of Secular and Ecclesiastical Treasures contains jewelry and regalia of the Holy Roman Empire and the Habsburgs. Modern collections are found in the Museum of Modern Art Ludwig Foundation (mumok) and the Secession museum. Collections of scientific, technical, and industrial interest are found in the Museum of Natural History Vienna, the Austrian Museum of Applied Arts (MAK), the Museum of Ethnology, and the Technical Museum Vienna.

The oldest Austrian academic research institution is the Austrian Academy of Sciences, whose traditions date to the early 18th century. More modern scientific foundations, notably the Körner Foundation, support scientific research and other cultural endeavours; their main support comes from government sources. A federal ministry of science and research was established in 1970; it is responsible for university institutions and for the advancement of scientific activities.

SPORTS AND RECREATION

Austria's situation in the Alps means that outdoor winter sports are a favourite pastime. Known as the birthplace of downhill skiing, the country is littered with ski areas. Mountain climbing and hiking also are popular, and thousands of well-marked trails crisscross the Alps. Residents of the lowlands enjoy thousands of venues —swimming pools, stadiums, riding arenas, bicycle paths, and other facilities—for a wide range of sports. Eastern Austria's rivers and lakes attract countless swimmers and boaters in the warmer months and skaters in winter.

Austria has sent teams to every Olympic Games since 1896, except the 1920 Games in Antwerp, Belgium. The country hosted the Winter Games in 1964 and 1976, both times in the Alpine city of Innsbruck. At Innsbruck in 1976, a young Austrian skier, Franz Klammer, set a world record for the men's downhill event. Since Klammer's time many other Austrian Olympians—among them the skiers Mario Reiter, Petra Kronberger, Günther Mader, Anita Wachter, and Hermann Maier—have continued the country's tradition of athletic excellence.

MEDIA AND PUBLISHING

Austria has several major independent newspapers, including three major dailies in Vienna, *Neue Kronen-Zeitung*, *Kurier*, and *Die Presse*. The leading provincial newspaper is *Salzburger Nachrichten*. Until the turn of the 21st century, radio and television were the monopoly of the Österreichischer Rundfunk (ORF), a state-owned corporation that enjoys political and economic independence. Several private local and regional radio stations have been licensed, although ORF still operates the country's main radio stations. ORF also operates a number of television channels.

CHAPTER 5

AUSTRIAN HISTORY: PREHISTORY TO THE PROBLEM OF THE AUSTRIAN SUCCESSION

In the territories of Austria, the first traces of human settlement date from the Lower Paleolithic Period (Old Stone Age). In 1991 a frozen human body dating from the Neolithic Period (New Stone Age) was discovered at the Hauslabjoch pass in the Ötztal Alps, on the Italian-Austrian border. At 5,300 years old, the so-called Iceman, nicknamed Ötzi, was the oldest intact mummy ever discovered. The archaeological material becomes richer and more varied for subsequent periods, giving evidence of several distinct cultures succeeding one another or coexisting. The Austrian site of Hallstatt gave its name to the principal culture of the Early Iron Age (c. 1100–450 BCE). Celtic tribes invaded the eastern Alps about 400 BCE and eventually founded the kingdom of Noricum, the first "state" on Austrian territory known by name. In the west, however, the ancient Raetian people were able to maintain their seat. Then, attracted by the rich iron resources and the strategic importance of the region, the Romans began to assert themselves. After an initially peaceful penetration during the last two centuries BCE, Roman troops finally occupied the country about 15 BCE, and the lands as far as the Danube River became part of the Roman Empire, being allotted to the Roman provinces of Raetia, Noricum, and Pannonia.

The Romans opened up the country by an extensive system of roads. Among the Roman towns along the Danube, Carnuntum (near Hainburg) took precedence over Vindobona (Vienna), while Lauriacum (Lorch; near the confluence of the Enns River and the Danube) belonged to a later period. Roman municipalities (*municipia*) also grew up at Brigantium (Bregenz), Juvavum (Salzburg), Ovilava (Wels), Virunum (near Klagenfurt), Teurnia (near Spittal), and Flavia Solva (near Leibnitz). North of the Danube the Germanic tribes of the Naristi, Marcomanni, and Quadi settled. Their invasions in 166–180 CE arrested the peaceful development of the provinces, and, even after their repulse by the emperor Marcus Aurelius, the country could not regain its former prosperity. In the 3rd century the Roman frontier defenses began to be hard-pressed by invasions from the Alemanni. Finally, in the 5th century, heavy attacks by the Huns and the eastern Germans put an end to the Roman provincial defense system on the Danube.

There is archaeological evidence of a Christian cult in this area from the 4th century, and the biography of St. Severinus by Eugippius constitutes a unique literary source for the dramatic events of the second half of the 5th century. At that time several Germanic tribes (the Rugii, Goths, Heruli, and, later, Langobardi) settled on Austrian territory. In 488 part of the harassed Norican population was forced to withdraw to Italy.

EARLY MIDDLE AGES

Following the departure of the Langobardi to Italy (568), further development was determined by the Bavarians in a struggle with the Slavs, who were invading from the east, and by the Alemanni, who settled in what is now Vorarlberg. The Bavarians were under the political influence of the Franks, whereas the Slavs had Avar rulers.

GERMANIC AND SLAVIC SETTLEMENT

At the time of their greatest expansion, the Slavs had penetrated as far as Niederösterreich (Lower Austria), Steiermark (Styria), Kärnten (Carinthia),

ALEMANNI

The Germanic people known as the Alemanni are first mentioned in historical sources in connection with the Roman attack on them in 213 CE. In the following decades, their pressure on the Roman provinces became severe; they occupied the Agri Decumates C. 260, and late in the 5th century they expanded into Alsace and northern Switzerland, establishing the German language in those regions. In Austria, they established settlements in the west, in modern-day Vorarlberg. In 496 they were conquered by Clovis and incorporated into his Frankish dominions.

The Alemanni were originally composed of fragments of several Germanic peoples, and they remained a loosely knit confederation of tribes in the Suebi group, which also included the Langobardi (Lombards) and others. Although several tribes put their military forces under the joint command of two leaders for the duration of a campaign, the different peoples generally found it difficult to combine, and they had nothing that could be called a central government. The French and Spanish words for Germany (Allemagne; Alemania) are derived from their name.

and eastern Tirol. After 624 the western Slavs rose against the Avars under the leadership of the Frankish merchant Samo, whose short-lived rule may also have extended over the territories of the eastern Alps. About 700 the Bavarian lands again bordered on Avar territory, with the lower course of the Enns forming the approximate frontier. On the death of the Frankish king Dagobert I (639), the Bavarian dukes from the house of Agilolfing became virtually independent.

Christianity had survived only here and there among the remnants of the Roman population when, about 600 and again about 700, Christian missionaries from the west became active, with the support of the Bavarian dukes. At the end of the 7th century, St. Rupert, who came from the Rhine, founded the church of Salzburg. When they were threatened once more by the Avars, the Alpine Slavs (Karantani) placed themselves (before 750) under the protection of the Bavarians, whose mission was extended to them. At the same time, Bavarian settlers penetrated into the valleys of Kärnten and Steiermark. Charlemagne, emperor of the neighbouring Franks, however, deposed the Bavarian duke Tassilo III, wiping out the Bavarian dukedom for a century. During the following years (791–796), Charlemagne led a number of attacks against the Avars and destroyed their dominion. Surviving Avars were made to settle in the eastern part of Lower Austria between the rivers of Fischa and Leitha, where they soon disappeared

from history, most probably mixing with the native population.

As was the usual Frankish practice, border provinces (Marken, or marches) were instituted in the newly won southeastern territories. The Avar March on the Danube and Lower and Upper Pannonia and Karantania were to form a border fortification, but this arrangement soon became less effective because of frequent disagreements among the nobility. To that unrest was added a threat from the Bulgarians and from the rulers of Great Moravia. Nevertheless, the process of Germanization and Christianization continued, during the course of which the churches of Salzburg and Passau came into conflict with the eastern mission, which was led by the Slav apostles Cyril and Methodius. The Frankish kingdom richly endowed the church and nobility with new lands, which came to be settled by Bavarian and Frankish farmers.

In 881 the beginning of incursions by the Magyars led to a first clash near Vienna. By 906 they had destroyed Great Moravia, and in 907 near Pressburg (Bratislava, Slovakia) the Magyars defeated a large Bavarian army that had tried to win back lost territory. Liutpold of Bavaria as well as Theotmar, the archbishop of Salzburg, were killed in battle. The Lower Austrian territories as far as the Enns River, and Steiermark as far as the Koralpe massif, fell under Magyar domination. Nevertheless, a certain continuity of German-Slav settlement was maintained so that, after the victory of the German king Otto I (later Holy Roman emperor) in 955 and the further repulse of the Magyars in the 960s, a fresh start could be made.

EARLY BABENBERG PERIOD

The first mention of a ruler in the regained territories east of the Enns is of Burchard, who probably was count (*burgrave*) of Regensburg. It appears that he lost his office as a result of his championship of Henry II the Quarrelsome, duke of Bavaria. In 976 his successor, Leopold I of the house of Babenberg, was installed in office. Under Leopold's rule the eastern frontier was extended to the Vienna Woods after a war with the Magyars. Under his successor, Henry I, the country around Vienna itself must have come into German hands. New marches were also created in what were later known as Carniola and Steiermark.

Wars against Hungarians and Moravians occupied the reign (1018–55) of Margrave (a count who ruled over a march) Adalbert. Parts of Lower Austria on both sides of the Danube were lost temporarily; after they were retaken, they became the so-called Neumark (New March), which for some time enjoyed independence—as did the Bohemian March to the north of the Babenberg territories. The position of the Babenbergs was at that time still a modest one; their territorial rights were no greater than those of other leading noble families. Their power within their own official sphere was further diminished by ecclesiastical immunities (Passau in particular but also Salzburg, Regensburg, and Freising), with numerous monasteries owning large territories as well.

Austria was repeatedly drawn into the disputes of the Investiture Controversy, in which Pope Gregory VII and King Henry IV (later Holy Roman emperor) fought for control of the church in Germany. In 1075 Margrave Ernest, who had regained the Neumark and the Bohemian March for his family, was killed in the Battle of the Unstrut, fighting on the side of Henry IV against the rebellious Saxons. Altmann, bishop of Passau, a leader of church reform and a champion of Gregory VII, influenced the next Babenberg margrave, Leopold II, to abandon Henry's cause. As a result, Henry roused the Bohemian duke Vratislav II against him, and in 1082 Leopold II was defeated near Mailberg, his territories north of the Danube devastated. The Babenbergs, however, managed to survive these setbacks. Meanwhile, the cause of church reform gained ground, with its centres in the newly founded monasteries of Göttweig, Lambach, and, in Steiermark, Admont.

Under Leopold III (1095–1136) the history of the Babenbergs reached its first culmination point. In the struggle between emperor and pope, Leopold avoided taking sides until a consensus had built up among the German princes that it was Emperor Henry IV who stood in the way of a final settlement. Then Leopold did not hesitate to side with Henry's rebellious son, Henry V, in 1106. For this he was rewarded with the hand of Henry V's sister Agnes, who had formerly been married to the Hohenstaufen Frederick I of Swabia. The intermarriage with the reigning dynasty not only increased Leopold's reputation but also no doubt brought him additional power. Leopold was even proposed as a candidate to the royal throne, but he declined. It was apparently his intention to concentrate on consolidating his position in Austria. He was the first Austrian margrave to describe himself as the holder of territorial principality (*principatus terrae*), and during his time Austrian common law was mentioned for the first time, another proof of the developing national consciousness.

Leopold's reputation with the clergy was high, and he was eventually canonized (1485). He gave generous endowments to religious communities, establishing the Cistercians at Heiligenkreuz, and he founded, or at least restored, the monastery of Klosterneuburg, which he then gave to Augustinian canons. In Klosterneuburg he built a residence in which he stayed even after he had acquired Vienna.

On the death of Leopold III, the Babenbergs were drawn into a conflict between the two leading dynasties of Germany, the Hohenstaufen and the Welfs; the Babenbergs took the side of the Hohenstaufen because of their family ties. In 1139 the German king Conrad III bestowed Bavaria, which he had wrested from the Welfs, on his half brother, Leopold IV. After the latter's untimely death, Henry II Jasomirgott succeeded to the rule of Austria and Bavaria.

The Holy Roman emperor Frederick I (Barbarossa) tried to put an end to the quarrel between the Welfs and the Hohenstaufen, and, in the autumn of 1156 at Regensburg, he arranged a compromise. Bavaria was restored to the Welf Henry III (the Lion), duke of Saxony, while the Babenbergs were confirmed in their rule of Austria, which was made a duchy, and were given the "three counties," the actual location of which is disputed. Also, the obligations of the dukes of Austria toward the empire were reduced. Their attendance at royal court days was called for only when court was held in Bavaria, and they were compelled to participate only in campaigns of the empire that were directed against Austria's neighbour —that is, Hungary. Henry II Jasomirgott and his wife, Theodora, a Byzantine princess, were granted succession through the female line and the right, in the event of the premature deaths of their children, to appoint a candidate for the succession. The Babenbergs also were given the right of approving the exercise of jurisdiction by other powers within the new duchy, permitting Henry to exert pressure against rival internal powers, secular as well as ecclesiastical. The rights of the duke were laid down by imperial charter (Privilegium Minus). For centuries, however, Austria continued to contain territorial dominions not ruled by the duke. Henry moved his residence to Vienna, where he also founded the monastery of the "Scottish" (actually Irish) monks.

Leopold III. Photononstop/SuperStock

LATER BABENBERG PERIOD

In 1192 the Babenbergs' territory was greatly extended when they won the duchy of Steiermark. In Steiermark the margraves of the family of the Otakars of Steyr had gradually asserted themselves —under conditions similar to those of the Babenbergs—over their rivals, the noble families of the Eppensteiner, Formbacher, and Aribonen. The most successful among Steiermark's margraves was Otakar III (reigned 1130–63). Then, in 1180, Emperor Frederick I, in the course of a renewed anti-Welf policy, raised Steiermark to the status of a duchy and granted it complete independence from Bavaria. A few years later a treaty of inheritance (Georgenberg; 1186) was concluded between the dukes Leopold V of Austria (reigned 1177–94), a son of Henry II Jasomirgott, and Otakar IV of Steiermark, the ailing last Otakar ruler. When Otakar died in 1192, Leopold succeeded him, and thus the Babenbergs came into the inheritance.

Except for a short intermission (1194–98), the reigning Babenberg thereafter ruled both duchies, Austria and Steiermark. Steiermark then included parts of the Traungau, which eventually was to become part of Upper Austria, and the province of Pitten, north of the Semmering Alpine pass, afterward assigned to Lower Austria. In logical continuation of the Babenberg policy, Leopold VI (the Glorious) and his successor, Frederick II (the Warlike), the last representative of the dynasty, extended their domains farther south, gaining fiefs in Carniola.

Before he inherited the duchy of Steiermark, Leopold V had taken part in the Third Crusade, during which, on the ramparts of Acre (modern 'Akko, Israel), he became involved in a quarrel with the English king Richard I (the Lion-Heart). Later, on his return journey to England, Richard tried to make his way through Austria in disguise but was recognized near Vienna, taken prisoner, and later handed over to the Holy Roman emperor Henry VI. England had to pay a heavy ransom, a share of which Leopold obtained and invested in the foundation, extension, and fortification of towns as well as in the stamping of a new coin, the so-called Wiener pfennig. The road connecting Vienna and Steiermark was improved, and the new town of Wiener Neustadt was established on its course to protect the newly opened route across the Semmering.

On Leopold V's death the Babenberg domains were divided between his sons for four years, until the death of one of them, Frederick I, in 1198. His brother Leopold VI, the most outstanding member of the family, then took over as sole ruler (1198–1230). This was a time of great prosperity for the Babenberg countries. In imperial politics Leopold VI again took sides with the Hohenstaufen, backing Philip of Swabia. In church matters he was a great supporter of the monasteries, founding a Cistercian monastery at Lilienfeld (c. 1206). He tried to concentrate patronage rights over ecclesiastical property in his own hands and took rigorous action against the heretics (the Cathari and Waldenses). He participated in several crusades in Palestine, Egypt, southern France (against the Albigenses), and Spain (against the Saracens). Leopold VI's efforts to emancipate Austria ecclesiastically by creating a separate Austrian bishopric in Vienna came to naught because of the opposition of the church in Passau and also in Salzburg; nor did his son Frederick II succeed in the same matter. Leopold VI played some role in imperial politics, bringing about the Treaty of San Germano between the Holy Roman emperor Frederick II and Pope Gregory IX (1230). He met his death in San Germano (now Cassino, Italy), and his body was transported to Lilienfeld for burial.

A change came about under the last representative of the dynasty, Frederick the Warlike, Leopold's son. His harsh internal policy and military excursions against neighbouring lands, together with his opposition to the emperor Frederick II, led in 1237 to the temporary loss of both Austria and Steiermark. The crisis, however, was overcome, and fresh opportunities were about to open for the duke when, on June 15, 1246, he was killed in battle against the Hungarians on the Leitha River. With him the male line of the family came to an end.

The political history of Austria from the end of the 10th century to the middle of the 13th is marked by the establishment and consolidation of territories. This process was most advanced in the Babenberg domains but was not confined to them. Dukes Herman (1144–61) and Bernhard (1202–56) of Kärnten achieved a comparable status, and Count Albert of Tirol (died 1253) moved in the same direction. The archbishops of Salzburg strove to eliminate all secular powers and patrons of their see, but, in the other territories, secular princes strengthened their rule.

Another milestone of this period was the completion of the colonization of the Austrian territories. New settlements were established by clearing the woods and advancing to more remote mountain areas. Several old and new settlements grew into market centres and towns and were eventually granted charters. The colonization movement also affected the ratio of the German to non-German

NIBELUNGENLIED

The Middle High German epic poem called the *Nibelungenlied* ("Song of the Nibelungs") was written *c.* 1200 by an unknown poet from the Danube region in what is now Austria. It is preserved in three main 13th-century manuscripts. Elements of great antiquity are discernible in the poem, traceable to Old Norse literature, stories in the *Poetic Edda,* and Scandinavian sagas. The principal characters are Prince Siegfried, Queen Brunhild, Princess Kriemhild, her brother King Gunther, and his henchman Hagen; the story focuses on deceit, revenge, and slaughter. Many variations and adaptations of the poem appeared in later centuries, including Richard Wagner's opera cycle *Der Ring des Nibelungen* (1853–74).

population. Except for some places in the Alpine regions, the Slavs were gradually assimilated, and the same held true of the remnants of the Roman population in Salzburg and northern Tirol.

The intellectual life of the period deserves mention. The Babenberg court was famous enough to attract some of the leading German poets. At the beginning of the 13th century, the saga known as the *Nibelungenlied* was written down by an unknown Austrian. Historical writing flourished in the monasteries. The era also produced first-rate Romanesque and early Gothic architecture.

LATE MIDDLE AGES

Upon the death of Frederick the Warlike, the Babenberg domains became the political objects of aspiring neighbours. The emperor and the pope also tried to intervene. Two female descendants of the Babenbergs, Frederick's niece Gertrude and his sister Margaret, were considered to embody the claims to the heritage. Gertrude married first the Bohemian prince Vladislav and afterward the margrave Hermann of Baden, who died in 1250. After Hermann's death, Otakar II, prince of Bohemia (from 1253 king) and a member of the house of Přemysl, married the widowed Margaret. Thereupon Hungarian forces intervened. Under the Treaty of Ofen (1254) Otakar was to rule Austria, while King Béla IV of Hungary received Steiermark. Troubles in Salzburg, stemming from a conflict between Bohemia and Hungary, inspired a rising among

Steiermark's nobles. Otakar intervened and in the Treaty of Vienna (1260) took over Steiermark as well. The state of anarchy that prevailed in Germany during this period proved advantageous to Otakar, who was granted Austria and Steiermark in fief from Richard, earl of Cornwall, the titular German king. The grant, however, was only by writ and was invalid according to German law. During the following years, Otakar's energetic rule met with growing opposition among the Austrian nobility. He introduced foreigners into important official positions, broke fortresses that had been erected without his consent, and dissolved his childless marriage with Margaret. Otakar had two of the opposition leaders, Otto of Meissau and Seifried of Mahrenberg, executed. The gentry and the inhabitants of the cities, on the other hand, generally favoured Otakar, who supported the churches and monasteries. To complete his success, Otakar gained Kärnten and Carniola, which Ulrich of Spanheim, duke of Kärnten, willed to him in 1269.

Reverses came only when Count Rudolf IV of the house of Habsburg was elected German king as Rudolf I on September 29, 1273. Cautiously but nevertheless energetically, Rudolf set out to undermine the powerful position Otakar had created for himself. He challenged the legitimacy of Otakar's acquisitions and finally placed the Bohemian king under the ban of the empire. In 1276 Rudolf and his allies invaded Austria, forcing Otakar to do homage and to renounce his claims to Austria. Two years later, while trying to recover what he had lost, Otakar was defeated by the united forces of Rudolf and the Hungarians and was killed on the battlefield near Dürnkrut (August 26, 1278).

ACCESSION OF THE HABSBURGS

As the German princes had not cared to give Rudolf adequate support against Otakar, he did not feel bound to them and set out to acquire the former Babenberg lands for his own house. In 1281 he made his eldest son, Albert (later Albert I, king of Germany), governor of Austria and Steiermark; on Christmas, 1282, he invested his two sons, Albert and Rudolf II, with Austria, Steiermark, and Carniola, which they were to rule jointly and undivided. As the Austrians were not used to being governed by two sovereigns at the same time, the Treaty of Rheinfelden (June 1, 1283) provided that Duke Albert should be the sole ruler. In 1282 Carniola had already been pawned to Meinhard II of Tirol (of the counts of Gorizia), one of the most reliable allies of Rudolf who, in 1286, was also invested with Kärnten.

At first the Habsburg rulers were far from popular in Austria. Albert's energetic and relentless rule aroused bad feeling, and the Swabian entourage that had arrived with the new dynasty to occupy key positions was despised by native nobles. There were conflicts with Bavaria, Salzburg, and Hungarian nobles who violated the Austrian frontier. After the death of King Rudolf (1291), all the neighbours and rivals of the Habsburgs and the counts of Gorizia united. Albert, however, succeeded in negotiating a peace with his most dangerous foes, the Hungarians and the Bohemians, and he broke the fortresses of the rebel nobility. Meanwhile, Meinhard II had stifled the uprising in Kärnten.

In 1292 Albert was passed over in the German election, and Adolf of Nassau was called to the throne. When Adolf fell out with the electoral princes, however, they went over to Albert, who had just subdued another rebellion in Austria. After Adolf was defeated and killed near Göllheim (1298), Albert had himself elected a second time. In his Austrian lands Albert's main concern was to provide for an effective administration, in which he was assisted by his privy councillors, most of whom were foreign. Records were set up to codify the prerogatives and returns of the ducal property. Eventually Albert did not spare the church, either. When the Přemysl family died out in 1306, Albert aspired to the Bohemian throne. He had his eldest son, Rudolf III, elected Bohemian king, but Rudolf died the following year. Albert was preparing for a new campaign when he was murdered by his nephew John and some accomplices in 1308

On Albert's death the anti-Habsburg movement flared up again in Austria, but his sons, Frederick I (the Fair) and Leopold I, managed to maintain control. Frederick stood for election as German king (as Frederick III), and for the next several years the Habsburg countries had to support the cost of the war with his rival, Louis IV of Bavaria, until 1322, when Frederick was defeated near Mühldorf. Earlier, another decisive battle had been lost by the Habsburgs to the Swiss at Morgarten in 1315. From that time on, the Habsburg domains in the territory south of the Rhine and Lake Constance began to crumble away. Frederick the Fair spent his last years in Austria and was buried in the Carthusian monastery of Mauerbach (1330). He seems to have been the first of the Habsburgs for whom Austria meant home. From his time on, Habsburg rule and Habsburg territories were known as the Austrian domains (*dominium Austriae*), a term that was replaced, in the course of the 14th and 15th centuries, by the new concept of the house of Austria.

After Frederick's death the Habsburgs were for some time ruled out as possible candidates for the German throne; but, under the brothers Albert II and Otto, Habsburg Austria received its first important accession of territory. In 1335 Kärnten and Carniola were acquired after the death of Henry of Gorizia, while, with the help of Luxembourg troops, Henry's daughter Margaret Maultasch managed to retain the Tirol. Albert and his brother Otto had not gotten on too well, but, when Albert came to rule on his own, he proved to be of sound judgment and keen on preserving the peace. It was a time of calamities: bad harvests, floods, earthquakes, and in 1348–49 the plague, which brought a persecution of the Jews; this was suppressed, however, by the duke. Albert arranged several tours around his domains to establish contacts with the populace and to improve jurisdiction. Two campaigns against the Swiss failed to yield any spectacular results, but they helped to consolidate the weakened Habsburg position. At his death in 1358 Albert left four sons. Though in 1355 a family ordinance had decreed that all the male members of the family were to rule jointly over the undivided domains, only the eldest of them, Rudolf, was then fit to rule. Throughout his short reign (1358–65), Rudolf IV showed himself extremely energetic and ambitious. He started to rebuild St. Stephen's Cathedral in the Gothic style, and he founded the University of Vienna (1365). With these two projects, he imitated and rivaled his father-in-law, the Holy Roman emperor Charles IV, at Prague.

In 1359 Rudolf's forged charter, the Privilegium Majus, by which he claimed immense privileges for Austria and its dynasty, as well as the title of archduke, caused a breach between him and the emperor Charles IV. Charles was not prepared to accept the Privilegium Majus to its full extent (although it later was sanctioned by Frederick III, the Habsburg king of Germany—and, from 1452, Holy Roman emperor—in 1442 and again in 1453). Upon news of the death of Margaret Maultasch's son, Duke Meinhard, in 1363, Rudolf prevailed upon Margaret to make over the Tirol to him. On this occasion the emperor backed the Habsburgs against the rulers of Bavaria, the Wittelsbachs, and the Tirol thus passed to the house of Austria.

DIVISION OF THE HABSBURG LANDS

Rudolf was succeeded in 1365 by his two brothers, Albert III and Leopold III. After some years of joint rule, however, they quarreled and in 1379, by the Treaty of Neuberg, partitioned the family lands. Albert, as the elder brother, received the more prosperous countries on the Danube (Upper and Lower Austria). The rest of the widespread domains fell to Leopold (including Steiermark, Kärnten, Tirol, the old Habsburg countries in the west, and central Istria). The treaty also contained several points on mutual wardship, preemption rights, and common titles, by which some connection between the two lines was to be preserved.

In 1382 the resourceful duke Leopold took advantage of the weak position of Venice in its war with Genoa and seized Trieste, which had broken away from Venice. His efforts to expand his rule in the west, however, were less successful, though he seemed lucky enough at first. Envisaging a connection between the original Habsburg territories in the west and the new domains in the Tirol, the Habsburgs looked for a foothold in the region west of the Arlberg (modern Vorarlberg). Neuberg on the Rhine was won in 1363 and Feldkirch in 1375. Another important acquisition was the city of Freiburg in the Breisgau region. But then Leopold came into conflict with the Swiss, which led to defeat and his death in the Battle of Sempach in 1386. An army of his brother, Albert III, was likewise defeated in the Battle of Näfels in 1388, and the Habsburgs suffered heavy territorial losses. Leopold's sons recognized the wardship of Albert, who acquired Bludenz and the Montafon Valley west of the Arlberg in 1394. In his own domains

Albert was forced to check the dynasty of the Schaunbergs (in Upper Austria), who tried to create an independent domain around Peuerbach and Eferding. Albert III especially favoured the city of Vienna as his capital, and it was because of his reorganization that the university Rudolf IV had founded there was able to survive.

After Albert's death in 1395, new Habsburg family troubles arose, differences that the treaties of Hollenburg (1395) and Vienna (1396) tried to settle. Under the Vienna treaty, the line of Leopold III split into two branches, resulting in three complexes of Austrian territories—a state of affairs that was to reappear in the 16th century. The individual parts came to be known by the names of Niederösterreich ("Lower Austria," comprising modern Lower and Upper Austria), Innerösterreich ("Inner Austria," comprising Steiermark, Kärnten, Carniola, and the Adriatic possessions), and Oberösterreich ("Upper Austria," comprising the Tirol and the western domains, known as the Vorlande, or Vorderösterreich [the Austrian provinces west of the Arlberg]).

In 1396 the Austrian estates, or diets, were first assembled to consider the Turkish threat; thereafter they were to play an important political role in Austria. In them the nobility usually took the lead, but they also included representatives of the monasteries, towns, and marketplaces. In the Tirol, in Vorarlberg, and, at times, in Salzburg, the peasants also sent their representatives to attend the diets. Because of the Habsburg partitions and frequent regencies, the estates were able to gain in importance. They did not obtain the right to pass laws, but they obstinately insisted on the privilege to grant taxes and duties.

After the short rule of Albert IV (1395–1404) and a troublesome tutelary regime (1404–11), Albert V came into his own, and with him the Danube countries again enjoyed a strong and energetic rule (1411–39). Albert, however, had married the daughter of the Holy Roman emperor Sigismund and was thus drawn into the Hussite religious wars, in the course of which the Austrian lands north of the Danube were ravaged. In the Austrian west, Duke Frederick IV of the Tirolean branch lost the Aargau to the Swiss but was able to assert himself in Tirol against a rebellion of his nobles.

When Sigismund died, Albert inherited his positions. In 1438 he was elected Hungarian king, with the German (as Albert II) and the Bohemian crowns to follow later. Albert no doubt had many of the qualities of a born ruler, but he died prematurely in 1439 on an unsuccessful campaign against the Turks. Soon thereafter his widow gave birth to a son and heir, Ladislas Posthumus, to whom Frederick V of Steiermark, as the senior member of the house, became guardian. Frederick also had Sigismund, the son of Frederick IV of Tirol, under his tutelage.

Thus began the long reign of Frederick V (as Holy Roman emperor he was to become Frederick III). His reign was marked by almost ceaseless strife with the estates, with his neighbours, and with his jealous family. When he tried unsuccessfully to take advantage of a conflict between the Swiss Confederates, the Tiroleans made Frederick release Duke Sigismund from tutelage (1446). In 1452, on his return from Rome, where he had been crowned emperor, his enemies at home and abroad forced him also to give up Ladislas, who was then the recognized king (as Ladislas V) of Hungary and Bohemia. The boy king's policies were made by Count Ulrich of Cilli. Ulrich was murdered at Belgrade, Serbia, in 1456, however, and a year later King Ladislas died. In Bohemia and Hungary, national kings came to power. Frederick now won himself a foothold in the Austrian domains on the Danube and succeeded in acquiring the rich estates and fiefs of Ulrich.

BURGUNDIAN AND SPANISH MARRIAGES

Maximilian I, the son of the emperor Frederick III, was married to the Burgundian heiress, Mary, at Ghent in 1477. By that tie to Burgundy, the Habsburgs became involved in long struggles with France. After Mary's death (1482), Maximilian, moreover, met with increasing difficulties in the Burgundian countries themselves. Meanwhile, another crisis had arisen in the eastern Habsburg domains. Disagreement about the Bohemian succession and a political error of Frederick III, who tried to install the former archbishop of Gran (now Esztergom, Hungary) at Salzburg, led Matthias I of Hungary to march against Austria. Vienna was besieged and finally taken by the Hungarians (1485), as was Wiener Neustadt (1487). The harried Maximilian came into even greater distress in the Low Countries, where the rebellious citizens of Brugge put him under arrest (1488). Sigismund, the Habsburg ruler of the Tirol, who was heavily encumbered by debts, planned to sell his country to the Bavarians. A complete breakdown of the house of Habsburg threatened, but Maximilian was ultimately released. He prevailed upon Sigismund to abdicate in his favour. In 1490 the Habsburgs were able to take over Lower Austria. Maximilian even attacked Hungary, but, in the Treaty of Pressburg (1491), he renounced claims to that country, though reserving his family's succession rights.

After the death of his father, Emperor Frederick III, Maximilian came into a heritage that surpassed the endowments of all his predecessors. Furthermore, his son, Philip I (the Handsome), who governed the Low Countries, was betrothed to the Spanish infanta Juana (later called Joan the Mad), and, through the unexpected deaths of male members of the Spanish dynasty, this marriage was to raise the Habsburgs to the throne of Spain. In the German empire as well as in Austria, Maximilian introduced sweeping administrative reforms that were the first steps toward a centralized administration. In 1508 Maximilian assumed the title of elected emperor, as he was unable to pass through hostile Venetian territory to go to Rome for his coronation,

and henceforth Rome and the pope had no more say in the creation of new Holy Roman emperors.

During Maximilian's last years, eastern politics again came to the fore. The great crusade he planned against the Turks, however, never materialized. In 1515 Maximilian arranged a double marriage between his family and the Jagiellon line that ruled Bohemia and Hungary, thus reviving earlier Habsburg claims to these countries. Maximilian's energetic reign added greatly to the prestige of the Habsburgs. Thus, his grandson Charles V was able to prevail against French opposition to inherit the imperial crown. Charles's younger brother, Ferdinand I, took over the rule of the Austrian countries but encountered the opposition of the estates, which he cruelly suppressed. In the agreements of Worms (1521) and Brussels (1522), Charles V formally handed over the Austrian lands to his brother. The subsequent years of Ferdinand's reign were troubled by peasant risings in the Tirol and in Salzburg, which were followed by similar upheavals in Inner Austria.

In the late medieval period, the Alpine lands were assembled by the Habsburgs into a monarchical union roughly comprising the territory of the modern Austrian state. The process of union was at times intercepted and hindered by the partitions among the dynasty. When the process was finished, however, the territories retained their individuality and their own legal codes. During this period the towns developed and prospered, but in the rural settlements a backward tendency had set in. Many settlements were abandoned, especially in Lower Austria. The leading classes lost interest in rural colonization as they found other and more-lucrative sources of income. Mining developed, but trade was impaired by political instability.

Until about 1450 the University of Vienna enjoyed some fame in the fields of theology and science. The literary culture of Austria was characterized by remarkable works, among them the rhyming chronicle of Otakar aus der Geul, the work of the abbot John of Viktring, the poetry of Oswald of Wolkenstein, and the works of the theologian and historian Thomas Ebendorfer. From the middle of the 15th century onward, Austria came under the influence of Italian humanism.

REFORMATION AND COUNTER-REFORMATION

The great 16th-century movement for the ethical and theological reform of the Catholic church, the Reformation, begun in Germany by Martin Luther in 1517, had important consequences in Austria. A number of Protestant sects took root there, and the religious and temporal power struggles between Catholics and Protestants became a leading force in Austria's political fortunes.

ACQUISITION OF BOHEMIA

The year 1526 saw the defeat and death of the Jagiellon king of Hungary and Bohemia, Louis II, who fell in the Battle of Mohács against the Turks. In view of the treaties of 1491 and 1515, Ferdinand I and the Vienna court envisaged Hungary and Bohemia and the adjoining countries falling to the Habsburgs. Thus, the union of Austria, Bohemia, and Hungary became the leading concept of Habsburg politics. After clever diplomatic overtures, Ferdinand was elected king of Bohemia (October 23, 1526). In Hungary, however, there was a split election; John (János Zápolya), voivode (governor) of Transylvania, was chosen by an opposition party, whereupon war broke out between the two candidates.

Ferdinand's troops in Hungary would have been in a stronger position had John not been assisted by the Turks under Süleyman I, sultan of the Ottoman Empire. In 1529 the Turks advanced as far as Vienna, which they besieged in vain. Another Turkish offensive came to a halt at Güns in western Hungary in 1532. Ferdinand, on the other hand, failed in his attempt to take Ofen (Hungarian: Buda), where the Turks had entrenched themselves. By about the middle of the century, the frontiers had become fixed. Hungary happened to be divided into three parts: the west and the north remained with the Habsburgs, the central part came under Turkish rule, and Transylvania and its adjoining territory were kept by John and his successors. This situation was anticipated in the truce of 1547 and became formalized in the Peace of Constantinople (1562).

During a short truce in the fighting against John and the Turks, Ferdinand started to reorganize Austrian administration. In 1527 he created new central organs: the Privy Council (Geheimer Rat), for foreign affairs and dynastic matters; the Court Council (Hofrat), as the supreme legal authority; the Court Chancery (Hofkanzlei), which served as the central office and only later dealt with internal affairs; and the Court Treasury (Hofkammer), for finance and budgeting. As the Court Treasury proved inefficient in the financing of the Turkish war, the Court Council of War (Hofkriegsrat) was established in 1556 to take care of the pay, equipment, and supplies of the troops, acquiring some influence on military operations as well.

ADVANCE OF PROTESTANTISM

The Protestant movement gained ground rapidly in Austria. The nobility in particular turned toward the Lutheran creed. For generations eminent families provided the protagonists of Protestantism in the Lower and Inner Austrian territories. The sons of the nobility were often sent to North German universities to expose them more fully to Protestant influence. From 1521, Protestant pamphlets were produced by Austrian printers. Bans on them, issued from 1523 onward, remained ineffective.

Among the peasant population, the Anabaptists had a stronger appeal than the Lutherans. However, as they had no support from the estates and because of their radicalism, the Anabaptists were persecuted from the start. In 1528 Balthasar Hubmaier, their leader in the Danube countries and in southern Moravia, was burned at the stake in Vienna. In 1536 another Anabaptist, the Tirolean Jakob Hutter, was burned at the stake in Innsbruck after he had led many of his followers into Moravia. Ferdinand, for his part, advocated religious reconciliation and looked for means to achieve it, but the dogmatic viewpoints proved irreconcilable. The Peace of Augsburg (1555) finally brought some respite in the religious struggles.

Charles V abdicated in 1556, and in 1558 Ferdinand I became Holy Roman emperor; thus, the leadership of the empire was taken over by the Austrian (German) line of the Habsburgs. Maximilian II, the eldest son, followed his father in Bohemia, Hungary, and the Austrian Danube territories (1564). The next son, Ferdinand, was endowed with Tirol and the Vorlande; Charles, the youngest of the brothers, received the Inner Austrian lands and took up residence in Graz. Maximilian was known for his Protestant leanings but was bound by a promise he had given his father to remain true to the Roman Catholic religion. The Protestants were therefore granted fewer concessions from him than they might have expected.

Meanwhile, Catholic counteractivity began, with the Jesuits particularly prominent in Vienna, Graz, and Innsbruck. A new generation of energetic bishops proved a great asset to the cause. It was also of some importance that the monasteries, though they had been deserted by many of their members and were struggling for existence, had not been secularized. On the Protestant side, it proved impossible to reconcile the various reforming movements. Social differences between them, especially between the nobility and the peasants, also stood in the way of a united Protestant front. The Counter-Reformation scored its first successes in Gorizia and Carniola, where Protestantism had remained insignificant. And, in other parts, official religious commissions started to replace the Protestant preachers with Catholic clergymen.

RUDOLF II AND MATTHIAS

Maximilian's successor as Holy Roman emperor and as archduke of Austria, his son Rudolf II (reigned 1576–1612), had been educated in Spain strictly in the Catholic faith. He had all Protestants dismissed from court service. The conversion of the cities and market centres of Lower Austria to Catholicism was conducted by Melchior Klesl, at that time administrator of the Vienna see but later to become bishop and cardinal. In Upper Austria, where the Protestants had their strongest hold, the situation remained undecided, with the Catholic governor Hans Jakob Löbl of Greinburg and the Calvinist Georg Erasmus of Tschernembl leading the opposing religious parties. When the future emperor

Ferdinand II (the son of Charles, the ruler of Inner Austria) took over in Steiermark, he proved to be the most resolute advocate of the Counter-Reformation. It was he who eventually succeeded in uprooting Protestantism, first in Inner Austria and then in the other Habsburg countries, with the exception of Hungary and Silesia.

From local skirmishes along the frontier, a long drawn-out war with the Turks developed (1592–1606). In 1598 Raab (now Győr, Hungary), which served as a bastion of Vienna, was temporarily lost; Gran, Veszprém (now in Hungary), and Stuhlweissenburg (now Székesfehérvár, Hungary) passed several times from one side to the other. The introduction of the Counter-Reformation in Hungary, moreover, resulted in a rising of Protestant elements under István Bocskay. But in 1606 at Vienna, a peace was concluded between Austria and the Hungarian estates. At Zsitvatorok another peace was negotiated with the Turks, who for the first time recognized Austria and the emperor as an equal partner.

Political disagreements between Emperor Rudolf, who, to an increasing degree, showed signs of mental derangement, and the rest of the family led to the so-called Habsburg Brothers Conflict. Cardinal Klesl in 1607 brought about an agreement between the younger relatives of the emperor to recognize his brother Matthias as the head of the family. As the conflicts with Rudolf persisted, Matthias strove to come to an understanding with the estates, which were mainly Protestant. The formation of opposing religious leagues in Germany, the Protestant Union and the Catholic League, added to the general confusion.

Matthias advanced into Bohemia, and, in the Treaty of Lieben (1608), Rudolf conceded to him the rule of Hungary, the Austrian Danube countries, and Moravia, while Matthias had to give up the Tirol and the Vorlande to the emperor. In 1609 the estates received a confirmation of the concessions that Maximilian II had made to them. The cities were guaranteed only in general terms that their old privileges should not be interfered with. At the same time, Rudolf II was forced to grant to Bohemia the so-called Letter of Majesty, which contained far-reaching concessions to the Protestants. After a final defeat of Rudolf in Bohemia in 1611, Matthias was crowned king of Bohemia.

Rudolf's death in 1612 finally ended the conflict.

After Matthias had been elected emperor, his principal councillor, Cardinal Klesl, tried in vain to arrange an agreement with the Protestants in Germany. The ensuing years were filled with wars in Transylvania, where Gábor Bethlen came to power. In the Peace of Tyrnau (1615) the emperor had to recognize Bethlen as prince of Transylvania, and, in the same year, he extended the truce with the Turks for another 25 years. In the meantime, war had broken out with Venice (1615–17) because of the pirating activities of Serb refugees (Uskoken) established on the Croatian coast. A settlement was reached in the Peace of Madrid. The situation in Bohemia then reached a critical point, the religious tensions in the country finding a vent in the Defenestration of Prague (May 23, 1618), in which two of the emperor's

MELCHIOR KLESL

The Austrian statesman Melchior Klesl (or Khlesl; born February 19, 1552, Vienna—died September 18, 1630, Vienna), who was bishop of Vienna and later a cardinal, tried to promote religious toleration during the Counter-Reformation in Austria. Converted from Protestantism by the Jesuits, he became an outstanding preacher and served as bishop of Vienna from the 1590s.

Klesl became the most trusted adviser of the Habsburg archduke Matthias, king of Hungary and of Bohemia, and helped to procure his patron's election as Holy Roman emperor (June 13, 1612). He was then appointed director of the privy council and was allowed by Matthias to conduct most of the secular political affairs of the empire. Klesl was made a cardinal secretly in 1615 and publicly the next year. He hoped to reconcile the religious factions within the empire by means of reciprocal concessions. His conciliatory attitude was resented by the German Catholic princes and by the archdukes Maximilian and Ferdinand (afterward emperor as Ferdinand II). When Klesl recommended concessions to the Bohemian Protestants, he was seized by the archdukes in 1618 and imprisoned. In 1627 Ferdinand II allowed Klesl to return as bishop to Vienna and restored most of his fortune.

regents were thrown from the windows of the Hradčany Palace.

THE BOHEMIAN RISING AND THE VICTORY OF THE COUNTER-REFORMATION

War became inevitable when Emperor Matthias died in 1619. Not that he had been master of the situation, but his death brought Ferdinand II, the most uncompromising Counter-Reformer, to the head of the house of Habsburg. Ferdinand was hard-pressed at first, as Bohemian and Moravian troops invaded Austria. A deputation of the estates of Lower Austria tried to make him renounce Bohemia in a peace treaty and demanded religious concessions for themselves, unsuccessfully. The Bohemians were forced to retreat, and imperial troops advanced into their country. The Bohemians deposed Ferdinand from the throne of Bohemia and elected Count Palatine Frederick V in his stead; two days later, however, Ferdinand II was elected Holy Roman emperor at Frankfurt (August 28, 1619).

War was the only means of resolving the issue. The conflict for the Bohemian crown developed into a European war —the so-called Thirty Years' War—when Spain, the Bavarian duke Maximilian I, and the Protestant elector of Saxony entered the struggle on the side of the emperor. The Upper Austrian estates rashly joined Frederick V, with the result that their country was occupied by the army of the Catholic League and afterward pledged to Bavaria. At the Battle of the White Mountain, Ferdinand II became master of Bohemia, Moravia, and Silesia, while Lusatia was pledged to Saxony. King Frederick fled to the Netherlands. The leaders of the Bohemian rising were executed, and other nobles who had compromised themselves lost their property. Many Protestants left the country. In the new constitution of 1627, Bohemia and its associated lands became a hereditary kingdom. The diets were not dissolved entirely, as the government wanted to make use of their administration, but their influence was restricted to financial matters.

After the death of Matthias, Ferdinand had also inherited the Danubian territories. Tirol, however, retained a special status under a new Habsburg *secundogeniture* (inheritance by a second branch of the house). Upper Austria, pledged to Bavaria, was disturbed by a great peasant rising. The Protestant peasants were defeated after heavy fighting, and in 1628 the country passed into the hands of the emperor again.

The Counter-Reformation was vigorously enforced in the Austrian domains. This led to the mass emigration of Protestants, including many members of the nobility. Most went to the Protestant states and to the imperial cities of southern Germany. After the Bohemian victory the war went favourably for the emperor, and the Peace of Lübeck (1629) seemed to secure the hegemony in Germany for the Habsburgs. But in 1629 Ferdinand's attempt in the Edict of Restitution (Restitutionsedikt) to establish religious unity by force throughout the empire provoked the violent opposition of the Protestants.

STRUGGLE WITH SWEDEN AND FRANCE

July 1630 saw intervention in Germany's religious strife from a different quarter —Sweden. In that month the Protestant Swedish king, Gustav II Adolf, landed on the Baltic coast of Pomerania. His purpose was to defend the Protestants against further oppression, to restore the dukes of Mecklenburg, his relatives, who had been driven from their lands by Ferdinand's forces, and perhaps to strengthen Sweden's strategic position in the Baltic. In the ensuing conflict, the German city of Magdeburg was destroyed by fire after it had been taken by the emperor's troops under General Johann Tserclaes, Graf (count) von Tilly (1631). The North German Protestants, who had so far remained undecided, consequently went over to the Swedes. After victories in the Battle of Breitenfeld and on the Lech River, the Swedish troops entered Bavaria.

During the subsequent period of the Thirty Years' War, Ferdinand adopted a rigorous and often unrelenting attitude, though he yielded a little when the Peace of Prague was being negotiated (1635). His successor, Ferdinand III (1637–57), was as loyal to Catholicism as his father had been but showed himself more of a realist. He was not able, however, to prevent the war from again dragging into Habsburg territory, so in 1645 even Vienna was threatened. The extremist party that had rejected all concessions lost its influence at the Vienna court, and two able diplomats, Maximilian, Graf von Trauttmansdorff, and Isaac Volmar, were entrusted with the representation of a weakened Austria at the German cities of Münster and Osnabrück, where extended negotiations were conducted until acceptable terms could be settled for Austria. In the Peace of Westphalia (1648), Austria lost its possessions in Alsace, and Lusatia had to be ceded for good to Saxony.

The peace in many respects marked the beginning of a new epoch. The Holy Roman Empire from then on was reduced to a loose union of otherwise independent states, and Habsburg politics shifted its emphasis, falling back entirely on the political, military, and financial resources of the hereditary Habsburg lands, now including also Bohemia. The new central organs and the administrative bodies of the territories took on much greater importance than the remaining institutions of the Holy Roman Empire. The emperor came to rely on a standing army rather than on troops provided by the German princes.

The heavy drain the religious wars had made on the population of the Austrian territories was compensated for by immigrants from the Catholic parts of the empire and by Croatian refugees from the southeast. The economic position of the peasants on the whole deteriorated. Many members of the nobility, as well as the church, acquired new property. In mining, boom and depression followed quickly upon each other. The loss of many experienced miners during the Counter-Reformation resulted in difficulties, but the government took several steps toward improving and extending the salt mines. In 1625 it founded the Innerberg Union, under which Steiermark's iron industry was reorganized. The emperor also tried to interfere with the trade organizations of the towns, though without much success. Trade and finance in the Austrian territories were dominated by foreign capital.

The cultural life of the period was also dominated by the religious struggle. In the field of education the schools of the denominational parties rivaled each other. In 1585 a Jesuit university was founded at Graz, while at Salzburg a Benedictine university was established (1623). Austrian humanists produced some outstanding works of poetry and historical writings, and the sovereigns were great patrons of the arts, but on the whole this was an epoch dominated by Italian and Western influences.

AUSTRIA AS A GREAT POWER

After the Thirty Years' War, Austrian rulers were understandably reluctant to enter into another military conflict. In 1654 Ferdinand IV, the eldest son of the emperor, died. His brother, the future emperor Leopold I, who had been destined for a church career, was then considered as heir to the throne and was recognized as such by Austria, Bohemia, and Hungary. In Germany, however, difficulties arose when France declared itself against Leopold. Nevertheless, following the death of Emperor Ferdinand, Leopold was finally elected (1658) after having conceded constitutional limitations that restricted his liberty of action in foreign politics. West German princes under Johann Philipp von Schönborn, archbishop of Mainz, formed the French-oriented League of the Rhine. At the same time, Austria was engaged in the northeast when it intervened in the war between Sweden and Poland (1658) in order to prevent the collapse of Poland. There were some military successes, but the Treaty of Oliva (1660) brought no territorial gains for Austria, though it stopped the advance of the Swedes in Germany.

During the Thirty Years' War the Turkish front had been quiet, but in the 1660s a new war broke out with the Turks (1663–64) because of a conflict over Transylvania, where a successor had to be appointed for György II Rákóczi, who had been killed fighting against the Turks. The Turks conquered the fortress of Neuhäusel in Slovakia, but the imperial troops succeeded in throwing them back. The Austrian military success was not, however, reflected in the terms of the Treaty of Vasvár: Transylvania was given to Mihály Apafi, a ruler of pro-Turkish sympathies. A minor territorial concession was also made to the Turks. The year after the Turkish peace, Tirol and the Vorlande reverted to Leopold I (1665), and the second period of the Habsburg partition (1564–1665) came to an end.

In Hungary dissatisfaction with the results of the Turkish war spread. Not only the Protestants, who were threatened by the Counter-Reformation, but also many Catholic nobles were alarmed by Habsburg absolutism. A group of Hungarian nobles and Steiermark's Count Hans Erasmus of Tattenbach entered into a conspiracy. The Austrian government, informed of their activities, had four of the ringleaders executed—an action that led to a rising by rebels known as Kuruzen (Crusaders).

In the meantime, the position of the Habsburgs in the west had again deteriorated. At first, Leopold I's leading statesmen, Johann Weikhart, Fürst (prince) von Auersperg (dismissed in 1669), and the president of the Court Council of War, Wenzel Eusebius, Fürst von Lobkowitz, remained rather passive in view of the expansionist policies of Louis XIV of France. They also stayed outside the Triple Alliance of Holland, England, and Sweden that was concluded in order to ward off the attacks of Louis against the Spanish Netherlands. When Louis actually invaded Holland, the emperor finally entered the war, but, in the ensuing Treaties of Nijmegen (1679), he had to cede Freiburg im Breisgau to France.

Another and still more menacing danger appeared in the southeast. After some deliberation the leader of the Hungarian rebels, Imre Thököli, had asked the Turks for help, whereupon the grand vizier Kara Mustafa Pasa organized a large Turkish army and marched it toward Vienna. Habsburg diplomats succeeded in concluding an alliance between Austria and Poland. Meanwhile, imperial troops under Charles IV (or V) Leopold, duke of Lorraine and Bar, tried to hold back the Turks but had to retreat. From July 17 to September 12, 1683, Vienna was besieged by the Turks. Deciding against a direct assault, the Turks had begun to drill tunnels underneath the bastions of the city when relief columns arrived from Bavaria, Saxony, Franconia, and Poland. King John III Sobieski of Poland took over the command of the relieving army, which descended upon the Turks and dispersed them. The emperor concluded a pact with Poland and the Venetian republic known as the Holy League. In 1685 Neuhäusel was won back, and in September 1686 Ofen (Buda) was captured despite fierce Turkish resistance.

In 1687 the Hungarian diet recognized the hereditary rights of the male line of the Habsburgs to the Hungarian throne. In 1688 Belgrade, Serbia, was conquered, and Transylvania was secured by imperial troops. Meanwhile, Louis XIV had begun an offensive against the German Palatinate that grew into the War of the Grand Alliance. This war meant that no further troops could be spared for the Turkish war, and in 1690 all recent conquests in the south, including Belgrade, were lost again. A victory of the imperial and the allied German troops under Margrave Louis William I of Baden-Baden near Slankamen, Serbia, (1691) prevented the Turks from advancing farther, but then the margrave was ordered to the Rhine front. Eventually Prince Eugene of Savoy took over the command and gained a decisive victory over the Turks in the Battle of Zenta (1697). After another offensive against Bosnia, the Turks finally decided to negotiate a peace. In the Treaty of Carlowitz (1699) Hungary, Transylvania, and large parts of Slavonia (now in Croatia) fell to the Habsburg emperor. Meanwhile, the war in the west, overshadowed already by the question of the Spanish succession, had come to an end with the Treaty of Rijswijk (1697).

WAR OF THE SPANISH SUCCESSION

From 1701 to 1714 Austria was involved in hostilities with France—the War of

The Battle of Blenheim in 1704 proved to be a significant victory for Austria during the War of the Spanish Succession. The English and Austrian army saved Vienna from Franco-Bavarian forces and served France their first major defeat in over 50 years. Universal Images Group/Getty Images

the Spanish Succession—over the heir to the Spanish throne. The childless king Charles II of Spain, a Habsburg, had willed all his possessions to a Bourbon prince —a grandson of Louis XIV of France. All those who disliked the idea of a French hegemony in Europe consequently united against the French. The emperor declared war (1701) and was immediately supported by Brandenburg-Prussia and Hanover. In the spring of 1702, England and Holland entered the war in the Grand Alliance against France. Louis XIV was able to win the electoral princes of Bavaria and Cologne as his allies. At this critical juncture another Hungarian rising, led by Ferenc II Rákóczi, occurred. The rebels were prepared to join forces with the enemies of Austria and for years engaged Austrian troops. The rebels even threatened Vienna, whose suburbs had to be fortified. In the war with France, imperial troops fought on four fronts: in Italy, on the Rhine, in the Spanish Netherlands, and in Spain. Much larger forces were mobilized than had been customary during the 17th century, and the financial drain on the imperial treasury was so heavy that the emperor had to resort to Dutch and English loans. When Bavaria entered the war on the side of the French, Austria was in further danger, until the Battle of Blenheim (1704), in which an English and Austrian army under the duke of Marlborough and Prince Eugene of Savoy defeated the French and Bavarian forces.

After a reign of 48 years filled with almost endless troubles, Emperor Leopold died in 1705. He was succeeded by his son, Joseph I (reigned 1705–11). In the religious quarrels the new emperor, an ally of Protestant states, showed great restraint and allowed himself to be guided mainly by political motives.

In 1703 Victor Amadeus II, duke of Savoy, who had left the French to go over to the Habsburgs, found himself in a critical situation; his capital, Turin, had come under French siege. An imperial army under Prince Eugene and reinforced by a Prussian contingent was sent to his aid and succeeded in uniting with the Savoyan forces and relieving Turin after a victorious battle (1706). At the beginning of the next year, an agreement was reached under which the French evacuated northern Italy. The same year, a smaller imperial army under Wirich, Graf (count) von Daun, conquered Spanish-ruled southern Italy, but an invasion of southern France, which the sea powers had instigated, failed. A quick success, however, fell to the Austrians in a campaign against the Vatican state over a conflict between the emperor and the Roman Curia concerning mutual feudal rights and caused by Pope Clement XI's rather pro-French leanings.

The allies were victorious in the Netherlands, winning the Battle of Oudenaarde and conquering Lille (1708). Paris seemed within easy reach. The Battle of Malplaquet (1709) was another victory for the allies, but they had to pay dearly for it. In the meantime, peace negotiations had foundered. After reverses in Spain and a political change in England, the alliance itself was in danger of falling apart. The situation was further aggravated by the death in 1711 of Emperor Joseph I, who left only daughters.

At this juncture, liquidation of the Hungarian rising became possible. Rákóczi, who in 1707 had declared the deposition of the Habsburgs, began to meet with growing opposition among his followers. Imperial troops forced Rákóczi to flee to Poland, and the rebels, who had been promised an amnesty and who were guaranteed religious liberty, made their peace in 1711. From then on the Vienna government tried to be more considerate of Hungary and its aristocracy.

The election of Charles VI as emperor was effected without any difficulties. The English left the coalition, and after a military reverse most of the Habsburgs' allies joined the treaties of Utrecht (1713–14). In the peace negotiations between Austria and France that were begun at Rastatt, Germany, Prince Eugene showed himself an unyielding and successful agent of Habsburg interests. Austria gained the Spanish Netherlands (henceforth known as the Austrian Netherlands), a territory corresponding approximately to modern Belgium and Luxembourg. These gains were somewhat impaired, however, by the Dutch privilege of stationing garrisons in a number of fortresses. In Italy, Austria received Milan, Mantua, Mirandola, the continental part of the Kingdom of Naples, and the isle of Sardinia. The Wittelsbachs of Bavaria regained their country, but the treaty contained an appendix that provided for the eventuality of Bavaria's being exchanged for the Netherlands. Of its gains, the northern Italian territories were of the greatest value to Austria; the possession of Naples and the Netherlands, on the other hand, posed considerable military and political risks.

PROBLEM OF THE AUSTRIAN SUCCESSION

The extinction of the Spanish line of the Habsburgs and the fact that the emperor Charles VI was the last male member of that house posed serious problems for the Habsburg territories, which, at the beginning of the 18th century, were held together mainly by the person of the sovereign, notwithstanding the fact that there were some institutions of central administration. A settlement was made in the form of a family ordinance. On April 19, 1713, Charles VI issued a decree, according to which the Habsburg lands should remain an integral, undivided whole. In the event of the Habsburgs' becoming extinct in the male line, the daughters of Charles or their descendants or, in default of any descendants of Charles, the daughters of Joseph I and their descendants and, after them, all other female members of the house, should be eligible for the succession. As the son that was born to the emperor in 1716 died after a few months and only daughters were born to him after that (Maria Theresa, 1717; Maria Anna, 1718; Maria Amalia, 1724), this Pragmatic Sanction (a term used to characterize a pronouncement by a sovereign on a matter of prime importance) became of great significance. Austrian diplomacy in the last decades of Charles's reign was directed toward securing acceptance of the

PRAGMATIC SANCTION OF EMPEROR CHARLES VI

On April 19, 1713, the Holy Roman emperor Charles VI promulgated a decree known as a Pragmatic Sanction that was intended to ensure that all his Habsburg kingdoms and lands descended as an integral whole without partition. It stipulated that his undivided heritage go to his eldest son, should he have one, or, failing a son, to his eldest daughter and then, if she should die without issue, to his deceased brother Joseph I's daughters and their descendants. A son was born to Charles in 1716 but died in the same year, and Charles's subsequent children were both daughters (Maria Theresa, born in 1717, and Maria Anna, born in 1718). Accordingly, in 1720, the Pragmatic Sanction was published, embodying Charles's decision of 1713. On its publication the decree received the assent of the individual estates of the Habsburg dominions, so that it came to be a constitutional law of the developing Habsburg monarchy and a bond between the lands belonging to the Holy Roman Empire (the Austrian and Bohemian lands) and the lands outside the empire (those under the crown of Hungary).

Austrian diplomacy in the last decades of Charles's reign was directed toward securing acceptance of the Pragmatic Sanction from all the European powers. Joseph I's daughters and their husbands (the electors of Saxony and Bavaria), the Diet of the Empire, Russia, Spain, Great Britain, France, Prussia, the Netherlands, Denmark, and Sardinia did in fact recognize the Pragmatic Sanction.

On the death of Charles VI in October 1740, however, the Pragmatic Sanction was promptly contested by two of the powers that had guaranteed it: Charles Albert of Bavaria and Frederick the Great of Prussia. The resultant War of the Austrian Succession cost the Habsburgs most of Silesia, part of the Duchy of Milan, and the duchies of Parma and Piacenza (Treaty of Aix-la-Chapelle, 1748). On the other hand, Maria Theresa was left in possession of the rest of the Habsburg inheritance, and her husband, Francis Stephen of Lorraine, was recognized as Holy Roman emperor, with the style of Francis I.

Pragmatic Sanction from all the European powers. It was published in 1720 and by 1722 had been recognized by the estates of all the Habsburg countries. Even the unanimous consent of the Hungarian diet was eventually obtained.

NEW CONFLICTS WITH THE TURKS AND THE BOURBONS

During the War of the Spanish Succession, the Ottoman Empire had remained neutral toward Austria. But the Turks had attacked the possessions of the Venetians on the Peloponnese and on the Ionian Islands. Austria tried to intervene and finally declared war. Prince Eugene defeated the Turks near the fortress of Peterwardein (Petrovaradin, now part of Novi Sad, Serbia) and conquered the strong bastion of Temesvár (now Timișoara, Romania) in 1716. In the summer campaign of 1717, Belgrade again came into the hands of the imperial troops after a battle was won against a Turkish relief army. In the Treaty of Passarowitz (1718), a frontier line was agreed upon that corresponded to the de facto situation. The Turks had to cede to the Austrians the Banat region, the Turkish part of Syrmia (Srem, now part of Vojvodina, Serbia), Walachia Minor as far as the Olt (Aluta) River, northern Serbia, Belgrade, and a strip of land along the frontier in northern Bosnia. A favourable trade agreement was also concluded.

During the Turkish war another crisis emerged. The Spanish minister Giulio Alberoni tried to initiate a policy of expansion in Italy. When Spanish troops landed in Sardinia and Sicily, the emperor formed an alliance with Great Britain and France, later joined by the Dutch Republic (the Quadruple Alliance). After the English defeated the Spanish fleet, Madrid recalled its troops from the disputed territories. Austria received the more prosperous Sicily in exchange for Sardinia, which fell to Savoy. Charles then agreed to recognize the Spanish Bourbons. The gains from the Quadruple Alliance plus those of the Treaty of Passarowitz gave the Habsburgs the largest territory they were ever to rule. Their domains were far from unified, however, with the individual provinces showing a wide national, economic, cultural, and constitutional diversity.

Trading interests soon interfered with the empire's alliance with the maritime powers of Britain and the Dutch Republic. At first the attempts of the Ostend Company, which was backed by Charles VI, to enter into trade with India were quite successful. Because of the antipathy of the maritime powers, however, it seemed advisable to find an alternative to trade with Dutch and British colonial markets in the vast transatlantic empire of Spain. In 1725 Charles entered into an alliance with Spain, whereupon France, Great Britain, and Prussia formed a rival alliance. But soon after Russia was won over to the Habsburg cause, Prussia changed sides. As the outbreak of a European war seemed imminent, attempts were made at the Congress of Soissons to relax political tensions. Spain abruptly changed its alliances and concluded a treaty (1729) with England and France, the Dutch Republic joining later. When Russia also began to waver, Prince Eugene tried to fall back on the traditional alliance with the maritime powers. After prolonged and difficult negotiations, Britain in 1731 accepted the Pragmatic Sanction, the emperor in return giving a promise not to marry his daughter Maria Theresa, the Habsburg heiress, to a prince who was himself heir to important domains. Austria finally dissolved the Ostend Company, having already suspended its charter in 1727. Charles VI then invested a great deal of energy in his endeavours to secure the recognition and the guarantee of the Pragmatic Sanction in the German diet. In this he was opposed by Bavaria and the elector of Saxony, but Austria finally obtained the guarantee of the Pragmatic Sanction at the Regensburg Diet (1732).

The question of the Polish succession led to a revival of the Austrian conflict with the Bourbon countries. Austria, with Prussia and Russia, favoured Augustus III of Saxony, the son of the deceased king, whereas France backed Stanisław I (Stanisław Leszczyński). On the military intervention of Russia in Poland, the Bourbons attacked Austria. The issue came to be mixed up with the problem of Lorraine; France dreaded that, on the impending marriage of Maria Theresa to Francis Stephen, duke of Lorraine, the latter's domains would be united with Austria's, and French plans for the acquisition of Lorraine would be thwarted. France, Sardinia, and Spain simultaneously opened the war against Austria in 1733. Prince Eugene, who was now aged, was able only to prevent a major success of the enemy on the Rhine. On the Italian front the Habsburgs fared even worse. The Battle of Parma ended undecided, but the Austrians were finally beaten near Guastalla in northern Italy. The small Austrian force that was stationed in southern Italy was unable to resist the Spanish attack, and Sicily and Naples were occupied by the Spaniards. In 1735 a Russian relieving corps reinforced the Habsburg front on the Rhine, and in northern Italy there were also a few successful operations of some local importance.

Direct contacts between Austria and France eventually led to the preliminary Peace of Vienna (October 3, 1735). Austria lost Naples and Sicily, which fell to a secondary branch of the Bourbons, and had to cede a tract of territory in Lombardy to Sardinia. As some compensation, Austria received Parma and Piacenza. Francis Stephen of Lorraine was promised Tuscany but had to renounce his hereditary duchy. On these conditions, France agreed to recognize the Pragmatic Sanction. The final peace was then concluded at Vienna in 1738.

Prince Eugene had died during the War of the Polish Succession. It soon proved disastrous that a successor of similar capacity was not found. During the second Turkish war of Charles VI (1737–39), Austria joined in the Turkish-Russian conflict but without coordination of military operations. The Austrians, furthermore, underrated the Turkish forces and were themselves reduced by epidemics. The fortress of Niš, Serbia, was taken but was lost again soon afterward. Peace negotiations conducted at Nemirov, Ukraine, were broken off, and the war went on. The Austrians lost another battle at Grocka, Serbia. Again peace negotiations were launched, in the course of which the larger part of the gains of the Peace of Passarowitz were lost. More disquieting even than the territorial losses was the loss in prestige. The epoch that had seen the rise of Austria to a great power thus ended with reverses.

SOCIAL, ECONOMIC, AND CULTURAL TRENDS IN THE BAROQUE PERIOD

The Thirty Years' War and the Turkish wars had resulted in the devastation of large parts of the country and in great losses among the population, which suffered further reduction during the plague years of 1679 and 1713. The territories that had been wrested from the Turks had to be resettled systematically by German and other immigrants. The initiative for resettlement projects came from the official bureaucracy, the settlements being concentrated mainly in the south of Hungary. During the period of religious conflicts, many Protestants had been exiled, but, in the 18th century, Protestants often were transported to the various underpopulated parts of the empire.

In the industrial and commercial fields, mercantilist ideas, encouraged by the government, were prominent from the 1660s. The situation of the peasantry was thoroughly unfavourable. Tentative measures in the reigns of Leopold I and Charles VI to protect the peasants had little effect. Certain "model industries" (mostly textile factories) were established but were only partly successful. The economic policy of the absolutist state also resulted in strong interference with trade organizations. The guilds were suppressed or at least debarred from the new manufactures.

Trade was encouraged but yielded only small gains for the state. Industrial and commercial undertakings were managed in part directly by the state but largely through privileged corporations or private persons. Of some importance were the first (1667) and the second (1719) Oriental trading companies and the Ostend Company (1722). Trade in the Mediterranean was also intensified. Promising colonial ventures in India were discontinued for political reasons, however, in the middle of the 18th century. Under Charles VI new roads came to be planned and built on a large scale.

The state was in permanent want of money. This was a period of perpetual war as well as great economic investments, both entailing excessive strain on state finances. At first the government resorted to rich bankers such as Samuel Oppenheimer and his successor Samson Wertheimer for funds. Soon, however, it attempted to establish state-controlled banking firms. The Banco del Giro, founded in Vienna in 1703, quickly failed, but the Vienna Stadtbanco of 1705 managed to survive; the Universalbancalität of 1715 was liquidated after a short period of operation.

After the victory of the Counter-Reformation, education was almost exclusively in the hands of the Roman Catholic Church. The grammar schools of the religious orders, especially of the Jesuits and the Benedictines, set a very high standard for the most part. In 1677 another university was established at Innsbruck, the theological school of which was to acquire some fame. Historical writing flourished, the most outstanding works being those of two Benedictine brothers, Bernard and Hieronymus Pez; Gottfried Bessel, abbot of Göttweig; and Leopold I's official historiographer, the Jesuit Franz Wagner. The Austrian Jesuits were famous for their scientific and geographic

GEORG RAPHAEL DONNER

The work of the Austrian sculptor Georg Raphael Donner (born May 24, 1693, Esslingen, Austria —died February 15, 1741, Vienna) marked the transition from the Baroque to the Neoclassical style. While studying for the priesthood in Heiligenkreutz, Donner met the sculptor Giovanni Giuliani and was encouraged to take up sculpture, working in Giuliani's studio and later entering the Vienna Academy. He lived in Salzburg for some years, later returning to Vienna, where he produced his masterpiece, the *Providence Fountain* (1738–39) on the Neuer Markt. The figures originally cast in lead, a technique favoured by the artist, were replaced in 1873 by copies in bronze. Other Donner works are the *Perseus and Andromeda Fountain* in the courtyard of the Vienna Rathaus and a statue of Emperor Charles VI in the Belvedere Castle, Vienna. The refined form and clear outline of his sculpture contrasted with the exaggerated Baroque style of his contemporaries and predecessors and helped bring about a change in sculptural style.

researches, most notably the exploration of China.

Among the achievements of Baroque poetry, mention should be made of Wolf Helmhart of Hohberg, whose works offer interesting insights into the life of the nobility, and of Katharina of Greiffenberg. The theatre of the Baroque was remarkable for the splendour of its decorations and the ingenuity of its stage machinery. The plays produced ranged from the elaborate Italian opera to the blunt humour of the popular play. Music attained an especially high standard, encouraged by three emperors who were themselves composers (Ferdinand III, Leopold I, and Joseph I). Charles VI was also a skillful musician, and he engaged the services of Johann Joseph Fux, who came from eastern Steiermark and developed into an important composer and teacher.

Austrian Baroque culture is most clearly revealed by the splendours of its architecture. At first the field was dominated by the Italians, but soon native architects stepped forth. Preeminent among them was Johann Bernhard Fischer von Erlach (whose works included the first plan of the Schloss Schönbrunn in Vienna, Karls Church in Vienna, and Kollegien Church in Salzburg) and his son Josef Emanuel Fischer von Erlach (who designed the Hof Library, in Vienna). They were rivaled by Jakob Prandtauer (whose works included monasteries in Herzogenburg and Melk) and especially by Johann Lucas von Hildebrandt (who designed the Schwarzenberg and Belvedere palaces in Vienna, Peters Church in Vienna, and the monastery of Göttweig). Among native sculptors, Georg Raphael Donner was the first in rank and quality of work. Fresco painting was best represented by Johann Michael Rottmayr from Salzburg, Daniel Gran from Vienna, and Paul Troger from the Tirolean Pustertal valley.

CHAPTER 6

FROM THE AUSTRIAN SUCCESSION TO THE SEVEN WEEKS' WAR

In October 1740 the Holy Roman emperor Charles VI, the last male Habsburg ruler, died and was succeeded by his daughter Maria Theresa, the young wife of the grand duke of Tuscany, Francis Stephen of Lorraine. Although no woman had ever served as Habsburg ruler, most assumed at the time that the succession would pose few problems because of Charles VI's diligent efforts to gain recognition for her. He had established a reasonably unified order of succession for all the lands under Habsburg rule (the Pragmatic Sanction) and, by making broad concessions to foreign powers and to the diets of the crown lands, had secured recognition of this act from most of the important constitutional units inside and outside the Habsburg lands. When he died, he had no reason to expect anything less than a smooth transition for his daughter.

FROM THE ACCESSION OF MARIA THERESA TO THE CONGRESS OF VIENNA

The challenge to that transition came from a surprising source—the kingdom of Prussia. For the previous 40 years, Prussia had been a fairly loyal supporter of the Habsburgs, especially in matters related to the Holy Roman Empire and in matters involving Poland.

WAR OF THE AUSTRIAN SUCCESSION

The Prussian king Frederick William I (reigned 1713–40) had created perhaps the most proficient, if not the largest, army in

Maria Theresa. DEA/ A. Dagli Orti/De Agostini/Getty Images

Europe but had displayed no eagerness to use it except in the service of the empire, and then only reluctantly. But Frederick William had died about five months before Charles VI, and his son and heir, Frederick II (later called the Great), had no reluctance to use his father's finely honed armed force. In December 1740 Frederick II invaded the Habsburg province of Silesia and thereby threatened not only to conquer the wealthiest of the Habsburg lands but also to challenge Maria Theresa's right to rule the rest of them, a challenge soon joined by other powers.

As Maria Theresa prepared to meet these threats, she found that the resources left by her father were meagre indeed. The War of the Polish Succession and the war against the Turks from 1737 to 1739 had drained the monarchy's financial and military resources and spread irresolution and doubt among its senior officials. The army sent forth to meet Frederick suffered defeat in the Battle of Mollwitz in April 1741. This defeat prompted the formation of an alliance of France, Bavaria, and Spain, joined later by Saxony and eventually by Prussia itself, to dismember the Habsburg monarchy. Faced by this serious threat, Maria Theresa called together her father's experienced advisers and asked them what she should do. Most argued that resistance was hopeless and recommended that she make the necessary sacrifices in order to reach as quick an accommodation with her enemies as possible, a policy endorsed by her husband. This counsel offended Maria Theresa, who regarded it as defeatism; commenting on this period later, she described it

as finding herself "without money, without credit, without an army, without experience, and finally without advice."

Maria Theresa had no intention of surrendering. She resolved to drive off her enemies and then to create a government that would never again suffer the humiliation she experienced at her accession. To begin, she reached a settlement with Frederick, ceding to him Silesia by the treaties of Breslau and Berlin in June and July 1742. She did so only to focus resistance on the French and Bavarians, who in late November 1741 had occupied Upper Austria and Bohemia, including the Bohemian capital, Prague. In the wake of these conquests by anti-Habsburg forces, in January 1742 the electors of the Holy Roman Empire rejected the candidacy of Maria Theresa's husband and chose as emperor Charles Albert of Bavaria (called Charles VII as emperor), the only non-Habsburg to serve in that capacity from 1438 to the empire's demise in 1806. Perhaps as a portent of his unhappy reign as emperor, on the day of Charles Albert's coronation in Frankfurt, Habsburg forces occupied his Bavarian capital of Munich, which they held until shortly before his death three years later.

The War of the Austrian Succession, as this conflict is called, continued until 1748. It rather quickly became a struggle of two alliance systems, with primarily France, Bavaria, Spain, and Prussia on one side and Austria, Great Britain, and the Dutch Republic on the other. Saxony and Sardinia began the war as members of the first alliance and later switched to the second. Russia joined Austria in a defensive accord in 1746, primarily to prevent Prussia from reentering the war after it had concluded the Treaty of Dresden with Austria in 1745.

The Treaty of Dresden and the Treaty of Aix-la-Chapelle in 1748 brought the various parts of the war to an end. Austria had to return some minor principalities in Italy to the Spanish Bourbons until such time as the Bourbon lines there became extinct and had to agree to a small frontier rectification in favour of Piedmont-Sardinia, but neither of these adjustments was of great consequence. For Austria the most serious loss was Silesia, which Maria Theresa found necessary to cede to Prussia first in 1742 and again in 1745. Losing Silesia opened the way to the rise of Prussia as the most serious rival of the Habsburgs in Germany. It also meant a considerable decrease in the proportion of Germans living within Habsburg lands, with important consequences in the rise of the national problem in the following century. Although as part of the cession Frederick II agreed to recognize the election of Francis Stephen of Lorraine as Holy Roman emperor Francis I in 1745, Maria Theresa never forgave his "rape" of Silesia; at the war's conclusion she immediately undertook preparations first to deter Frederick from coveting more of her lands and then to take Silesia back.

Perhaps the most important result of the war for Austria, however, was the very fact that the monarchy was not dismembered. Nor did it become a satellite state under the tutelage of other great powers. The outcome of the War of the Austrian Succession, except for the loss of Silesia, was a genuine defensive victory that proved to the world that Austria represented more than an agglomeration of lands under the same rule, acquired by wars and marriage contracts. In the two centuries since Ferdinand I had become king in Bohemia, Hungary, and Croatia, as well as regent in the so-called hereditary lands, a certain cohesion between the major historical units had been clearly established.

FIRST REFORMS, 1748–56

Maria Theresa determined from the outset of her reign that the Habsburg monarchy would never again be perceived as too weak to defend itself. Consequently, even while the war was under way she had been studying reforms, and when it ended she immediately began implementing them. First and foremost was reform of the army. Maria Theresa proposed establishing an effective standing army of 110,000 men—60,000 more than in her father's day and 30,000 more than the Prussian peacetime army of Frederick William I. She also tried to encourage her nobility to take a greater interest in serving in the officer corps, creating a school for officers called the Theresianum at Wiener Neustadt and introducing military orders as rewards for good service.

Maria Theresa realized, however, that no military reform would be effective without financial reform, and in this area she achieved her greatest accomplishments.

Before Maria Theresa came to the throne, Habsburg finances were to a great extent based on the contributions offered by each of the monarchy's crown lands, or provinces. The crown lands were governed by estates sitting in diets (parliamentary bodies made up of representatives of the nobility, the church, and the towns). These bodies negotiated annually with the ruler regarding the amount of taxes (i.e., the contribution) that each crown land would pay to the central government. Following the advice of Friedrich Wilhelm, Graf (count) von Haugwitz, a Silesian who had fled the Prussians in 1741, Maria Theresa proposed negotiating with each diet only every 10 years, setting the amount to be collected annually for an entire decade. The estates were generally not happy with the proposal, but she made certain that each agreed to it in one form or another. The results were a steady income upon which reliable budgets could be based and an erosion in the power of the diets—which, although never abolished, lost much of the influence they had held in the past.

Following the military and financial reforms came other changes, generally in administrative matters. Although these reforms were subjected to many modifications and changes throughout Maria Theresa's reign and after, the result was a government far more centralized than it had ever been before.

SEVEN YEARS' WAR

While Maria Theresa and her advisers focused on internal reform, her new state chancellor, Wenzel Anton, Graf (count) von Kaunitz (subsequently Fürst [prince] von Kaunitz-Rietberg and Maria Theresa's most important adviser until her death in 1780), laid the diplomatic preparations for the reconquest of Silesia. The result in 1756 was the "reversal of alliances," a treaty system intended to isolate Prussia. With the two sets of irreconcilable enemies being France and Great Britain on the one hand and Prussia and Austria on the other, the reversal refers to Austria's abandoning Great Britain as an ally in favour of France and Prussia's abandoning France as an ally in favour of Great Britain. However, it may be argued that the switch was made possible by Empress Elizabeth of Russia's determination to do in Frederick II and Frederick's seeking out Great Britain to intercept a Russo-British accord. In any case, when war erupted in 1756, Austria, France, and Russia seemed to have formed an alliance that Prussia, with only Britain as a friend, could never resist.

The ensuing conflict was the Seven Years' War, the great war of the mid-18th century. Undoubtedly, its most important result occurred not on the European Continent but in Europe's colonial empires, where British forces decisively defeated the French, paving the way for British control of Canada and the eventual domination of India. On the Continent, Austria, France, and Russia could never bring their united strength to bear effectively on Prussia. Prussia fended off all its enemies by exploiting its economic and human resources about as well as any 18th-century power could, by taking advantage of internal lines, and by virtue of Frederick II's military genius. But it did so at considerable cost. In October 1760 a Russian force reached Berlin, and by 1761 Frederick himself was so discouraged that he was contemplating abdication as the only way to salvage his beleaguered state.

Although it was not obvious at the time, for all intents and purposes the war ended with the death of Empress Elizabeth in January 1762. Her successor, Peter III, worshipped Frederick II and was determined not only to end Russia's war against Prussia but also to join Prussia in fighting against Austria and France. Before he could implement such a radical change in policy, however, he was deposed by conspirators supporting his wife, Catherine II (later called the Great), and their policy was simply to end the war. With Russia out of the conflict and France defeated throughout the world, Maria Theresa and her advisers could see no alternative but to negotiate a settlement with Prussia based on the status quo ante (Treaty of Hubertusburg, 1763), meaning that once again Prussia retained Silesia.

REFORMS, 1763–80

Maria Theresa's second period of reform was more important than the first, because it carried with it elements of centralization and change that were portents of the kind of government, society, and economy that would emerge in the 19th century and mature in the 20th. As modern as some of these elements were, the government that introduced them was not thinking of long-range goals but was dealing with immediate problems, the most important being recovery from the Seven Years' War. The area requiring urgent attention was finance. The cost of the Seven Years' War had added so much debt to the treasury that, for the remainder of Maria Theresa's reign, servicing that debt while providing for the costs of defense and governmental operations became the obsession of many of her advisers.

Financial need led Maria Theresa and her statesmen into other fields. All realized that financial recovery to a great extent depended on an improved economy, and they introduced a number of measures to make it better. Foreign workers and artisans with skills in the manufacture of various articles were recruited from the Low Countries, the Italian lands, and Germany and settled throughout the monarchy. Farmers came from western Europe for settlement in some of the more remote lands of the monarchy that had been badly depopulated, mainly in southern and eastern Hungary. Some important sectors of the economy, such as textiles and iron making, were freed from guild restrictions. And in 1775 the government created a customs union out of most of the crown lands of the monarchy, excluding some of the peripheral lands and the kingdom of Hungary, which was not joined to Austria in a customs union until 1851.

The basically mercantilist policy of Charles VI's reign and earlier was revised in line with the influence of physiocratic and so-called populationist theories. Thenceforward human labour, and not precious metal, was gradually to become the yardstick of national wealth. This led, on the one hand, to restrictions on emigration and, on the other, to an easing of some imports that were not considered competitive with domestic industries.

Financial and economic reforms also had an impact upon society. Maria Theresa's government was fully aware that most taxes came from society's lower elements, and so it was eager to make certain that those lower elements had the wherewithal to bear their burden. In 1767 she imposed a law on Hungary regulating the rights and duties of the serfs and their lords with the intent of bettering the condition of the peasants, which was not good at all. This law suffered somewhat because the lords themselves were responsible for implementing it, but it was later codified into the Hungarian statutes in 1790–91 and remained the basic law regarding the status of the serfs until their final emancipation in 1848. In response to a serf revolt in 1774 protesting not only oppression but also hunger, Maria Theresa issued a law in Bohemia in 1775 that restricted the aristocratic practice of exploiting the work obligations of the peasantry. She also had plans drawn up to change the dues of the peasantry from various forms of service to a strictly rent-paying system. Such a system was introduced on lands owned by the crown, but she did not enforce its extension to privately held lands.

Maria Theresa also introduced a system of public education. The motivation for this reform came from concern both that the Roman Catholic Church in Austria was no longer maintaining public morality properly and that certain changes in the 18th-century economy required that Austria provide a better-educated work force. It is often assumed that the great mass of the people in Austria at this time were serfs working on the lords' lands, owing various work and money dues, and thus—while suffering oppression—at least forming a fairly stable society. In fact, by the late 18th century the vast majority of the rural population was made up of cottars, gardeners, and lodgers who owed minimal feudal duties and who depended on nonagricultural occupations for their survival. These people represented a proto-industrial work force, but they also represented an ignorant and potentially ill-disciplined rural population. Compulsory education was a method of instilling a good work ethic and a sense of morality in them. In 1774 Maria Theresa issued the General School Regulation for the Austrian lands, establishing a system of elementary schools, secondary schools, and normal schools to train teachers. The implementation of this regulation was difficult owing to a lack of teachers, resistance on the part of lords and peasants alike, and a shortage of funds. Despite these obstacles, however, 500 such schools had opened by 1780.

FOREIGN AFFAIRS, 1763–80

The great change in Maria Theresa's foreign policy after 1763 was her reconciliation to the loss of Silesia. Although as a result Maria Theresa and her advisers focused their attention for the most part on domestic affairs, a few foreign matters offered the monarchy opportunities for territorial gain and in two cases carried the threat of renewed warfare. In 1768 the old matter of the fate of the Ottoman Empire appeared again, this time in the form of a Russo-Turkish war and the possibility that Russia would not simply defeat the now-decaying Ottoman state but would replace it as the Habsburg neighbour in the southeast, a condition the Habsburgs wanted to prevent even at great cost. By 1771 Kaunitz was so fearful that this possibility was becoming a probability that he recommended that Austria form an alliance with the Turks to fight the Russians, an idea resisted by Maria Theresa, who still regarded the Turks as infidel predators in Europe.

The threat of war diminished, however, owing to the intervention of Frederick II, who suggested as a solution to the crisis the annexation of Polish territory by the three great eastern European powers and the maintenance of the Ottoman Empire in its entirety in Europe. Austria agreed to this suggestion, although Maria Theresa herself did so most reluctantly. She believed that the difficulties she had had at the beginning of her reign had been brought on by the refusal of the European powers to respect the territorial integrity of their fellows and that, by agreeing to the partition of Poland, she was in fact endorsing the same kind of cynical, parasitical policy that had caused her such grief and that she had regarded as so heinous in 1741. However, as Kaunitz warned her, refusal to take part would not only continue the threat of war but also weaken the monarchy relative to its two powerful neighbours, who had no compunction about adding land and taxpayers to their rolls while Austria received nothing. Consequently, in 1772, Austria, Prussia, and Russia participated in the First Partition of Poland, which added the Polish province of Galicia to the monarchy.

In 1775, following the initiative of Joseph II, Maria Theresa's son, who had joined her as coruler after the death of her husband, the monarchy wrested the province of Bukovina from the Turks. The province served as a convenient connection between Galicia and Transylvania.

In 1778 one of Kaunitz's initiatives, to trade the distant Austrian Netherlands for nearby Bavaria, led to a third war with Prussia. This War of the Bavarian Succession, however, featured virtually no military contact between the two powers, because Maria Theresa, who for a time had left most of the policy making to her chancellor and her son, intervened directly with her old enemy Frederick II and concluded with him the Treaty of Teschen. The treaty resulted in a few minor territorial adjustments—especially the addition of Bavarian territories east of the Inn River to Upper Austria—but above all in the canceling of the proposed swap of the Austrian Netherlands for Bavaria.

REIGN OF JOSEPH II

Maria Theresa died in 1780 and was followed by Joseph II. The problem of succession had caused Maria Theresa considerable grief in her early years, and she had vowed to create not only governmental institutions to protect her lands but familial ones as well, most notably by making certain that there would never again be a shortage of Habsburgs to rule the monarchy (after her marriage, the official name of the family changed from Habsburg to Habsburg-Lorraine). She gave birth to 16 children, the oldest male being Joseph. . Upon the death of Francis I in 1765, Joseph had become emperor and co-regent, but Maria Theresa kept most of the authority in her hands, a condition that led to frequent clashes between the strong-willed mother and the strong-willed son.

When Joseph became sole ruler, he was determined to implement his own policies. One was broadening church reform. Joseph's role as church reformer has been the subject of considerable debate. In Austrian history the term Josephinism generally means subjecting the Roman Catholic Church in the Habsburg lands to service for the state, but the origins and extent of such subjection have generated controversy. Both Maria Theresa and Joseph were devoutly Roman Catholic, but both also believed in firm state control of ecclesiastical matters outside of the strictly religious sphere. To improve the economy, Maria Theresa ordered restrictions on religious holidays and prohibited the taking of ecclesiastic vows before the 24th birthday. She insisted that clerics be subject to the jurisdiction of the state in nonecclesiastical matters and that the acquisition of land by the church be controlled by the government. She took action against the Society of Jesus (Jesuits), but only in 1774, after the pope had ordered its suppression.

Joseph's most radical measures in church matters were the Edict of Toleration (1781) and his monastic reforms. The edict and the legislation

EDICT OF TOLERATION

On October 19, 1781, the Holy Roman emperor Joseph II promulgated a law known as the Edict of Toleration (German: Toleranzpatent) that granted limited freedom of worship to non-Roman Catholic Christians and removed civil disabilities to which they had been previously subject in the Austrian domains. It also maintained a privileged position for the Catholic Church. In an edict of January 2, 1782, sometimes also called the Toleranzpatent, Joseph regulated the status of Jews in the Habsburg territories, freeing them from many discriminatory restrictions.

attached to it gave Lutherans, Calvinists, and Orthodox Christians near equality with Roman Catholics and gave Jews the right to enter various trades as well as permission to study at universities. In this respect, the difference between Joseph and his mother was fundamental. While Maria Theresa regarded Protestants as heretics and Jews as the embodiment of the Antichrist, Joseph respected other Christian denominations, believed Jews did good service for the state, and had at least entertained the thought of an Austrian church independent of Rome.

As to the monasteries, Joseph held that institutions not engaged in useful work for the community—above all agriculture, care of the sick, and education—should be dissolved. Consequently, about a third of the Austrian monasteries ceased to exist, their former members being ordered to learn skills adapted to secular life. The property of the dissolved institutions was used to pay for the upkeep of parishes and to finance the establishment of new parishes.

Control of church discipline and church property were further tightened by Joseph; seminaries for the training of the clergy were secularized. He even tried, without success, to simplify the Roman Catholic liturgy. Many of his religious policies were discontinued in the reaction that followed, but the Edict of Toleration and the monastic reforms remained.

Another of Joseph's famous reforms was the abolition of serfdom, which was not quite a total abolition but certainly changed considerably the status of the peasants. In November 1781 he issued a decree allowing any peasant to move away from his village, to engage in any trade of his choosing, and to wed whomever he wished, all without asking permission of his lord. Labour service required of a peasant's children was abolished, except for orphans. Initially these new freedoms applied only to the lands of the Bohemian crown, but over the next few years they were applied to the other Austrian lands and in 1785 to Hungary, the land that had been exempt from most reforms in the Theresian period. Joseph issued decrees providing for peasant appeals to the central government for redress of grievances; this was to make certain that the feudal courts, controlled by the lords, could not sabotage these reforms by issuing decisions against peasants who wanted to exercise their new rights. Such changes were preludes to Joseph's most daring reform, a proclamation in 1789 that all land, whether held by nobleman or commoner, would be taxed at the same rate of 12 $^2/_9$ percent of its appraised value and that all dues and services paid by a peasant to his lord would now be commuted to a cash payment not to exceed 17 $^2/_9$ percent of the peasant's production.

To muster popular support for these and other reforms, Joseph II in 1781 also substantially eased official censorship, which had been a characteristic of Theresian rule that had undergone a good bit of criticism even in the 18th century. His immediate purpose was to generate support for his religious policies by unleashing those popular writers eager to condemn Roman Catholic clericalism and especially the pope, and for the first few years he was not disappointed. These very writers soon began to find fault with Joseph's policies, however, and the emperor began to respond in ways that reduced considerably the initial liberalization. Censorship was reimposed, and in 1786 he issued secret instructions to the police to concentrate their attention on monitoring public opinion at all levels of society. By 1789 the police reports contained almost exclusively news on agitators and potential unrest.

Toward the end of Joseph's reign, there was indeed increasing dissatisfaction. Religious elements were unhappy with many of his reforms, and both lords and peasants were apprehensive about what his agricultural changes would mean for their future. Moreover, a few other policies had inspired resistance. In 1784 he informed the Hungarian government that its official language, Latin, was not effective for modern government and, since Hungarian was spoken by only part of the population of that kingdom, that the language of government from then on would be German. That language would be used in the central offices immediately, in the county offices after one year, and in the local offices after three. Government employment and even membership in the Hungarian Diet would be open to German speakers only. Although it was designed to facilitate administration, many Hungarians interpreted this

language ruling to be a threat to their entire culture and spoke out enthusiastically against it. To add to the Hungarians' horror, Joseph refused to submit to a coronation in Hungary lest he have to swear to uphold laws that he did not wish to, and then he had the sacred crown of the kingdom moved to Vienna.

By 1787 resistance to Joseph and his government was intensifying. One Habsburg possession that had escaped reforms during the reign of Maria Theresa and Joseph was the Austrian Netherlands, which ruled itself under its own laws. In January and March 1787 Joseph simply swept away the constitution of the Austrian Netherlands and announced that from then on it would be ruled according to absolutist principles, just like the other provinces of the monarchy. Resistance simmered in the Austrian Netherlands until 1789, when it boiled over into open revolt, forcing the administration there to flee to safety in the duchy of Luxembourg. By that time there also were rumours of rebellion in Hungary and in Galicia, and for a period it appeared as if revolution might erupt in many parts of the monarchy.

Joseph's reforms might not have generated as much opposition had it not been for his foreign policy. Joseph was not especially aggressive in foreign affairs, but he did follow the anti-Prussian advice of his and his mother's old chancellor, Kaunitz, and that advice ended in misfortune. Kaunitz firmly believed that Austria could check Prussia only with the help of Russia. Consequently, in 1781 he and Joseph negotiated with Catherine the Great a pact that provided for Russian help for Austria in case of war with Prussia. In exchange, Austria promised to help Russia in case of war with the Ottoman Empire. Confident of her diplomatic and military strength, Catherine then engaged in a series of provocations toward the Turks that resulted in 1787 in a declaration of war by the sultan. Although Joseph had no real desire to participate in this war, his treaty obligations with Russia required him to do so. At first the war went poorly. In 1788 the Austrians waited for the Russians to take the offensive in Romanian lands—which they failed to do—only to be themselves attacked by the Turks and sent scurrying north from the Danube in an effort to reconsolidate their lines. Joseph himself was present on this campaign, which did no one any good. He could not inspire his officers to be more aggressive, and he became quite ill, so much so that he returned to Vienna in late 1788 in an effort to recover. The campaign in 1789 went much better, resulting in the Austrian conquest of the important fortress of Belgrade at the confluence of the Sava and Danube rivers and in a joint Austro-Russian offensive in Moldavia and Walachia that drove the Turks all the way to the Danube.

But by this time all the unfortunate consequences of Joseph's domestic and foreign policies were bearing down on him. The war itself caused an outpouring of popular agitation against his foreign policy, the people of the Austrian Netherlands rose in outright revolution, and reports of trouble in Galicia increased. Finally, it was Hungary that broke Joseph's spirit. In 1788 he had to convoke the old county assemblies to ask for recruits and supplies to fight the war. The noblemen who made up these assemblies replied with protests and demands that the old constitution be restored and that Joseph submit to coronation in the traditional Hungarian manner. Even the Hungarian chancellery, the ministry in the central government in charge of Hungarian affairs, recommended that Joseph yield to these wishes of his constituents.

Faced with these difficulties, Joseph revoked many of the reforms that he had enacted earlier. In a letter of January 1790 he emphasized his good intentions in enacting his new laws in Hungary and then revoked all of them except the Edict of Toleration, the laws related to the status of peasants, and the monastic reforms. He agreed to call the Hungarian Diet—but not too soon, given the dangerous international situation—and he consented to return the crown to Hungary and to his own coronation as that country's king. The crowning never came to pass, however, for Joseph died the following month.

CONFLICTS WITH REVOLUTIONARY FRANCE

Joseph was succeeded by his younger brother, Leopold II. Leopold's reign (1790–92) was a short one, which many believe was quite unfortunate for the Habsburg monarchy because, had he lived, he might have been able to salvage many of Joseph's reforms. In addition, evidence indicates that he planned to introduce a measure of popular representation into the Habsburg government that might have given the monarchy greater stability as it encountered the challenges of industrialization, nationalism, liberalism, and democracy that became increasingly compelling in the next century.

Prior to his accession, Leopold had gained a considerable reputation as an enlightened prince of the Italian state of Tuscany, a land ruled directly by Maria Theresa's husband and then passed to the second Habsburg son (*secundogeniture*). When he became emperor, Leopold saw as his primary task ending the war with the Turks as quickly as possible. That, he believed, would relieve a great deal of the strain in domestic matters so that he could slowly implement a reform program of his own.

By the time of Leopold's accession, the Turkish war had become somewhat complicated—not in a military sense but in a diplomatic one. In 1788 Prussia and Great Britain had formed a coalition to put pressure on Austria and Russia to conclude the war with little or no compensation. This pressure carried with it the threat of war if the two eastern empires did not comply. In 1789 Joseph had wanted to reach such an agreement, but he could not convince Kaunitz to do so, and Kaunitz still had great influence. Leopold, however, did not hesitate to cast aside the

old chancellor's advice. Two weeks after he reached Vienna, Leopold notified the king of Prussia that he sought an accommodation based on the status quo ante, an accommodation reached in April 1790. The war was effectively over, although peace with the Turks was not concluded until August 1791 (Treaty of Sistova).

Initially Leopold accepted the cancellation of many of Joseph's reforms and the increasing authority of the secret police under the guidance of Johann Anton, Graf (count) Pergen. But soon the new emperor began to twist this apparent reaction into something far more progressive. In 1790 and 1791 there came to him a number of petitions from the lower classes of society demanding redress of various grievances. Leopold welcomed these petitions and began to cite them as reasons for introducing some changes in the nature of government, including providing greater representation for the lower orders in the provincial diets and placing the police under the rule of the law, a proposal that caused Pergen to resign. In fact, Leopold adopted a proposal of Joseph von Sonnenfels, an official often considered the leading enlightened political theorist in the monarchy, to make the police a service institution rather than an instrument of control. He put them in charge of local health measures and authorized them to settle minor disputes so that people would not have to go to law courts with petty arguments.

Apparently, in early 1792 Leopold was beginning to take steps to extend representation in the provincial diets to virtually all classes in society. Clearly he did not intend to establish a constitutional monarchy, but he believed that, by drawing the nonprivileged classes into the government, he could check the resistance of the privileged classes and at the same time create a constituency that would support an improved kind of enlightened absolutism. Whatever he had in mind, however, did not come to pass, for he died prematurely on March 1, 1792.

Succeeding Leopold was his much less able but longer-lived eldest son, Francis II (known as Holy Roman Emperor Francis II until 1806 and as Francis I, emperor of Austria, from 1804 to 1835). Francis's foremost problem was significantly different from those that had faced his father and uncle. The domestic situation was settled again, but foreign matters had become increasingly perilous owing to events in France. The French Revolution had erupted in the summer of 1789, and the initial Austrian policy had been essentially to leave France alone. Indeed, Leopold had at first made some approving remarks about the changes in France, and Kaunitz had noted that at least France would not be a serious force in international affairs for some time. The event that changed these passive responses was the flight to Varennes, when King Louis XVI and his wife, Marie-Antoinette (the youngest daughter of Maria Theresa and therefore sister of Joseph and Leopold and aunt of Francis), fled Paris in June 1791 for the safety of the Austrian Netherlands. They reached the French border town of

Varennes, where they were recognized and placed under arrest; later they were returned to Paris.

The flight to Varennes proved to monarchical Europe that, despite protestations to the contrary, the French king did not approve the course of the revolution and in fact had become a prisoner of it. As a result, Leopold and King Frederick William II of Prussia issued a joint declaration (the Declaration of Pillnitz, August 1791) expressing concern about the developments in France. The French government, now acting without the king, interpreted this declaration as a threat to its sovereignty and responded with a series of provocations—answered in kind by Austria and Prussia—that led to a French declaration of war on Austria in April 1792.

The declaration of war inaugurated a period of 23 years of almost continuous conflict (or preparation for conflict) between Austria and France. During that time Austria and France fought five wars for a total of 14 years, and Austria lost all of them but the last. At one time (1809–12), Austria was stripped of all its Italian possessions, the Austrian Netherlands, its western German lands, its access to the Adriatic Sea, and the portion of Poland that it had acquired in the Third Partition in 1795. In 1804 Francis added to his titles that of emperor of Austria, but he did so because he anticipated being stripped of his most venerated title of Holy Roman emperor, which he indeed was in 1806 at the insistence of Napoleon I (who had had himself declared emperor of

France in 1804). French armies occupied Vienna twice, and in 1810 the Habsburgs had to endure the indignity of giving the hand of one of Francis's daughters, Marie-Louise, to Napoleon in marriage.

For the first two wars, that of the First Coalition (1792–97) and that of the Second Coalition (1799–1800), Austrian policy was guided by Franz Maria, Freiherr (baron) von Thugut, the only commoner to reach the rank of minister of foreign affairs in the history of the Habsburg monarchy. Thugut was an experienced diplomat and knew France very well, and he was convinced that the French Revolution represented a threat to the traditional European powers less in ideological terms than in terms of pure military might. He believed that the revolution had somehow reinvigorated an almost moribund French state and had resurrected its military power to a surprising—and dangerous—degree. Therefore, he looked upon the war against Revolutionary, and later Napoleonic, France as akin to the wars against France in the time of Louis XIV. In other words, what was required was a coalition of the great and small European powers to resist what was fundamentally French aggression.

Regardless of his interpretation of the France he was fighting, his efforts ended in failure. In the War of the First Coalition, both Prussia and Spain dropped out in 1795, and for the next two years Austria carried the brunt of the struggle with some help from Britain. In 1797 serious defeats at the hands of the young Napoleon Bonaparte in Italy forced Austria to seek peace. By the Treaty of Campo Formio (October 1797), Austria gave up the Austrian Netherlands and Lombardy but acquired much of Venice.

Thugut was convinced that war would begin again soon, and for the next one he secured Russia as an ally. The War of the Second Coalition began in 1799 when Bonaparte was in Egypt and the French government was in crisis, and it looked for a time as if the Austro-Russian forces would win. However, a terrible defeat inflicted upon the coalition in Switzerland, followed by recrimination and blame heaped upon each ally by the other, resulted in Russia's leaving the alliance as the campaign of 1799 ended. Thugut convinced Francis to continue the struggle, which ended in significant Austrian defeats at Marengo in Italy and at Hohenlinden in Germany in 1800 and in the ouster of Thugut himself in early 1801. Austria sued for peace, which came in the Treaty of Lunéville (February 1801), by which Austria agreed to the cession of the left bank of the Rhine to France (originally a provision of the Treaty of Campo Formio) and recognized French domination of the Austrian Netherlands, Switzerland, and Italy.

From 1801 to 1805, the Austrian government again focused on internal reform, especially in finances. The ongoing wars had cost a great deal of money, and the debt had risen to an astonishing degree. However, most of the expenses of the wars had been paid for by printing paper money, massive amounts of which were in circulation by 1801. Most merchants had accepted this paper money at face value during much of the 1790s, and there is evidence that some of it was invested in technology and industry, suggesting that Austria enjoyed at this time its first hint of industrial revolution. Unfortunately, by 1801 merchants were doubting the value of the currency they received, and inflation assumed serious proportions. From 1801 to 1805 many proposals were advanced to reduce the debt and curb inflation, but none succeeded in doing so.

The other major area of reform was military, and here hope for success seemed higher because the genuine Austrian military hero of the time, Archduke Charles, brother of the emperor, undertook the task of improving the armed forces. He reduced the time of service for all ranks, curbed harsh disciplinary measures, and introduced a number of administrative changes. Yet he firmly believed that an army of long-serving and well-drilled enlisted men was the key to success, and he did not advocate the introduction of the draft that had led to such an incredible increase in the size of the French armies since 1794.

CONFLICTS WITH NAPOLEONIC FRANCE

When the Austrians took the field against the French in 1805, the army was still inadequately equipped, insufficiently trained, under strength, and indifferently led. The war itself had come about owing to miscalculations by the foreign ministers, who firmly believed that an alliance with Russia in late 1804 would deter rather than encourage Napoleon from attacking either of the eastern empires. Napoleon had gathered his major force along the French Atlantic coast for a possible invasion of Great Britain, and the Austrian statesmen believed that, even should they receive news that Napoleon was marching east, the Austrian and Russian armies could easily unite before he could bring his forces to central Europe.

They were wrong. In one of his most brilliant strategic moves, Napoleon marched his army quickly into Germany (and not into Italy, where the Austrians had anticipated he would go and where Archduke Charles had collected the largest Habsburg force). Napoleon surrounded an Austrian army at the city of Ulm, compelled it to surrender, and advanced to Vienna itself, which he took in November 1805. He then moved into Moravia, to Vienna's northeast, where he met a remnant of the Austrian army and the oncoming Russians. He defeated both at the famous Battle of Austerlitz on December 2, 1805. Austria concluded peace immediately (Treaty of Pressburg, December 26, 1805), while Russia continued the war. In this treaty Austria gave up Venice to Napoleon's Italian kingdom, Tirol to Bavaria, and a number of other lands to Napoleon's clients. It did receive the former archbishopric of Salzburg (secularized in 1803); however, this territory would come under French administration (1809–10) and then Bavarian rule (1810–15) before finally becoming a permanent part of Austria after the Napoleonic Wars.

The next period of peace, 1806–09, again saw Austrian preparations for war, this time directed by a Rhineland German in Habsburg service, Johann Philipp, Graf (count) von Stadion. Like others before him, Stadion believed that Austria could not make any long-term accommodation with Napoleon because he represented a mortal danger to monarchical Europe. He believed also that Napoleon could be defeated only by large armies, which he regarded as the secret to France's success. He thus proposed that the Austrians raise large armies, but he knew that the monarchy could not finance increases in the kind of armies that it had used in the past. Therefore, he proposed to supplement the regular troops with trained reserves and militia.

Stadion also realized, however, that, while costing less than long-serving regulars, reserves and militiamen needed reasons to fight. Consequently, he initiated martial appeals of various kinds tailored to various elements of society. The most famous of these was an appeal to nationalism, especially German nationalism. Some scholars point out the

BATTLE OF AUSTERLITZ

The Battle of Austerlitz, also called the Battle of the Three Emperors, which took place on December 2, 1805, was one of Napoleon's greatest victories. It was the first engagement of the War of the Third Coalition. Napoleon's 68,000 troops defeated almost 90,000 Russians and Austrians nominally under General M.I. Kutuzov, forcing Austria to make peace with France (Treaty of Pressburg) and keeping Prussia temporarily out of the anti-French alliance.

The battle took place near Austerlitz in Moravia (now Slavkov u Brna, Czech Republic) after the French had entered Vienna on November 13 and then pursued the Russian and Austrian allied armies into Moravia. The arrival of the Russian emperor Alexander I virtually deprived Kutuzov of supreme control of his troops. The allies decided to fight Napoleon west of Austerlitz and occupied the Pratzen Plateau, which Napoleon had deliberately evacuated to create a trap. The allies then launched their main attack, with 40,000 men, against the French right (south) to cut them off from Vienna. While Marshal Louis Davout's corps of 10,500 men stubbornly resisted this attack, and the allied secondary attack on Napoleon's northern flank was repulsed, Napoleon launched Marshal Nicolas Soult, with 20,000 infantry, up the slopes to smash the weak allied centre on the Pratzen Plateau. Soult captured the plateau and, with 25,000 reinforcements from Napoleon's reserve, held it against the allied attempts to retake it. The allies were soon split in two and vigorously attacked and pursued both north and south of the plateau. Some 15,000 of the allied men were killed and wounded and 11,000 were captured, while Napoleon lost 9,000 men. The remnants of the allied army were scattered. Two days later Francis I of Austria agreed to a suspension of hostilities and arranged for Alexander I to take his army back to Russia.

irony that the first official appeals to modern German nationalism came from the Habsburg government, which would be the primary foe of German nationalism in the 19th century and in some ways the victim of it in the 20th. But the Habsburg government under Stadion's direction did not limit its appeals to German nationalism to inspire its militia. It issued calls to patriotism, love of the emperor, provincialism, and xenophobia, plus appeals to Czechs, Slovenes, Hungarians, and Poles. Often the inspirational appeals to non-Germans were simply translations of the appeals to Germans with the appropriate words replaced with references to the correct national group.

In any case, it was for naught. Inspired by the popular resistance of the Spanish people to Napoleon, Stadion appealed to his own people in 1809 to go to war. The declaration came in April, and the French army occupied Vienna in May. However, on May 21–22, at Aspern, across the Danube from Vienna, Archduke Charles and the regular Austrian army inflicted the first defeat Napoleon was to suffer on the field of battle. They did not take advantage of it, however; Napoleon regrouped and defeated Archduke Charles in July in the Battle of Wagram, just a few miles from Aspern. At the Treaty of Schönbrunn (October 1809), the monarchy surrendered considerably more territory but at least remained in existence.

After 1809, foreign policy and to some extent domestic policy passed into the hands of Klemens, Graf von Metternich (later given the title of Fürst [prince]), who would steer the monarchy's ship of state for the next 40 years. Unlike his predecessors in charge of foreign policy, Metternich believed that the only hope for the continued existence of the monarchy was to seek accommodation with Napoleon. It was he who arranged the marriage of Marie-Louise, and it was he who convinced Francis to send troops to take part in Napoleon's invasion of Russia in 1812.

Even when Napoleon suffered his thunderous defeat in Russia, Metternich was by no means eager to join his former allies in pursuing the defeated French. The main reason was that by this time Metternich had come to the conclusion that the key to the future security of the monarchy was not the restoration of the Europe of 1789 but rather the creation of an effective balance of power among the great European states. In his view, a completely victorious Russia would be just as great a threat to Austria as a completely victorious France. His goal was to arrange an agreement between Russia and Napoleonic France that would establish each one as a counterweight to the other while restoring an independent Habsburg monarchy and Prussia between them. Metternich sought this goal through the first half of 1813, but Napoleon would agree to no concessions. So in August 1813, Austria formally declared war on France.

In the ensuing War of Liberation, Austria assumed the leading role. It provided the greatest number of troops to the allied forces, in addition to their commander, Karl Philipp, Fürst zu

Schwarzenberg, and his brilliant staff officer, Joseph, Graf Radetzky. Metternich, however, never sought to vanquish Napoleon utterly, because he still distrusted Russian ambition as much as he did that of the French. He could never convince Napoleon to accept his views, however, and Austria in the end took part in Napoleon's defeat and exile to the island of Elba in 1814.

In September 1814 the congress to conclude the quarter century of war gathered in Vienna under Metternich's chairmanship. In terms of territory, Metternich gladly relinquished claims to the old Austrian Netherlands and the various Habsburg possessions in Germany for a consolidated monarchy at the centre of Europe. Austria regained its lands on the Adriatic and in the area that is now Austria, which it had previously lost, and it won considerable territory in Italy, including Lombardy, Venetia, Tuscany, and Modena.

But in Germany Metternich worked his greatest magic. He had no intention of restoring the old Holy Roman Empire but wished to create instead a system that could defend itself against both France and Russia and keep Prussia under control. His solution was the German Confederation, a body comprising 35 states and 4 free cities, with Austria assuming the presidency. Such an institution, in Metternich's eyes, would give Austria far more influence in Germany than it had had under the old Holy Roman Empire.

While Metternich arranged central Europe as best he could, the four victorious powers—Austria, Prussia, Russia, and Great Britain—pledged to maintain the peace settlement, thereby establishing what is known as the Concert of Europe. Moreover, each monarch in Europe pledged allegiance to a Christian union of love, peace, and charity. This "Holy Alliance" was the brainchild of Alexander I of Russia; Metternich knew that it was little more than sentiment, but he welcomed it as a statement he could exploit to persuade other monarchs to do his bidding. With the end of the Congress of Vienna, Metternich became the "coachman of Europe" and would remain so for some time.

THE AGE OF METTERNICH

The 33 years after the end of the Napoleonic Wars are called in Austria —and to some extent in all of Europe—the Age of Metternich. The chief characteristics of this age are the onset of the Industrial Revolution, an intensification of social problems brought on by economic cycles of boom and bust, an increasingly mobile population, more demands for popular participation in government, and the rising tide of nationalism, all watched over by governments intent upon preserving the social, political, and international status quo.

Metternich was the symbol of those forces eager to preserve the status quo. In the debate about his policies, some have argued that Metternich was little more than an oppressive, reactionary but opportunistic statesman, eager to snuff out sparks of revolution and liberalism wherever he could detect them. Moreover,

From 1814 to 1815, representatives from across Europe convened at the Congress of Vienna, an assembly that met in Vienna to reorganize Europe after the Napoleonic Wars. The major powers, including Austria, were represented there, as were many minor states. DEA Picture Library/De Agostini/Getty Images

his much vaunted direction of the other powers in preserving the European order was really a mask for maintaining Habsburg influence in international affairs far out of proportion to the power that the monarchy actually possessed. Others contend that Metternich was one of the first philosophical conservatives, basing his social and political policies on coherent principles of orderly and cautious change in the context of good

government and his diplomatic policies on maintaining stability by convincing the great powers of their mutual interests in preserving the European order as it then existed.

In international affairs, Metternich's Concert of Europe did not last long. Within a few years after the Congress of Vienna, it had become clear that the five great powers simply did not have sufficiently similar interests or goals to cooperate on every issue that came before them. After European congresses at Troppau, Laibach, and Verona (1820–22) granted permission to Austria to deal with revolutions in Italy and to France to do the same in Spain, Britain announced its withdrawal from the Concert of Europe, proclaiming that it wanted no more to do with the conservative Continental powers. Likewise, a revolution in France in 1830 weakened that country's link to Metternich's system, and he even had trouble with Russia, which was greatly upset by Ottoman persecution of Orthodox Christians during the movement for Greek independence (1821–30).

In domestic matters, Metternich may have desired good government, but his reputation as an oppressor gained considerable credence after 1815. Protests against conservative policies by a gathering of German students (at the Wartburg Festival) in 1817 and the assassination of a conservative playwright (August von Kotzebue) in 1819 led, under Metternich's guidance, to the German Confederation's adopting the Carlsbad Decrees, a set of laws placing German and Austrian universities under strict control. Harsh censorship was imposed, and a commission was established at Mainz to investigate all student societies for subversives. Teachers, writers, and students suspected of liberal views were blacklisted throughout Germany and Austria. In 1824 the German Federal Diet renewed these provisions for an indefinite period and in 1832 and 1833 expanded them at Metternich's behest.

Metternich's name was also equated with suppressing liberalism and radicalism in Italy. In 1821 Austrian troops put down risings in Naples and Piedmont; in 1831 rebellions in Parma, Modena, and the Papal States likewise ended in suppression by Austrian soldiers. The Austrian regime became the nemesis of the Carbonari and Young Italy, two movements associated with Italian nationalism and republicanism that were enormously popular among educated Italians.

Whereas Metternich's name is often equated with oppression, he in fact was not eager to impose harsh and unrelenting rule in his own state or in others. Metternich believed that the best government was absolutism (the political doctrine and practice of unlimited, centralized authority and absolute sovereignty, as vested especially in a monarch or dictator), but he believed that it was best because it guaranteed equal justice and fair administration for all. In the Habsburg monarchy and in the Italian governments he saved from revolution, he advocated reforms that would provide good government for the people. In many places his appeals went unheeded—in the Papal States, for example—and even in Austria his influence in domestic affairs weakened considerably as time went on. In 1826 Emperor Francis appointed Franz Anton, Graf (count) von Kolowrat, minister of state, and he steadily reduced Metternich's influence in internal policy. In 1835 Francis died and was succeeded by his son Ferdinand, whose feeblemindedness necessitated the creation of a "state conference" to rule the monarchy. It consisted of two of Ferdinand's uncles and his brother, along with Kolowrat and Metternich, as permanent members. High policy tended to drift, because the two archdukes were nonentities and Kolowrat and Metternich were usually at odds with one another.

While Metternich and his colleagues focused most of their attention on political activity, the monarchy was by no means standing still in economic and social matters. By the 1820s Austria was experiencing its first sustained industrial development. While many have regarded Austria's exclusion from the Zollverein, the German customs union created by Prussia in the 1820s and '30s, as permanently retarding Austria's economic advancement, in fact, by the 1840s, Austrian production of pig iron, coal, cotton textiles, woolens, and foodstuffs was growing at a faster rate than that of the Zollverein. Advocates of political liberalism may have suffered at this time, but those of economic liberalism were gaining ground. After Francis's death in 1835, practically all restrictions on new enterprises, especially those engaged in commerce, were lifted.

Most people still lived on the land, but even there changes were under way. As growing cities created markets for more and more agricultural goods, producers began to focus on agriculture for profit instead of for subsistence. Along with industrial crops such as sugar beets and flax, old crops such as wheat, vegetables,

wine, and livestock were grown more and more for the commercial market. The social impact of these changes in agriculture became starkly apparent in 1848, when the final abolition of serfdom was encouraged by some of the landholding nobility, who were relying more and more on wage labour to work their estates and no longer wanted the obligations associated with having serfs.

Aiding these new economic efforts were the beginnings of an Austrian infrastructure of railroads and water transport. The first railroad on the European Continent appeared between Linz (Austria) and Budweis (now Ceské Budejovice, Czech Republic); it was a horse-drawn railway between the Danube and the Moldau (Vltava) rivers, which in fact was a connection between the Danube and the Elbe river systems. In 1836 work began on a steam railway heading north from Vienna, and by 1848 the monarchy contained more than 1,000 miles (1,600 km) of track. Canals were not a feature of Habsburg transportation because of poor terrain, but steam navigation began on the Danube in 1830 and expanded quickly.

REVOLUTION AND COUNTERREVOLUTION

The year 1848 was a time of European-wide revolution. A general disgust with conservative domestic policies, an urge for more freedoms and greater popular participation in government, rising nationalism, social problems brought on by the Industrial Revolution, and increasing hunger caused by harvest failures in the mid-1840s all contributed to growing unrest, which the Habsburg monarchy did not escape. In February 1848, Paris, the archetype of revolution at that time, rose against its government, and within weeks many major cities in Europe did the same, including Vienna.

As in much of Europe, the revolution of 1848 in the Habsburg monarchy may be divided into the three categories of social, democratic-liberal, and national, but outside Vienna the national aspect of the revolution fairly soon overshadowed the other two. On March 13, upon receiving news of the Paris rising, crowds of people, mostly students and members of liberal clubs, demonstrated in Vienna for basic freedoms and a liberalization of the regime. As happened in many cities in this fateful year, troops were called out to quell the crowds, shots were fired, and serious clashes occurred between the authorities and the people. The government had no wish to antagonize the crowds further and so dismissed Metternich, who was the symbol of repression, and promised to issue a constitution.

From that beginning to the end of October 1848, Vienna ebbed and flowed between revolution and counterrevolution, with one element or another gaining influence over the others. In mid-May the Habsburgs and their government became so concerned about the way matters were going that they fled Vienna, although they did return in August when it appeared that more-conservative elements were asserting control. The emperor issued a constitution in April providing for an elected legislature, but when the legislature met in June it rejected this constitution in favour of one that promised to be more democratic. As the legislature debated various issues over the summer and autumn, the Habsburgs and their advisers regrouped both their confidence and their might, and on October 31 the army retook Vienna and executed a number of the city's radical leaders. By this time the legislature had removed itself to Kremsier (now Kroměříz, Czech Republic) in the province of Moravia, where it continued to work on a constitution. It finished its work there, issued its document, and was promptly overruled and then dismissed by the emperor.

Although the assembly in the end did not create a working constitution for Austria, it did issue one piece of legislation that had long-lasting influence: it fully emancipated the peasantry. The conservative regime that followed kept and implemented this law.

In other parts of the monarchy, the revolution of 1848 passed quickly through a liberal-democratic to a national phase, and in no place was this more evident or more serious than in Hungary. Joseph II's effort to incorporate Hungary more fully into the monarchy, along with the early 19th century's rising national awareness throughout Europe, had a profound impact upon the aristocratic Hungarians who held sway in the country. Modern nationalism made them even more intent on preserving their cultural traditions and on continuing their political domination of the land. Consequently, after 1815 the Hungarian nobility engaged in a number of activities to strengthen the Hungarian national spirit, demanding the use of Hungarian rather than Latin as the language of government and undertaking serious efforts to develop the country economically. The revolution in Paris and then the one in Vienna in March 1848 galvanized the Hungarian Diet. Under the leadership of a young lawyer and journalist named Lajos Kossuth, the Hungarian Diet demanded of the sovereign sweeping reforms, including civil liberties and far greater autonomy for the Hungarian government, which would from then on meet in Pest (Buda and Pest were separate cities until 1873, when they officially merged under the name Budapest). Under great pressure from liberal elements in Vienna, the emperor acceded to these wishes, and the Hungarian legislators immediately undertook creating a new constitution for their land.

This new constitution became known as the March Laws (or April Laws) and was really the work of Kossuth. The March Laws provided for a popularly elected lower house of deputies, freedom for the "received religions" (i.e., excluding Jews), freedom of the press, peasant emancipation, and equality before the law. As the Hungarians set up their new national government based on these principles, they encountered from some of the minority nationalities living in their land the kind of resistance they had offered the Austrians. A characteristic of the new regime was an intense pride in being Hungarian, but the population in the Hungarian portion of the Habsburg monarchy was 60 percent non-Hungarian. And in 1848 all the talk about freedom and constitutions and protection of one's language and culture had inspired many of these people as well. But Kossuth and his colleagues had no intention of weakening the Hungarian nature of their new regime; indeed, they made knowledge of Hungarian a qualification for membership in parliament and for participation in government. In other words, the new government seemed as unsympathetic to the demands and hopes of its Serbian, Croatian, Slovak, and Romanian populations as Vienna had been to the demands of the Hungarians.

In March 1848 the Habsburgs made an appointment that would lead to war with the Hungarians; they selected as governor of Croatia Josip, Graf (count) Jelačić, well known for his devotion to the monarchy, for his dislike of the "lawyers' clique" in Pest, and for his ability to hold the South Slavs in the southern portion of the monarchy loyal to the crown. Jelačić did not disappoint Vienna. One of his first acts was to reject all authority over Croatia by the new Hungarian government, to refuse all efforts by that government to introduce Hungarian as a language of administration, and to order his bureaucrats to return unopened all official mail from Pest. He also began negotiations with the leadership of the Serbs to resist Hungarian rule together.

From April to September 1848 the Hungarian government dealt with its minority nations and with the government in Austria on even terms, but then relations began to deteriorate. The return of the Habsburgs to Vienna in August, the more conservative turn in the government there that the return reflected, and Austrian military victories in Italy in July prompted the Habsburg government to demand greater concessions from the Hungarians. In September, military action against Hungary by Jelačić and his Croats prompted the Hungarian government to turn power over to Kossuth and the Committee of National Defense, which immediately took measures to defend the country. What then emerged was open warfare between regular Habsburg forces and Jelačić on the one hand and the Hungarians on the other.

The war was a bloody affair, with each side dominating at one time or another. In April 1849 the Hungarian government proclaimed its total independence from the Habsburgs, and in that same month the Austrian government requested military aid from Russia, an act that was to haunt it for years to come. Finally, in August 1849, the Hungarian army surrendered, and the land was put firmly under Austrian rule. Kossuth fled to the Ottoman Empire, and from there for years he traveled the world denouncing Habsburg oppression. In Hungary itself many rebel officers were imprisoned, and a number were executed.

A second serious national rising occurred in Italy. Since 1815 many Italians had looked upon the Habsburgs as foreign occupiers or oppressors, so when news of revolution reached their lands, the banner of revolt went up in many places, especially Milan and Venice. Outside the Habsburg lands, liberal uprisings also swept Rome and Naples. In Habsburg Italy, however, war came swiftly. In late March, answering a plea from the Milanese, the kingdom of Sardinia, the only Italian state with a native monarch, declared war on the emperor and marched into his lands.

The Habsburg government in Austria was initially willing to make concessions to Sardinia, but it was strongly discouraged from doing so by its military commander in Italy, the old but highly respected and talented Field Marshal Radetzky, who had been the Austrian chief of staff in the war against Napoleon in 1813–14. In July 1848 Radetzky proved the value of his advice by defeating the Sardinians at Custoza, a victory that helped restore confidence to the Habsburg government as it faced so many enemies. Radetzky reimposed Habsburg rule in Milan and Venice, and in March 1849 he defeated the Sardinians once again when they invaded Austria's Italian possessions.

Besides the Hungarians and the Italians, the Slavic peoples of the monarchy also responded to the revolutionary surge, although with less violence than the other two. In June 1848 a Pan-Slav congress met in Prague to hammer out a set of principles that all Slavic peoples could endorse. The organizer of the conference was the great Czech historian František Palacký (most of the delegates were Czech), who not only had called for the cooperation of the Habsburg Slavs but also had endorsed the Habsburg monarchy as the most reasonable political formation to protect the peoples of central Europe. Upon being asked by the Germans to declare himself favourably disposed to their desire for national unity, he responded that he could not do so because it would weaken the Habsburg state. And in that reply he wrote his famous words: "Truly, if it were not that Austria had long existed, it would be necessary, in the interest of Europe, in the interest of humanity itself, to create it."

Unfortunately, the Pan-Slav congress met in a highly charged atmosphere, as young inhabitants of Prague likewise had been influenced by revolutions elsewhere and had taken to the streets. In the commotion, a stray bullet killed the wife of Field Marshal Alfred, Fürst (prince) zu Windischgrätz, the commander of the forces in Prague. Enraged, Windischgrätz seized the city, dispersed the congress, and established martial law throughout the province of Bohemia.

The Germans themselves also experienced a certain degree of national fervour, but in their case it was part of a general German yearning for national unification. Responding to calls for a meeting of national unity, in May 1848 delegates from all the German states met at Frankfurt to discuss a constitution for a united Germany. Made up primarily of the commercial and professional classes, this body was indeed distinguished and was looked upon by the German princes as an important gathering. To prove its respect for tradition, the Frankfurt parliament selected the emperor's uncle, Archduke Johann, as head of a provisional executive power and in September selected another Austrian, Anton, Ritter (knight) von Schmerling, as prime minister.

Despite this deference to Austria's prominent men, a major question the parliament addressed was whether to include Austria in the new Germany. Those who favoured doing so argued that a new Germany could accept the German-speaking provinces of the monarchy but not the non-German lands (the *Grossdeutsch*, or large German, position). Those against contended that the Austrian monarchy could never divide itself along ethnic lines and so favoured the exclusion of Austria altogether (the *Kleindeutsch*, or small German, position). Implicit in the latter position was that the new Germany would be greatly influenced if not dominated by Prussia, by far the most important German state next to Austria. In October 1848 the delegates agreed to invite the Austrian German lands to become part of the new Germany, but only if they were disconnected from non-German territory. This so-called compromise was really a victory for the *Kleindeutsch* supporters, who knew that the Austrian government would reject the invitation because it would never willfully break the monarchy apart.

In the end neither position prevailed, because the Frankfurt parliament was unable to unify Germany. All the German states finally rejected its proposals, and in April 1849 it dissolved. Nonetheless, it had created the impression that, when the new Germany did emerge, it would do so under the aegis of Prussia and with the exclusion of Austria.

NEOABSOLUTIST ERA

All things considered, the revolution across the empire had not accomplished much. Absolutism seemed firmly entrenched, and the political clock seemed to have been set back to the 18th century. And yet a regime so badly shaken as Austria's could not hope to rule unchallenged in the future. The unresolved social, constitutional, and national issues became more intense, and new changes were soon in the offing.

The period 1849–60 is called the Neoabsolutist era because it was the last effort by an Austrian emperor to provide good government by relying solely on bureaucratic effectiveness. In doing so, it was the legitimate descendant of the governments of Joseph II and Metternich. The emperor in this case was Francis Joseph, who in December 1848 had succeeded at the age of 18 to the throne in a deal engineered by Felix, Fürst (prince) zu Schwarzenberg, an able and iron-willed opponent of the 1848 revolutionaries and a proponent of strong central government. Francis Joseph had not been the heir, but Schwarzenberg contended that too many promises to revolutionaries had been made in the name of Ferdinand and the true heir, Francis Joseph's father, Francis Charles, and so only his son could rule without making compromises. Francis Joseph thus became emperor and ruled for the next 68 years, dying in the midst of World War I at the age of 86.

Under Francis Joseph and Schwarzenberg, order was restored. Schwarzenberg died in 1852, and the new regime passed largely to the direction of Alexander, Freiherr (baron) von Bach, minister of the interior and a competent bureaucrat. Despite its reputation as a repressive instrument, Bach's government was not without positive accomplishments. It established a unified customs territory for the whole monarchy (including Hungary), composed a code for trades and crafts, completed the task of serf emancipation, and introduced improvements in universities and secondary schools. In this period, economic growth continued its slow but steady pace, which had characterized the monarchy before 1848 and would continue to do so after 1860.

The regime's policies on other matters were more typically reactionary. Freedom of the press as well as jury and public trials were abandoned, corporal punishment by police orders restored, and internal surveillance increased. The observation of the liberal reformer Adolf Fischhof that the regime rested on the support of a standing army of soldiers, a kneeling army of worshippers, and a crawling army of informants was exaggerated but not entirely unfounded. One of the more backward developments was the concordat reached with the papacy that gave the church jurisdiction in marriage questions, partial control of censorship, and oversight of elementary and secondary education. Priests entrusted with religious education in the schools had the authority to see to it that instruction in any field, be it history or physics, did not conflict with the church's teachings.

The neoabsolutist regime came to an end because of its foreign policy. In the mid-1850s the matter that dominated the foreign offices of the European states was the Crimean War, a struggle that pitted an alliance system of Britain, France, the Ottoman Empire, and the Kingdom of Sardinia against Russia. Since the mid-18th century, Austrian statesmen had generally agreed that it was better to have as the monarchy's southeastern neighbour a weak Ottoman Empire than any strong power—especially Russia. So, in this war the monarchy declared its neutrality but also insisted that Russia not advance into the Ottoman provinces of Moldavia and Walachia, which lay to the east of the Austrian Empire. This policy had two deleterious results: it alienated Russia, which had helped the monarchy put down the Hungarian revolution, and it did not befriend France, which would in 1859 support Sardinia in its war of Italian unification against the Austrians.

It was the Austro-Italian war of 1859 that humiliated Austria and ended Bach's system. First securing support from Napoleon III of France, Sardinia provoked a woefully unprepared Austria into war and then invited France to come to the Italian kingdom's assistance. The Austrians suffered two major defeats at Magenta and Solferino and concluded peace. The monarchy gave up Lombardy and kept Venetia, but, more important, it lost its influence in Italy. The Habsburgs had no say in the events of 1860 and 1861 that led to the proclamation of a unified Italy under the rule of the kings of Sardinia.

CONSTITUTIONAL EXPERIMENTATION

Internally, the defeats in Italy convinced Francis Joseph that neoabsolutism had failed. Clamour for economic, political, and even military rejuvenation became irresistible. In March 1860 Francis Joseph ordered that the Reichsrat, an empirewide, purely advisory council of state, be enlarged by the addition of 38 members proposed by the provincial diets and selected by the crown. Its main task was to advise the emperor on the composition of a new constitution. The body divided into two groups rather quickly. One, made up mostly of German-speaking delegates, wished to create a strong central parliament and to continue to restrict the power of the provincial governments. The other, made up of conservative federalists who were largely Hungarian, Czech, and Polish nobles, wished to weaken the central government and give considerable power to the provinces. The emperor sided with the federalists, who persuaded him to

SEVEN WEEKS' WAR

The Seven Weeks' War (also called the Austro-Prussian War,) began in June 1866. It was fought between Prussia on the one side and Austria, Bavaria, Saxony, Hanover, and certain minor German states on the other and ended in a Prussian victory, which meant the exclusion of Austria from Germany. The issue was decided in Bohemia, where the principal Prussian armies met the main Austrian forces and the Saxon army, most decisively at the Battle of Königgrätz. A Prussian detachment, known as the army of the Main, meanwhile dealt with the forces of Bavaria and other German states that had sided with Austria. Simultaneously, a campaign was fought in Venetia between the Austrian army of the south and the Italians, who had made an alliance with Prussia.

The 1866 campaign was a carefully planned stage in the unification of Germany under Prussia's Hohenzollern dynasty, of which Otto von Bismarck was the principal agent. The issue was clear-cut: Prussia deliberately challenged Austria for the leadership of the German Confederation. Prussia had challenged Austria in 1850, but the complete failure of its mobilization in that year compelled the acceptance at Olmütz of the somewhat humiliating terms of Austria. Since then Prussia, with Bismarck as statesman, Count Helmuth von Moltke as strategist, and Count Albrecht von Roon as army organizer, had prepared methodically for a fresh challenge. The actual pretext found by Bismarck in 1866 was a dispute over the administration of Schleswig and Holstein, which Austria and Prussia had seized from Denmark in 1864 and had since held jointly. Diplomatic exchanges began in January and military preparations a little later, but hostilities did not actually break out until the middle of June.

By the alliance with Italy, Bismarck contrived to divert part of the Austrian forces to the south. This advantage, together with that of Prussia's modernized army discipline, resulted in a Prussian victory; the war was formally concluded on August 23 by the Treaty of Prague. The treaty assigned Schleswig-Holstein to Prussia. The latter also annexed Hanover, Hesse-Kassel, Nassau, and Frankfurt outright, thus acquiring the territory that had separated the eastern and the western parts of the Prussian state. By the Peace of Vienna (October 3, 1866) Austria ceded Venetia for transfer to Italy. Prussia's victory in the war enabled it to organize the North German Confederation.

accept their position mainly with historical and not ethnic arguments, and he proclaimed by decree a constitution called the October Diploma (1860). The constitution established a central parliament of 100 members and gave it advisory authority in matters of finance, commerce, and industry. Authority in other internal matters was assigned to the provinces. Foreign policy and military issues remained the domain of the emperor.

No one was happy with the October Diploma. The German centralists opposed it for giving too much authority to the provinces, and the federalists, particularly the Hungarians, opposed it for not restoring fully the old rights and privileges of the crown lands. Faced with such opposition, Francis Joseph abandoned the Diploma and four months later issued the February Patent (1861), officially a revision of the Diploma. This document provided for a bicameral system: an empirewide house of representatives composed of delegates from the diets and a house of lords consisting partly of hereditary members and partly of men of special distinction appointed for life. Furthermore, a separate parliamentary body for the non-Hungarian lands was established.

The February Patent restored much authority to the central government and so made the centralists happier, but it only antagonized further the federalists, now led enthusiastically by the Hungarians. Resistance was so great that by 1865 the constitution was considered unworkable, and Francis Joseph began negotiations with the Hungarians to revise it. In the meantime, a form of government by bureaucracy ran the country.

These constitutional issues received a significant jolt by another failure of Habsburg foreign policy. After the disbandment of the Frankfurt National Assembly in 1849, the German Confederation founded in 1815 had resumed its work, but the question of German unification had not gone away. In 1862 this issue gained an unlikely champion in the appointment of Otto von Bismarck as prime minister of Prussia and later chancellor of the German Empire. Bismarck was a Prussian patriot and a loyal subject of his king. While definitely not a German nationalist, he was determined to extend Prussia's power and authority into the German lands, and he knew that Prussia could expand its influence in Germany only at Austria's expense. From 1862 to 1866 he conducted a remarkably deft foreign policy that succeeded in isolating Austria from possible allies in Europe.

By exploiting issues in the German Confederation, Bismarck was able in 1866 to force Austria into a position that could only be resolved by war. The conflict is known as the Seven Weeks' War or the Austro-Prussian War. On July 3, 1866, the two armies clashed in this struggle's only major Austro-Prussian battle, the Battle of Königgrätz, or Sadowa as it is known in Austrian histories. Although the battle was hard fought on both sides, the arrival of an extra Prussian force toward the end of the day decided it in favour of Prussia. Afterward, peace came quickly, because neither side wanted the war to continue. As Austria had been excluded from the future of Italy in 1859, so it was now excluded from the future of Germany. The German Confederation came to an end, and Prussia was allowed a free hand in reorganizing northern Germany as it wished. Moreover, Italy had joined Prussia against Austria and, although defeated on land and sea, received Venetia, Austria's last possession in Italy, for its loyalty. Internally, the war meant that the government had to reach a constitutional arrangement for the remainder of its possessions.

CHAPTER 7

AUSTRIA-HUNGARY

The economic consequences of the defeat in the war of 1866 made it imperative that the constitutional reorganization of the Habsburg monarchy, under discussion since 1859, be brought to an early and successful conclusion. Personnel changes facilitated the solution of the Hungarian crisis. Friedrich Ferdinand, Freiherr (baron) von Beust (later Graf [count] von Beust), who had been prime minister of Saxony, took charge of Habsburg affairs, first as foreign minister (from October 1866) and then as chancellor (from February 1867). By abandoning the claim that Hungary be simply an Austrian province, he induced Emperor Francis Joseph to recognize the negotiations with the Hungarian politicians (Ferenc Deák and Gyula, Gróf [count] Andrássy) as a purely dynastic affair, excluding non-Hungarians from the discussion.

AUSGLEICH OF 1867

On February 17, 1867, Emperor Francis Joseph restored the Hungarian constitution. A ministry responsible to the Hungarian Diet was formed under Andrássy, and in May 1867 the diet approved Law XII, legalizing what became known as the Ausgleich ("Compromise"). This was a compromise between the Hungarian nation and the dynasty, not between Hungary and the rest of the empire, and it is symptomatic of the Hungarian attitude that led Hungarians to refer to Francis Joseph and his successor as their king and never their emperor

Emperor Francis Joseph on horseback. Keystone-France/Gamma Keystone/Getty Images

In addition to regulating the constitutional relations between the king and the Hungarian nation, Law XII accepted the unity of the Habsburg lands for purposes of conducting certain economic and foreign affairs in common. The compromise was thus the logical result of an attempt to blend traditional constitutional rights with the demands of modern administration. In December 1867 the section of the Reichsrat representing the non-Hungarian lands of the Habsburg empire (known as the *engerer* Reichsrat) approved the compromise. Though after 1867 the Habsburg monarchy was popularly referred to as the Dual Monarchy, the constitutional framework was actually tripartite, comprising the common agencies for economics and foreign affairs, the agencies of the kingdom of Hungary, and the agencies of the rest of the Habsburg lands—commonly but incorrectly called "Austria." (The official title for these provinces remained "the kingdoms and lands represented in the Reichsrat" until 1915, when the term "Austria" was officially adopted for them.)

Under the Ausgleich, both parts of the Habsburg monarchy were constitutionally autonomous, each having its own government and a parliament composed of an appointed upper and an elected lower house. The "common monarchy" consisted of the emperor and his court, the minister for foreign affairs, and the minister of war. There was no common prime minister and no common cabinet. Common affairs were to be considered at the "delegations," annual meetings of representatives from the two parliaments. For economic and financial cooperation, there was to be a customs union and a sharing of accounts, which was to be revised every 10 years. (This decennial discussion of financial quotas became one of the main sources of conflict between the Hungarian and Austrian governments.) There would be no common citizenship, but such matters as weights, measures, coinage, and postal service were to be uniform in both areas. There soon developed the so-called *gemeinsamer* Ministerrat, a kind of crown council in which the common ministers of foreign affairs and war and the prime ministers of both governments met under the presidency of the monarch. The common ministers were responsible to the crown only, but they reported annually to the delegations.

The Ausgleich for all practical purposes set up a personal union between the lands of the Hungarian crown and the western lands of the Habsburgs. The Hungarian success inspired similar movements for the restoration of states' rights in Bohemia and Galicia. But the monarch, who only reluctantly had given in to Hungarian demands, was unwilling to discontinue the centralist policy in the rest of his empire. Public opinion and parliament in Austria were dominated by German bourgeois liberals who opposed the federalization of Austria. As a prize for their cooperation in compromising with the Hungarians, the German liberals were allowed to amend the 1861 constitution known as the February Patent; the Fundamental Laws, which were adopted in December 1867 and became known as the

December constitution, lasted until 1918. These laws granted equality before the law and freedom of press, speech, and assembly; they also protected the interests of the various nationalities, stating that

> all nationalities in the state enjoy equal rights, and each one has an inalienable right to the preservation and cultivation of its nationality and language. The equal rights of all languages in local use are guaranteed by the state in schools, administration, and public life.

The authority of parliament was also recognized. Such provisions, however, were more a promise than a reality. Although parliament, for instance, did theoretically have the power to deal with all varieties of matters, it was, in any case, not a fully representative parliament (suffrage was restricted, and it was tied to property provisions until 1907). In addition, the king was authorized to govern without parliament in the event that the assembly should prove unable to work. Austrian affairs from 1867 to 1918 were, in fact, determined more by bureaucratic measures than by political initiative; traditions dating from the reign of Joseph II, rather than capitalist interests, characterized the Austrian liberals.

DOMESTIC AFFAIRS, 1867–73

After the December constitution had been sanctioned, Francis Joseph appointed a new cabinet, which was named the "bourgeois ministry" by the press because most of its members came from the German middle class (though the prime minister belonged to the Austrian high aristocracy). In 1868 and 1869 this ministry was able to enact several liberal reforms, undoing parts of the concordat of 1855 between Austria and the papacy. Civil marriage was restored; compulsory secular education was established; and interconfessional relations were regulated, in spite of a strong protest from the Roman Catholic Church. In 1870 the Austrian government used the promulgation of the dogma of papal infallibility as pretext for the total abrogation of the concordat.

The progressive legislation of the bourgeois cabinet stood in sharp contrast to its inability to cope with the demands of the non-German nationalities. In 1868 the Czechs and the Poles issued declarations demanding a constitutional status analogous to that of the Hungarians. The government in Vienna did give the Poles in Galicia a considerable amount of self-government, which was later used to Polonize the Ruthenian minority. In 1871 a ministry for Galician affairs was set up, and the Poles remained the staunchest supporters of the Austrian government well into World War I.

The bourgeois ministry was split into a liberal-centralist and a conservative-federalist faction; its members could not reach an agreement on policies to be adopted. The liberal members of the cabinet opposed Czech demands; the conservatives were willing to consider them. Francis Joseph, indignant because of the anticlerical policy of the liberals, dismissed his prime minister, Karl, Fürst (prince) von Auersperg, in 1868 and replaced him with the conservative Eduard, Graf (count) von Taaffe, his boyhood friend. A period of indecision nevertheless persisted. The emperor wavered between the liberals, whose anticlericalism and parliamentarianism he disliked but with whom he sympathized in their centralist, German-oriented policy, and the conservatives, whose political legislation he favoured but who aroused his fears by their demands for federalization. Neither Taaffe nor his successors Leopold Hasner, Ritter (knight) von Artha (1870), and Alfred, Graf Potocki (1870–71), could solve the Czech problem.

The Franco-German War of 1870–71 temporarily diverted public attention from the Czech demands. Opinion was divided strictly along lines of nationality: Austro-Germans celebrated the victories of the Prussian army, whereas the Slavs were decidedly pro-French. The Austrian government remained neutral because conflicting international interests had blocked Austro-French negotiations (which had culminated in a meeting of Francis Joseph and French emperor Napoleon III at Salzburg in 1867). The victory of Prussian chancellor Otto von Bismarck and the establishment of the German Empire under the leadership of the Prussian king gave finality to the results of the 1866 Austro-Prussian War. Austria was definitely excluded from the German scene, and a reorientation of dynastic interests seemed a logical consequence. Francis Joseph decided to explore the possibility of satisfying the Czechs with some measure of federalism. On February 5, 1871, he appointed as prime minister Karl Siegmund, Graf von Hohenwart, a staunch clericalist. The driving mind in Hohenwart's cabinet was the minister of commerce, Albert Schäffle, an economist whose socialism may not have appealed to the emperor but whose federalism did.

As a first step toward conciliation with the Czechs, the cabinet dissolved parliament and the provincial diets. When the Bohemian elections improved the federalist position, Hohenwart proceeded to deal directly with the Czechs, copying in certain measure the method used to conclude the compromise with Hungary. Secret talks with the Czech leaders František Ladislav Rieger and František Palacký led Francis Joseph to issue an imperial rescript on September 12, 1871, promising the Czechs recognition of their ancient rights and showing his willingness to take the coronation oath. The Czechs answered this rescript on October 10, 1871, by submitting a constitutional program of 18 articles, called the Fundamental Articles. According to this program, Bohemian affairs should be regulated along the principles of the Hungarian compromise, raising Bohemia to a status equal to Hungary. With this, Hohenwart, who had been up against violent German opposition from the first day of his appointment, aroused Hungarian resistance, too. Andrássy, fearing that the Czech program could incite minority groups in Hungary, convinced Francis Joseph that the stability of the Habsburg monarchy was endangered by the Czech program. On October 27, 1871, Hohenwart was dismissed, and Francis Joseph returned the government to the hands of the German liberals.

The new Austrian prime minister, Adolf, Fürst von Auersperg, entrusted the key ministries of his cabinet to university professors and lawyers. The "ministry of doctors," as it was nicknamed, concentrated on legal and administrative reform and tried to strengthen German control in parliament. After the dismissal

COUNT ANDRÁSSY

The Hungarian prime minister and Austro-Hungarian foreign minister (1871–79) Gyula, Count Andrássy (born March 3, 1823, Kassa, Hungary, Austrian Empire [now Košice, Slovakia] —died February 18, 1890, Volosco, Istria, Austria-Hungary [now in Croatia]), helped create the Austro-Hungarian dualist form of government. As a firm supporter of Germany, he created, with the imperial German chancellor Otto von Bismarck, the Austro-German alliance of 1879, which became the cornerstone of Austria's foreign policy until the monarchy's eventual collapse in 1918.

A member of the radical Hungarian reform party under Lajos Kossuth, Andrássy entered the Hungarian Diet in 1847. He commanded a battalion in the revolt against Austria of 1848–49. Fleeing into exile on Hungary's surrender, he was condemned in absentia to death and was hanged in effigy, but he obtained an amnesty in 1857 and returned. Andrássy thereafter supported Ferenc Deák in the negotiations leading to the dualist compromise of 1867. Appointed Hungarian prime minister and defense minister (February 17, 1867), he was largely responsible for the final constitutional negotiations between Austria and Hungary.

Viewing the Slavs as a threat to his country, Andrássy became a staunch supporter of dualism and opposed Karl Siegmund von Hohenwart's scheme (1871) to raise the constitutional status of the lands of the Bohemian crown. He further cultivated relations with Germany as a counterweight to Russia and opposed the destruction of Turkey, which would have resulted in tremendous gains for the Slavic powers. On his insistence, Austria remained neutral during the Franco-German War of 1870–71.

When Emperor Francis Joseph abandoned his policy of revenge against Prussia, Andrássy became Austro-Hungarian foreign minister (November 14, 1871). During his tenure Austria-Hungary's international position was strengthened considerably. He tried to avoid an increase in the monarchy's Slavic population, but, to prevent Russia from profiting alone from the Balkan crisis beginning in 1875, he agreed at the Congress of Berlin (1878) to Austria's occupation of Bosnia and Hercegovina. This act, highly unpopular in both Austria and Hungary, contributed to his decision to resign (October 8, 1879). The previous day, however, he signed the fateful Austro-German alliance that was to link these two great powers until the end of World War I.

After his retirement, Andrássy remained in public life as a member of Hungary's upper house. His younger son and namesake also became a distinguished Austro-Hungarian political leader.

of Hohenwart, the Czechs turned to passive resistance, withdrawing from the Bohemian diet and again abstaining from attendance at the parliament in Vienna. This gave the government the chance to weaken the federalist position by introducing a bill for electoral reform. Instead of the existing modus, whereby the diets selected the deputies that were sent to parliament, the new bill set up electoral districts, each of which was to elect one deputy directly to the Reichsrat. The new system, however, preserved the old division of the electorate into *curiae* (socioeconomic classes), making parliament in this way a representation of German bourgeois interests.

The political victory of German capitalism took place at the very moment of a severe economic crisis. The opening of the Vienna International Exhibition of 1873 was seen as a manifestation of the material progress and economic achievements of the Habsburg monarchy. The so-called *Gründerjahre*, or years of expansive commercial enterprise during the late 1860s and early 1870s, however, were characterized not only by railroad and industrial expansion and the growth of the capital cities of Vienna and Budapest but also by reckless speculation. Warning signs of an imminent crisis were disregarded, and in May 1873, soon after the opening of the exhibition, the stock market collapsed.

The ensuing depression forced the government to abandon some liberal bourgeois principles. The state took over the railroads and instituted public-works projects in an attempt to alleviate popular distress. The government survived the crisis, however, and German liberal political rule continued for five more years. German liberalism would pass into eclipse not because of economic or domestic crisis but as a consequence of its opposition to foreign expansion.

A far-reaching consequence of the stock market crash of 1873 was the permeation of anti-Semitism into Austrian politics. Jews were accused of being responsible for the speculative stock market activities, even though official investigations proved that many elements of the population, including some ministers and aristocrats, had participated in the *Gründungsfieber*, or "speculative fever," and the attendant scandals.

INTERNATIONAL RELATIONS: THE BALKAN ORIENTATION

After his appointment as foreign minister on November 14, 1871, Andrássy conducted the foreign affairs of Austria-Hungary with the intention of preserving the status quo. Discarding the anti-Bismarck bias of his predecessor, Beust, he sought the friendship of the German Empire in order to strengthen his position in a possible confrontation with Russia over problems in the Balkans. The Dreikaiserbund (Three Emperors' League) of 1873, by which Francis Joseph and the German and Russian emperors agreed to work together for peace, gave expression to this policy and made a change of the status quo in the Balkans dependent on German consent.

The continuing decline of Ottoman power encouraged the Balkan nations in their opposition to Turkish rule, and in 1875 there were revolts and upheavals. Andrássy failed to induce the Ottoman government to adopt a reform program, and by 1876 Russian intervention seemed imminent. Russia offered to join with Austria-Hungary in partitioning the Balkans between them, but Andrássy believed that Austria-Hungary was a "saturated state" unable to cope with more nationalities and lands, and for a time he resisted the offer. He was aware, however, that Russia could not be restrained altogether; thus, through Bismarck's mediation, there were concluded two secret agreements, at Reichstadt (now Zákupy, Czech Republic) in July 1876 and at Budapest in January 1877, whereby Russia gave up its plans for a "great partition" and settled for the territory of Bessarabia and, in return, acquiesced in Austria-Hungary's acquiring Bosnia and Herzegovina. Austria-Hungary and Russia agreed to refrain from intervention for the time being, and it was only when great-power mediation proved unable to settle the conflict between Serbia and the Ottoman Empire that Russia declared war on the Ottoman Empire in April 1877, after having again secured Austro-Hungarian neutrality.

In February 1878, with the war won, the Russians did not content themselves with Bessarabia and, in the Treaty of San Stefano, violated Austria-Hungary's Balkan interests by creating a large independent Bulgaria. Having Great Britain as an ally in his opposition to the Russian advance in southeastern Europe and Bismarck as an "honest broker," Andrássy managed at the Congress of Berlin in July 1878 to force Russia to retreat from its excessive demands. Bulgaria was broken up again, Serbian independence was guaranteed, Russia retained Bessarabia, and Austria-Hungary was allowed to occupy Bosnia and Herzegovina. Military occupation of those two provinces turned out to be more than the expected mere formality. It took 150,000 Habsburg troops and several weeks of fighting before the lands were under Habsburg authority. Since no agreement could be reached on whether the newly acquired lands should aggrandize the Hungarian or the Austrian part of the monarchy, they were placed under the jurisdiction of the common Habsburg ministry of finance.

DOMESTIC AFFAIRS, 1879–1908

The German liberals had opposed the Balkan policy of Andrássy, and, out of fear that the Slav element in the monarchy would be strengthened by the addition of a new Slav population, they voted against the occupation of Bosnia and Herzegovina—in this way withdrawing support from the government. When Prime Minister Auersperg resigned, the era of German liberal predominance came to an end. In 1879, the same year in which an alliance with the German Empire (known as the Austro-German, or Dual, Alliance) bound the Habsburg monarchy to Germany's foreign policy, the reappointment of Taaffe as Austrian prime minister signified a reorientation in domestic affairs. From 1879 onward, the German element in the Habsburg monarchy was on the defensive, fighting stubborn and senseless rearguard actions against the Slav drive for political and national equality.

POLITICAL REALIGNMENT

Taaffe first tried to form a cabinet above parties. It was to include even the liberal Karl, Lord von Stremayr, who had presided over a caretaker government after Auersperg's resignation. The situation in parliament decisively changed when Taaffe persuaded the Czechs in 1879 to give up their boycott. Taaffe then governed with the support of a conservative coalition, including Slavs, German aristocrats, and clericals, which gave itself the name of the Iron Ring. In April 1880, language ordinances were issued that made Czech and German equal languages in the "outer [public] services" in Bohemia and Moravia. In 1882 the University of Prague was divided, giving the Czechs a national university. In the same year, an electoral reform reduced the tax requirement for the right to vote from 10 to 5 florins, thus enfranchising the more prosperous Czech peasants and weakening the hold of the German middle class.

Despite the conservative character of the government, political life in the Habsburg monarchy underwent a decisive change during the Taaffe period. The traditional party lineup decomposed, and new alignments and parties formed that were essentially radical and aggressive. From 1890 well into the 1920s, political life in Austria was dominated by three movements that originated in the 1880s: Pan-Germanism, Christian Socialism, and Democratic Socialism.

In German Austria, especially in Vienna, moderate liberals were increasingly challenged by extremist groups—notably German nationalists. In 1882 their "Linz program" proposed the restoration of German dominance in Austrian affairs by detaching Galicia, Bukovina, and Dalmatia from the monarchy, by reducing relations with Hungary to a purely personal union under the monarch, and by establishing a customs union and other close ties with the German Empire. This Pan-Germanic program found its chief protagonist in Georg, Ritter (knight) von Schönerer, a deputy to the Reichsrat, who also introduced a note of anti-Semitism into German nationalism. Although his version of extreme chauvinism and racialism never attracted more than a small number of followers, in a modified and moderate way Pan-Germanism and anti-Semitism became the ideological support of the bureaucracy and officer corps; though these elements did not favour union with Germany, they did feel that the Habsburg monarchy had the task of bringing German culture to the "inferior" non-German nationalities.

While Schönerer and Pan-Germanism appealed to the educated classes, Karl

LINZ PROGRAM

Named for its town of origin in Upper Austria (German: Oberösterreich), the Linz program was an expression of German nationalist radicalism within Austria-Hungary. It was drafted in 1882 by the extreme nationalist Georg Ritter von Schönerer and subsequently by Victor Adler, Engelbert Pernerstorfer, Robert Pattai, and Heinrich Friedjung. Their main hope was to centralize the administration under German leadership while removing Slavic areas from the Austrian Empire. They demanded autonomy for Galicia (the northeasternmost part of the empire) under its Polish inhabitants and for Dalmatia (in part the coastal territory of modern Croatia) under its Italian minority, though they were ready to add the two to Hungary if the Magyars, many of whom disliked the Dual Monarchy, supported the Germans in Austria. The program degenerated into anti-Slav sentiment, specifically a dispute over the administrative partition of Bohemia. Other demands of the Linz program were for extended franchise, progressive taxation, and protective legislation for the poorer sections of the community.

Lueger transformed the Christian Socialism of Karl, Freiherr (baron) von Voegelsang, into a political organization that appealed to small shopkeepers, artisans, tradesmen, and lower bourgeois circles of Vienna and the surrounding countryside. The workers' movement, formerly a concern of welfare and adult-education societies, also transformed itself into a political party. Although workers' movements had been weakened in Austria by personal rivalries and government persecution, in 1889 at a conference in Hainfeld, Victor Adler managed to unite the competing Marxist groups into the Social Democratic Party.

Taaffe continued to seek compromises between nationalities that were becoming increasingly radical in their demands. The Slav orientation of the Taaffe cabinet did not satisfy the Czechs, for example, but rather encouraged a mood of belligerence; because the moderate Old Czechs failed to live up to radical demands, the nationalistic Young Czechs were able to gain support from the electorate. In 1890 Taaffe tried to negotiate an agreement between the Old Czechs and the German liberals, whereby Bohemia would be divided for administrative and judicial purposes along lines of nationality, but he was balked by the more chauvinistic Young Czechs and German nationalists, and his efforts led to riots in Prague in 1893.

When Emil Steinbach joined Taaffe's cabinet as minister of finance in 1891, he encouraged Taaffe and the emperor to try electoral reform as an instrument of breaking nationalist opposition. It was hoped that, by extending the franchise, nationalistic antagonism could be allayed and the growing unrest among urban workers could be placated. On October 10, 1893, the government introduced a suffrage bill that would have given the vote to virtually every literate adult male (while preserving the traditional system of voting in *curiae*). Conservative groups of all nationalities joined forces against this bill, and, under pressure from the Hungarian government, Taaffe had to resign on November 11, 1893.

Though failing in political matters, the cabinet had introduced some economic reforms. Between 1888 and 1892 a system of cooperative banks for farmers was organized, the taxation system was revised, Austrian currency was stabilized by a return to the gold standard, and the florin was replaced by the crown, which remained the Austrian currency until 1924. The Taaffe government is also remembered for social-reform legislation; the laws of 1884 fixed the maximum working day at 11 hours, outlawed the employment of children under 12, required a Sunday rest day for workers, and set up compulsory insurance against accidents and sickness.

POLITICAL TURMOIL

The franchise question continued to dominate Austrian domestic affairs and became closely welded to the nationality conflicts. The next Austrian prime minister, Alfred, Fürst (prince) zu Windischgrätz (grandson of the Windischgrätz who seized Prague in 1848), sought to win the support of parliament by forming a cabinet in which the clerical conservatives, the Poles, and the German liberals were represented. They were united, however, only in opposition to universal suffrage. Each

minister defended his national cause, and the ministry was torn by ceaseless conflict. The end came in June 1895, when the government fulfilled an old promise and introduced Slovene classes into the grammar school at Cilli (now Celje, Slovenia) in Steiermark. Because the school had been exclusively German, this was regarded as a grave blow to the German cause, and the German liberals resigned, forcing Windischgrätz himself to resign.

Embittered by the conduct of the German liberals, Francis Joseph on October 2 entrusted the task of solving Austria's problems to a Polish aristocrat, Kasimir Felix, Graf (count) von Badeni, known as a "strong man" for the high-handed way in which he had acted as governor of Galicia. Little noticed at the time, the appointment of Badeni as Austrian prime minister symbolized the breakdown of German control over the Habsburg monarchy. For the first time in Habsburg history, Germans controlled none of the key positions of government. Not only the prime minister but also the finance minister (Leo, Ritter [knight] von Biliński) and the foreign minister (Agenor, Graf Gołuchowski, who had succeeded Gusztáv Siegmund, Graf Kálnoky von Köröspatak, in May 1895) came from the Polish part of the empire.

Badeni managed to induce parliament to accept a compromise franchise bill that introduced qualified universal male suffrage but preserved the system of class voting (a fifth *curia* was even added). The shortcomings of the new system enraged the parties representing the masses of the population. By 1897, however, elections held on the basis of the new suffrage had strengthened the radical elements in the Reichsrat; the Young Czechs, for instance, had completely overwhelmed the conservative Old Czechs.

In the 1870s and '80s, decisive economic changes with far-reaching social consequences had occurred in the Habsburg lands. Though remaining primarily agrarian, they had undergone an industrialization that had resulted in an unprecedented growth of urban centres. Vienna, which had about 430,000 inhabitants in 1851, had become a metropolis of 1,800,000 by the turn of the 20th century, and this phenomenon was paralleled in other areas, especially in Bohemia, which had become the industrial centre of the western part of the Habsburg lands. These socioeconomic developments naturally began to affect politics. From 1890 on, the advance of the Social Democrats and the Christian Socialists caused considerable tension in Vienna. In October 1894 the Social Democrats held their first impressive orderly mass demonstration in the capital, and the communal elections of 1895 made the Christian Socialists the strongest party in Vienna, ending the long liberal rule. When the emperor refused to confirm Karl Lueger, the popular leader of the Christian Socialists, as mayor of Vienna, there were demonstrations and protests. Not until Lueger was elected mayor for the fifth time did Francis Joseph agree to confirm him, in April 1897.

Counting on support from the Slav and conservative parties in parliament, Badeni dared to take up the Bohemian-language question again. In April 1897 he issued a famous language ordinance that introduced Czech as a language equal to German even in the "inner service"—i.e., for communications within government departments. This decision meant that civil servants in Bohemia and Moravia would have to be able to speak and write Czech as well as German. Since many Germans refused to learn Czech, the ordinance put them at a definite disadvantage in Bohemia's administration. The publication of the ordinance provoked violent German reactions: university professors signed resolutions of protest, mass meetings incited the public, and German deputies in the Reichsrat began to obstruct all legislative activities. The protest reached its climax in November 1897, when parliamentary sessions turned into bedlam, and popular protests against Badeni led to street demonstrations. The mass protest was not restricted to Vienna. It was even worse in some German towns in Bohemia; in Graz, clashes between soldiers and the masses ended in the death of one demonstrator.

To pacify the public, Francis Joseph gave in; on November 28, 1897, he dismissed Badeni and asked Paul, Freiherr (baron) Gautsch von Frankenthurn, a former minister of education, to form a government out of the German parties of parliament. Gautsch's attempts to appease the Germans ran into obstruction from the Czechs. The scene of violence shifted from Vienna to Prague and from the Reichsrat to the Bohemian diet. In March 1898 Gautsch was replaced by the former governor of Bohemia, Franz Anton, Fürst zu Thun und Hohenstein, who failed within a year. Of his successors neither Manfred, Graf Clary und Aldringen, who formally revoked the Badeni language ordinance, nor Heinrich Wittek, who headed a short-lived cabinet of a few weeks, managed to solve the nationality problem.

On January 18, 1900, Francis Joseph asked Ernest von Koerber, a former minister of the interior, to form a new cabinet. Koerber was the only commoner to be appointed prime minister by Francis Joseph. As a leading bureaucrat, he formed his ministry from the ranks of other bureaucrats, concentrating in subsequent years on the administration of public affairs and economic programs rather than trying to deal with political problems. First by imperial decree and then, after some political bargaining, by consent of parliament, Koerber carried through a program of economic expansion, social legislation, and administrative reform; among his reforms was the liberation of the press from government and police control. By devious politicking, he managed to keep government activities free from national strife, but he could not prevent national emotions from becoming more and more extremist. The national conflict came to be fought over educational matters, and in the final years of Koerber's government the desire for national universities aroused

the sentiments of Italians, Slovenes, and Ruthenians—turning the traditional Czech-German conflict into a multinational one. In December 1904 Koerber's various maneuverings faltered, and he was driven from office by a combination of parties.

The political climate in Austria was further complicated by the worsening of relations between the emperor and the Hungarian government. Hungarian separatists had agitated for the separation of the Habsburg army, and when Francis Joseph used an address to the troops at Chłopy (now in Poland) in 1903 for an unequivocal reaffirmation of the common and unified character of his army, a controversy developed that had repercussions in the Austrian half of the Dual Monarchy. The plan to use universal suffrage—for which popular demand had strongly increased since the Russian Revolution of 1905—to break the opposition in Hungary actually furthered the cause of political democracy in Austria.

ELECTORAL REFORM

Gautsch, who had been reappointed as prime minister, oversaw a bill that would instate universal franchise in Austria. This first bill, introduced to parliament in February 1906, ran into the opposition of the middle-class and conservative parties that still controlled parliament. Nevertheless, imperial interest and popular pressure—the Social Democrats had organized mass rallies to support the bill—combined to overcome parliamentary opposition. After Gautsch resigned in March 1906 and his successor, Conrad, Fürst (prince) von Hohenlohe-Schillingsfürst, failed to master the situation, Max Wladimir, Freiherr (baron) von Beck (Austrian prime minister from June 1906), managed to carry the bill through parliament. In January 1907 Francis Joseph sanctioned the law, which gave the vote to every male over age 23 and abolished the *curiae*.

The returns of the election of 1907 made the Germans inescapably a minority in parliament, with 233 members, though they certainly remained the strongest national group. (The Czechs could count on 107 seats, the Poles 82, the Ruthenians 33, the Slovenes 24, the Italians 19, the Serbs and Croats 13, and the Romanians 5.) Universal suffrage also brought the expected decline of the chauvinistic parties. The Young Czechs and the Pan-Germans were reduced to small factions without parliamentary influence, while the Christian Socialists and the Social Democrats returned as the two strongest parties out of more than 30 represented in parliament; the socialist delegation in the Austrian parliament was, in fact, larger than in any other country. The Austrian constitution, however, did not force the emperor to form his government according to the composition of the parliament. Neither the Social Democrats nor the Christian Socialists acquired any significant influence on the shaping of Austrian government affairs.

Beck remained in office and satisfied the Christian Socialists with some concessions but for the most part based his policy on the support of the conservative parties. In 1905 the diet of Moravia had succeeded in finding a compromise between German and Czech national demands, and it was hoped that a similar compromise could be achieved for Bohemia. But, within a short time, national conflicts got the upper hand again, and parliamentary debate and public opinion were once more excited by national strife. In 1908, however, international complications diverted attention from domestic affairs.

FOREIGN POLICY, 1878–1908

The occupation of Bosnia and Herzegovina in 1878 had reasserted Habsburg interests in Balkan affairs. Facing the possibility of conflict with Russia in this area, Austria-Hungary had looked for an ally, with the result that in 1879 Austria-Hungary and the German Empire had joined in the Austro-German (or Dual) Alliance, by which the two sovereigns promised each other support in the case of Russian aggression. The signing of the Dual Alliance was Andrássy's last act as foreign minister, but the alliance survived as the main element in the international position of the Habsburg monarchy until the last day of the empire. Under Andrássy's successors, Habsburg foreign policy continued its conservative course.

In 1881 an alliance with Serbia, which after the Congress of Berlin (1878) had

AUSTRO-GERMAN ALLIANCE

An agreement often called the Dual Alliance, the Austro-German Alliance (1879) was a pact between Austria-Hungary and the German Empire in which the two powers promised each other support in case of attack by Russia, and neutrality in case of aggression by any other power. Germany's Otto von Bismarck saw the alliance as a way to prevent the isolation of Germany and to preserve peace, as Russia would not wage war against both empires. The addition of Italy in 1882 made it the Triple Alliance. The agreement remained an important element of both German and Austro-Hungarian foreign policy until 1918.

turned to Austria-Hungary for protection, made this Balkan state a satellite of the Habsburg monarchy. The Three Emperors' League (comprising Russia, Germany, and Austria-Hungary) of the same year brought Russian recognition of Habsburg predominance in the western part of the Balkan Peninsula. The signatories of this alliance promised to consult one another on any changes in the status quo in the Ottoman Empire, and, while Russia was given assurances that its position regarding Bulgaria and the Straits (the Dardanelles, the Sea of Marmara, and the Bosporus) would be recognized, Austria-Hungary received from Russia the promise that there would be no objection to a possible annexation of Bosnia and Herzegovina in the future.

The Three Emperors' League was an important element in the structure of alliances that German chancellor Bismarck set up to stabilize Europe. Having decided to rely on Austria-Hungary as the fundamental partner in international affairs, Bismarck had to try to neutralize all the areas in which the Habsburg monarchy might be drawn into a conflict. It was essential to avoid being involved in a controversy at an inopportune moment and in a region of little interest to Germany. Bismarck therefore attempted to lessen the possibility of a conflict between Austria-Hungary and Russia by making them partners in the Three Emperors' League. And when, in 1882, Italy approached Germany to find a partner in its anti-French policy, Bismarck used the opportunity to neutralize another European trouble spot. He told the Italian foreign minister that the road to Berlin led through Vienna, with the result that the Triple Alliance (comprising Italy, Germany, and Austria-Hungary) was signed in May 1882. It was primarily a defensive treaty against a French attack on Italy or Germany. It further stated that, in the event of any signatory coming to war with another power, the partners of the alliance would remain neutral. The treaty did not settle the problems still existing between the Habsburg monarchy and the

Italian kingdom, but for Bismarck it sufficed that they were neutralized.

In 1883 Bismarck acted again to reduce the danger of war in "Europe's backyard" by arranging a defensive agreement between Austria-Hungary and Romania. The Triple Alliance and the Romanian Alliance not only strengthened the international status quo but also gave security to the internal order of the Habsburg monarchy by weakening the irredentist movements in Transylvania and the Italian parts of Austria-Hungary.

The deterioration of German-French relations in the following years convinced Bismarck of the indispensability of the Triple Alliance, and he made every effort to force Vienna to renew the alliance in 1887. By threatening to withdraw protection against Russian aggression, Bismarck forced the Austro-Hungarian foreign minister Kálnoky to consent to his demands, but there can be no doubt that Austria-Hungary was impeded in its national interests by having to adapt its foreign policy to the German and Italian demand for the isolation of France. Although Kálnoky succeeded during the negotiations in avoiding any new obligation in western Europe, he was less successful in defending more-immediate Austrian interests. He managed to evade the Italian request for the support of an active Italian colonial policy, but he was unable to keep Italy out of involvement in Balkan affairs. It might be that, in view of his own conservative and defensive policy, he saw an advantage in having

Italy as a third partner in the maintenance of the status quo against possible Russian expansion. At any rate, it was on Kálnoky's initiative that the original Italian demand for a declaration in favour of the status quo along the Ottoman coasts and the Adriatic and Aegean seas was extended to the interior of the Balkan Peninsula. On top of this, Kálnoky granted the Italians the right to ask for compensation in case of any change in the territorial status quo without defining this term. In a certain way, all the differences and clashes between Austrian and Italian Balkan policy in the first decade of the 20th century can be traced to the introduction of this clause (later formulated in Article VII of the treaty) at the renewal of 1887.

In the same year, Bismarck built around the Triple Alliance a system of alliances and agreements that amounted to complete isolation of France and obliged the major European powers to guarantee the status quo along the borders of the Ottoman Empire. The First and Second Mediterranean Agreements of 1887 joined Great Britain to the powers (Austria-Hungary and Italy) interested in blocking Russia from the Straits and enabled Kálnoky to abandon direct agreements with Russia. The Three Emperors' League of 1881 was allowed to expire, and Austria-Hungary was thus left without any formal understanding with Russia. Gołuchowski, who followed Kálnoky as foreign minister in 1895, decided that direct relations with

Russia should be renewed. In April 1897 Francis Joseph and Gołuchowski visited St. Petersburg. The agreements signed as a result of this initiative aimed to exclude Italy from Balkan affairs and sought to entrust preservation of the Balkan order to the bilateral cooperation of the two eastern monarchies rather than to a multilateral alliance system. Thus, the final years of the 19th century were marked by a change from static continental policy to a more dynamic world policy, and the ensuing mobility in international relations reduced the value of the Triple Alliance.

The Austro-Russian agreements of 1897 came to bear in 1903, when a major revolt occurred in Macedonia. After a meeting between Tsar Nicholas II and Francis Joseph in October 1903, their foreign ministers drafted a reform program for the Ottoman Empire. A mutual neutrality agreement was added in 1904, leaving Austria-Hungary a free hand in the event of a conflict with Italy and enabling Russia to turn and face Japan.

Explicitly excluded from the agreement with Russia were Balkan conflicts. When King Alexander of Serbia was assassinated in a military revolt in 1903 and the Obrenović dynasty was replaced by the Karadjordjević, Serbian relations with the Habsburg monarchy deteriorated. The Serbs adopted an expansionist policy of unifying all South Slavs in the Serbian kingdom, and, in order to block a Serbian advance, the Habsburg monarchy applied economic pressure. In 1906 all livestock imports from Serbia into Austria-Hungary were prohibited. This conflict, the so-called Pig War, did not crush Serbia but rather pushed it into the Russian camp.

When, in 1906, Gołuchowski was replaced as foreign minister by the former ambassador to St. Petersburg, Alois, Graf (count) Lexa von Aehrenthal, a turning point in Austrian foreign policy was signaled. Aehrenthal made a belated effort to free Austria-Hungary from its submission to German interests and to engage in a dynamic Balkan policy. A first step was his proposal for the construction of a railroad through the Sandžak of Novi Pazar, a strip of land that separated Serbia from Montenegro. The combined Russian and Serbian opposition forced Aehrenthal to abandon the project temporarily and made it clear that any advance in the Balkans would probably result in war with Serbia and perhaps with Russia as well.

The danger of such a conflict arose within a short time. In July 1908, after a revolution in the Ottoman Empire, the Young Turk movement announced the reform of the Ottoman constitution. Afraid that this constitutional change could undermine the Habsburg position in Bosnia and Herzegovina, which nominally were still under Ottoman suzerainty, Aehrenthal decided to use the opportunity to fortify the Austro-Hungarian position in the Balkan Peninsula. In September 1908 he met with the Russian foreign minister, Aleksandr, Count Izvolsky, and secured, so he thought, Russian approval of the proposed annexation in return for Austria's support in having the Straits opened to Russian warships. On October 6, 1908, the annexation was announced, immediately bringing a violent reaction from Serbia. When Izvolsky found that his plans for the Straits were opposed by Great Britain and France, he retracted his tentative support of Austria and supported the Serbian position. The situation became serious, and for a while war seemed imminent. Franz, Freiherr (baron) Conrad von Hötzendorf, the chief of the general staff of the Habsburg monarchy, who had long advocated preventive war, pushed for an aggressive move, but Aehrenthal had apparently never planned more than going to the brink of war. In March 1909 a German ultimatum forced the Russians to withdraw their support from Serbia, and, since the Turkish government had agreed to the annexation of Bosnia and Herzegovina in return for a monetary compensation, Serbia also had to come to terms with the Habsburg monarchy. The Bosnian crisis was settled, but the Serbs felt their national pride deeply wounded and continued to stir unrest in the South Slav provinces of the Habsburg monarchy.

LAST YEARS OF PEACE

The annexation crisis had repercussions among the other Slav nationalities in the monarchy. For several years Czechs had been attracted by the Pan-Slav movement, and in July 1908 a Pan-Slav congress was held in Prague. During the diplomatic crisis of the following winter, the Czechs unabashedly took the side of the Serbs, and, on the day of the 60th anniversary of Francis Joseph's accession to the throne, martial law had to be declared in Prague. National strife broke out all over the monarchy, and parliamentary activities were all but blocked by filibustering and the riotous activities of the deputies. Austrian Prime Minister Beck had resigned in November 1908; his successor, Richard, Freiherr (baron) von Bienerth, after having accomplished little with a cabinet of civil servants, tried to appease the nationalities by including *Landsmannminister* (national representatives) in his cabinet (February 1909).

Obstruction in parliament continued. The Germans, in control of the government and the central administration, continued to assign to the monarchy the role of an outpost of German culture; the Slavs increasingly wanted to make Austria the home of Slav national aspirations. The Czech agrarian leader František Udržal stated in parliament: "We wish to save the Austrian parliament from utter ruin, but we wish to save it for the Slavs of Austria, who form two-thirds of the population." A population census taken in 1910 more or less confirmed the Slav claim: out of the 28,324,940 inhabitants of the western half of the Austro-Hungarian Empire, nearly 36 percent regarded themselves as Germans, whereas more than 60 percent regarded themselves as Slavs—nearly 18 percent as Poles, about 13 percent as Ruthenians, about 23 percent as Czechs or Slovaks, nearly 5 percent as Slovenes, and almost 3 percent as Serbs or Croats. (Less than 3 percent identified themselves as Italians.) Slav predominance was weakened by the attitude of the Poles, who remained loyal to the central government, allowing the national conflict to assume the character of a primarily Czech-German quarrel.

Even the Social Democratic Party could not overcome nationalist antagonism. In 1899, at the party congress at Brünn (now Brno, Czech Republic), the Social Democrats had presented a national reform program based on democratic federalism, which would have granted the right of national decisions to territorial units formed on a basis of nationality. Karl Renner and Otto Bauer, who later became leaders of German-Austrian socialism, drafted various programs for the solution of the nationality problem in books published between 1900 and 1910. But these efforts could not prevent the socialists from splitting along national lines too, and in 1910 the Czech socialists declared themselves independent of the Social Democratic Party.

Such national differences weakened the socialist position in the elections of 1911. More than 50 parties had competed in the campaign, and, since the German nationalist parties had allied in the Deutscher Nationalverband (German National League), they managed to return to parliament as the strongest single party, gaining 104 seats out of 516. The Christian Socialists, weakened by personal rivalry, suffered heavy losses, winning only 76 seats. The Social Democrats received 44 seats and the Czech Social Democrats 24. The Czech parties were badly divided, with those representing the Czech middle class gaining 64 seats. Prime Minister Bienerth found himself unable to form a workable ministry, and he was replaced by Gautsch, reappointed for the third and final time, who tried to reconcile the Germans and the Czechs.

For a while negotiations seemed quite successful, but extremist incidents deadlocked the talks, and the Gautsch cabinet was replaced by a new ministry headed by Karl, Graf (count) von Stürgkh, in November 1911. Unable to deal with the nationality problem in a parliamentarian fashion, Stürgkh repeatedly suspended the Reichsrat. It was characteristic of the general political climate in Europe that Stürgkh had to concentrate his legislative program on the improvement of Austrian armament, for international crises overshadowed the nationality conflict.

CONFLICT WITH SERBIA

Since the Bosnian crisis of 1908–09, Austrian diplomats had been convinced that war with Serbia was bound to come. Aehrenthal died in February 1912, at a moment when an Italian-Turkish conflict over Tripoli (now in Libya) had provoked anti-Turkish sentiment in the Balkan states. Leopold, Graf (count) von Berchtold, who directed Austro-Hungarian foreign policy from 1912 on, did not have the qualities required in such a critical period. Aehrenthal had been able to silence the warmongering activities of Conrad, the Habsburg chief of staff who continued to advocate preventive war against Italy and Serbia, but Berchtold yielded to the aggressive policies of the military and the younger members of his ministry. During the Balkan Wars (1912–13), fought by the Balkan states over the remnants of the Ottoman Empire, Austria-Hungary twice tried to force Serbia to withdraw from positions gained by threatening it with an ultimatum. In February and October 1913, military action against Serbia was contemplated, but in both instances neither Italy nor Germany was willing to guarantee support. Austria-Hungary ultimately had to acquiesce in Serbia's territorial gains. But by supporting Bulgaria's claims against Serbia, Austria-Hungary also had alienated Romania, which had shown resentment against the Habsburg monarchy because of the treatment of non-Hungarian nationalities in Hungary. Romania thus joined Italy and Serbia in support of irredentist movements inside the Habsburg monarchy. By 1914, leading government circles in Vienna were convinced that offensive action against the foreign protagonists of irredentist claims was essential to the integrity of the empire.

In June 1914 Archduke Francis Ferdinand, the heir of Francis Joseph, participated in army maneuvers in the provinces of Bosnia and Herzegovina, disregarding warnings that his visit would arouse considerable hostility. When Francis Ferdinand and his wife were assassinated by the Bosnian Serb nationalist Gavrilo Princip at Sarajevo (Bosnia and Herzegovina) on June 28, 1914, the Austro-Hungarian foreign office decided to use the opportunity for a final reckoning with the Serbian danger. The support of Germany was sought and received, and the Austro-Hungarian foreign office drafted an ultimatum putting the responsibility for the assassination on the Serbian government and demanding full satisfaction. The attitude of the foreign office was shared by Conrad and the Austrian prime minister, Stürgkh, but it was opposed by the Hungarian prime minister, István, Count Tisza, who wanted an assurance that a military move against Serbia would not result in territorial acquisitions and thus increase the Serb element in the monarchy. His demand satisfied, Tisza joined the advocates of war.

In ministerial meetings on July 15 and 19, a deliberately provocative ultimatum was drafted in words that supposedly excluded the possibility of acceptance by Serbia. The ultimatum was handed to the Serbian government on July 23. The Serbian answer, handed in on time on July 25, was declared insufficient, though Serbia had agreed to all Austro-Hungarian demands except for two that, in effect, entailed constitutional changes in the Serbian government. These demands were that

Archduke Francis Ferdinand and his wife, Sophie, riding through Sarajevo shortly before they were assassinated by a Bosnian Serb nationalist in 1914. The event was a precipitating cause of World War I. Henry Guttmann/Hulton Royals Collection/Getty Images

certain unnamed Serbian officials be dismissed at the whim of Austria-Hungary and that Austro-Hungarian officials participate, on Serbian soil, in the suppression of organizations hostile to Austria-Hungary and in the judicial proceedings against their members. In its reply, the Serbian government pointed out that such demands were unprecedented in relations between sovereign states, but it nevertheless agreed to submit the matter to the international

Permanent Court of Arbitration or to the arbitration of the Great Powers (comprising France, Germany, Great Britain, and Russia, in addition to Austria). On receiving this reply, the Austro-Hungarian ambassador left Belgrade (Serbia), severing diplomatic relations between the two countries.

Foreign Minister Berchtold and his government were clearly determined to make war on Serbia, regardless of the fact that such action might result in war between the Great Powers. While the European governments frantically tried to offer compromise solutions, Austria decided on a fait accompli. On July 28, 1914, Berchtold asked Francis Joseph to sign the declaration of war, informing him that

> it cannot be excluded that the [Triple] Entente powers [Russia, France, and Great Britain] might make another move to bring about a peaceful settlement of the conflict unless a declaration of war establishes a fait accompli [eine klare Situation geschaffen].

In the meantime, the German government had taken control of the situation. Placing German strategic and national plans over Austro-Hungarian interests, Germany changed the Balkan conflict into a continental war by declaring war against Russia and France.

WORLD WAR I

The German declaration of war subordinated the Austro-Serbian conflict to the German aim of settling its own rivalries with France and Russia. According to the terms of the military agreement between Germany and Austria-Hungary, the Austro-Hungarian army had to abandon plans to conquer Serbia and instead protect the German invasion of France against Russian intervention. The setbacks that the Austrian army suffered in 1914 and 1915 can be attributed to a large extent to the fact that Austria-Hungary became a military satellite of Germany from the first day of the war, though it cannot be denied that the Austrian high command proved to be quite incompetent. The Austro-Hungarian chief of staff, Conrad, had clamoured for preventive war since 1906, but, when he received his chance in July 1914, it turned out that the Austrian army had no plans for an expeditious offensive. Similarly, after Italy entered the war on the side of the Allied Powers in May 1915, Conrad was unprepared. The fact that only after the Germans had taken command could the Russian front be stabilized did little to enhance the prestige of the Austrian government.

In July 1914 parliament was out of session, and the Austrian prime minister, Stürgkh, refused to convene it. This and the military censorship established immediately after the outbreak of the war concealed the discontent of the non-German population. While German public opinion in Austria had welcomed the war enthusiastically, and while some Polish leaders supported the war out of anti-Russian feeling, the Czech population openly showed its animosity. The Czech leader Tomáš Masaryk, who had been one of the most prominent spokesmen of the Czech cause, emigrated to western Europe in protest. Karel Kramář, who had supported the Pan-Slav idea, was tried for high treason and found guilty on the basis of shaky evidence. German nationalism was riding high, but in fact the German

Austrians had little influence left. In military matters they were practically reduced to executing Germany's orders; in economic affairs the Hungarians, who controlled the food supply, had the decisive influence. The Hungarian prime minister, Tisza, who had opposed the war in July 1914, became the strongman of the empire. On his advice Foreign Minister Berchtold was dismissed in January 1915, and the foreign office was again entrusted to a Hungarian, István, Count Burián. But Burián failed to keep Italy and Romania out of the war. German attempts to pacify the two states by concessions were unsuccessful because Francis Joseph was unwilling to cede any territory in response to the irredentist demands of the two nations. How little the outward calm in the Habsburg lands corresponded to the sentiment of the population became apparent when Stürgkh was assassinated in October 1916 by Friedrich Adler, the pacifist son of Victor Adler, the leader of Austrian socialism. Francis Joseph made Koerber prime minister once again, but Koerber had no chance to develop a program of his own.

On November 21, 1916, Francis Joseph died, leaving the throne and the shaky empire to his 29-year-old grand-nephew, Charles (I), who had had little preparation for his task until he became heir apparent on the death of Francis Ferdinand. Full of the best intentions, Charles set out to save the monarchy by searching for peace in foreign affairs and by recognizing the rights of the empire's non-German and non-Hungarian nationalities. Charles relied heavily on the advice of politicians who had had the confidence of Francis Ferdinand. He dismissed Koerber in December 1916 and made Heinrich, Graf (count) von Clam-Martinic, a Czech aristocrat, prime minister. At the foreign office he replaced Burián with Ottokar, Count Czernin.

When parliament was reconvened in May 1917, it became manifest how far internal disintegration of the Habsburg monarchy had progressed. Parliament again became the stage of unrelenting national conflicts. Finding so little support from the Czech side, Charles turned back to the German element, and in June 1917 he made Ernst von Seidler, once his tutor in administrative and international law, prime minister. Although he tried to appease the Czechs, the stubborn insistence of the Germans not to yield any of their prerogatives made reform of the empire impossible.

At the same time, various moves to get Austria-Hungary out of the war ended in failure. After a U.S. offer of general mediation had miscarried in December 1916, Charles tried through secret channels to deal directly with the Triple Entente powers. In the spring of 1917 an exchange of peace feelers took place through the mediation of his brother-in-law, Sixtus, Fürst (prince) von Bourbon-Parma, but Italy's unwillingness to abandon some of the concessions granted to it in the 1915 Treaty of London (by which Italy joined the Allies) made these talks abortive. Similarly, negotiations with Allied representatives carried on in Switzerland brought no results.

Since the Austro-Hungarian government was unable to extricate itself from the Dual Alliance, which tied Austria-Hungary to Germany, France and England ceased to have regard for the integrity of the Habsburg monarchy. Furthermore, the revolutionary events in Russia in 1917 and the entry of the United States into the war introduced a new, ideological element into Allied policy toward the German-led coalition known as the Central Powers. The German-directed governments represented an authoritarian system of government, and national agitation in the Habsburg lands assumed the character of a democratic liberation movement, winning the sympathies of western European and American public opinion. From early 1918 the Allied governments began to officially promote the activities of the émigrés from Austria, foremost among them the Czech leader Masaryk, and in April 1918 the Congress of Oppressed Nationalities was organized in Rome.

But the collapse of the Habsburg monarchy cannot be ascribed to the Allied policy of supporting the independence claims of the Habsburg nationalities, which was only a belated adjustment to the changed conditions within Austria-Hungary. From the summer of 1917, the activities of the nationalist movements within the empire made the situation increasingly untenable. Two days before U.S. Pres. Woodrow Wilson proclaimed his Fourteen Points—one of which demanded the reorganization of the Habsburg monarchy in accordance with the principles of national autonomy—the Czechs demanded outright independence (January 6, 1918). Within a month Polish and South Slav deputies, together with the Czechs, presented to the Reichsrat a program demanding the establishment of independent constituent assemblies for nationally homogeneous areas.

END OF THE HABSBURG EMPIRE

As World War I raged and the national independence movement reached its final stage, another destabilizing development manifested itself. From 1915 on, the supply situation had worsened increasingly, and by January 1918 there were dangerous shortages, especially of food. Prompted by the difficult food situation and inspired by the Bolshevik victory in Russia, a strike movement developed in the Habsburg lands. Demands for more bread and a demand for peace were combined with nationalist claims resulting in open opposition to the government. The strikes among the civilian population were followed by mutinies in the army and navy. In January and February 1918 the army and the government succeeded in suppressing the social unrest and antiwar demonstrations. But, from the same date, the national opposition movement gathered momentum.

The hopes that the government soon placed on peace settlements with the eastern states were not fulfilled. The treaties of Brest-Litovsk with Ukraine (signed in February 1918) and with Soviet Russia (March 3, 1918) as well as the Treaty of Bucharest, which established peace with Romania (May 7, 1918), did not alleviate the supply situation and irritated the Poles because of certain provisions of the Ukrainian settlement.

In April 1918 Czernin was replaced as foreign minister by Burián. This change resulted from the conflict between Czernin and Charles over the desirability and possibility of Austria's concluding a separate peace with the Allies. When Charles's secret overtures to the Allies in 1917 were revealed by French premier Georges Clemenceau, the Germans were outraged, and Czernin was dismissed on their orders. Burián returned to the foreign office on April 16 and immediately reported to the German high command at Spa (Belgium), where he and Charles had to assure the German emperor, William II, of their unchanging loyalty. While this act of submission satisfied the German Austrians, it further incensed the Slav opposition.

In May 1918 a Slav national celebration in Prague demonstrated the strength of the independence movements. But Charles and the German elements in the central government were still not aware of the extent of the disintegration. In July 1918 Prime Minister Seidler resigned, and his successor, Max Hussarek, Freiherr (baron) von Heinlein, began a belated effort to reorganize the Habsburg monarchy. Hussarek's efforts to federalize the empire in the moment of imminent military defeat unintentionally turned out to provide the basis for the formal liquidation of the Habsburg monarchy. On October 16, 1918, Charles issued a manifesto announcing the transformation of Austria into a federal union of four components: German, Czech, South Slav, and Ukrainian. The Poles were to be free to join a Polish state, and the port of Trieste was to be given a special status. The lands of the Hungarian crown were to be excepted from this program.

Within a few days, national councils were established in all the provinces of the empire, and for all practical purposes they acted as national governments. The Poles proclaimed the union of all Poles in a unified state and declared their independence at Warsaw on October 7; the South Slavs advocated union with Serbia; and on October 28, the Czechs proclaimed the establishment of an independent republic. The dissolution of the Habsburg monarchy was thus consummated by the end of October 1918—that is, before the war actually ended.

It was impossible for the country to survive another winter of hostilities, and on September 14, 1918, Burián published an appeal to all belligerents to discuss the possibilities of ending the war. When this move was opposed by the Germans as well as by the Allies, Burián tried for a separate peace settlement for Austria-Hungary. On October 14 he sent a note to President Wilson asking for an armistice on the basis of the Fourteen Points. On October 18 the

U.S. secretary of state, Robert Lansing, replied that, in view of the political development of the preceding months and, especially, in view of the fact that the new country of Czechoslovakia had been recognized as being at war with the Central Powers, the U.S. government was unable to deal on the basis of the Fourteen Points anymore. On October 27 Gyula, Gróf (Count) Andrássy (the son of the former foreign minister Andrássy), who had replaced Burián three days before as foreign minister, sent a new note to Wilson; in asking for an armistice, he declared full adherence to the statements set forth in the U.S. note of October 18, thus explicitly recognizing the existence of an independent Czechoslovak state. From this moment, it remained only to liquidate the war.

On October 22 Heinrich Lammasch, a renowned authority in the field of international law and a respected pacifist, formed a new cabinet. He hoped to save the Habsburg monarchy by drawing up a federative structure. Instead, however, he found himself charged with the task of supervising the dissolution of the empire and bringing about an orderly transfer of power. The government could not influence events outside Vienna any longer, and from October 30 it was even challenged in the central agencies by the German-Austrian state council.

Hostilities were ended by an armistice signed on November 3, 1918. The Austro-Hungarian high command, which had blundered into the war unprepared in 1914, did little better at its conclusion. Owing to inaccuracies in the wording of the documents, more than 300,000 Austro-Hungarian soldiers were taken prisoner by the Italian army.

For some days, the government hoped that, in spite of the secession of the Slav areas, the Habsburg dynasty could survive in the remaining lands. But even the German Austrians had lost faith in the Habsburgs, and, with revolutionary agitation on the rise and republican passion widespread, Charles adhered to the advice of Lammasch and decided to waive his rights to exercise political authority. On November 11, 1918, he issued a proclamation acknowledging "in advance the decision to be taken by German Austria" and stating that he relinquished all part in the administration of the state. The declaration of November 11 marks the formal dissolution of the Habsburg monarchy.

CHAPTER 8

THE AUSTRIAN REPUBLIC

On October 21, 1918, the 210 German members of the Reichsrat of Austria formed themselves into the National Assembly for German-Austria, and on October 30 they proclaimed this an independent state under the direction of the State Council (Staatsrat), composed of the leaders of the three main parties (Social Democrats, Christian Socialists, and German Nationalists) and other elected members. Revolutionary disturbances in Vienna and, more important, the news of the declaration of a republic in Germany forced the State Council on the republican path. On November 12, the day after Charles's abdication, the National Assembly resolved unanimously that "German-Austria is a democratic republic" and also that "German-Austria is a component part of the German republic." Under the title of chancellor, the socialist Renner became head of a coalition government, with Bauer, the acknowledged spokesman of the left wing of the Social Democrats, as foreign secretary. On November 22 the territory of the republic was further defined: the National Assembly claimed for the new state all the Habsburg lands in which a majority of the population was German. It also claimed the German areas of Bohemia and Moravia.

FIRST REPUBLIC AND THE ANSCHLUSS

From the first day, the republic was faced with the disastrous heritage of the war. Four years of war effort and the breakup of the Habsburg empire had brought economic exhaustion and chaos. The resulting social distress and poverty inspired revolutionary activities, making bolshevism appear the greatest danger to the new republic, especially after a Soviet republic was established in Hungary at the end of March 1919.

EARLY POSTWAR YEARS

The Austrian Social Democrats were determined to resist bolshevism with their own forces without making an alliance (as the German Social Democrats did) with the old order. The Volkswehr (People's Guard) was organized and was twice effective (April 17 and June 15) against communist attempts at a putsch. Bauer and fellow socialist leader Friedrich Adler staked their popularity on defeating the communist agitation in the workers' and soldiers' councils, which had been set up on the Soviet model. By mid-1919, political and social order was restored on parliamentary lines, and the Communist Party relapsed into insignificance.

More dangerous was the tendency of the Länder (states) to break away from Vienna or to claim almost complete independence. Though the principal motive of this was reluctance to send food supplies to Vienna, it also represented a genuine social, political, and ideological conflict: the administration of the industrialized capital was socialist controlled, while the states, being predominantly agrarian, remained conservative and faithful to the Roman Catholic tradition. This difference was aggravated by the fact that the Habsburg monarchy had

been the only bond between the German Austrian lands; with the abdication of the emperor, no symbol of loyalty common to all states remained. Vorarlberg voted for union with Switzerland in May 1919, and Tirol also attempted to secede.

In February 1919, elections for a constitutional assembly were held. The Social Democrats were returned as the largest single party, with 69 seats. The Christian Socialists won 63 and the German Nationalists 26. When this assembly met (March 4), it had to make wide concessions to federalism in order to appease the states. In exchange, Vienna was elevated to the rank of a state, and the mayor was made the equivalent of a state governor. This proviso subsequently enabled socialist-controlled Vienna to pursue an autonomous policy, even though the Bundesregierung ("federal government") was controlled by the conservative parties from 1920 to 1934.

The constituent assembly also settled the constitution of the federal republic (October 1, 1920). The State Council was abolished, and a bicameral legislative assembly, the Bundesversammlung, was established. The Bundesrat (upper house) was to exercise only a suspensive veto and was to be elected roughly in proportion to the population in each state. This represented a defeat for the federal elements in the states, which had wanted the Bundesrat to exercise an absolute veto and to be composed of equal numbers of members from each state. The Nationalrat (lower house) was to be elected by universal suffrage on a basis of proportional representation. The Bundesversammlung in full session elected the president of the republic for a four-year term, but the federal government, with the chancellor at its head, was elected in the Nationalrat on a motion submitted by its principal committee; this committee was itself representative of the proportions of the parties in the house.

The foreign policy of Bauer and the representatives of the major political parties had insisted firmly on Anschluss ("union") with Germany, and, as late as 1921, unauthorized plebiscites held in the western provinces returned overwhelming majorities in favour of the union. But Article 88 of the Treaty of Saint-Germain (1919), signed by Austria and the Allied Powers, forbade Anschluss without the consent of the League of Nations and stipulated that the republic should cease to call itself Deutschösterreich (German-Austria); it became the Republik Österreich (Republic of Austria). The Austrian claim for the German-speaking areas of Bohemia and Moravia was denied by the Saint-Germain peace conference, and Austria also had to recognize the frontiers of Czechoslovakia along slightly rectified historical administrative lines. On Austria's southern frontier, the newly created Kingdom of Serbs, Croats, and Slovenes threatened armed invasion until it was decided that the border question should be settled by a plebiscite, which, on October 10, 1920, returned a majority of 59 percent in

favour of Austria. The German-speaking districts of western Hungary were to be ceded to Austria outright, but Austria, in the face of Hungarian resistance, was obliged to hold a plebiscite. The area of Sopron was finally restored to Hungary.

After the elections of February 1919, Renner had formed another coalition government; however, following a government crisis in the summer of 1920, a caretaker cabinet under the Christian Socialist Michael Mayr was formed. This was the government that prepared the draft of the constitution and introduced it into parliament. After its approval, new elections were held on October 17, 1920. The Christian Socialists were returned as the strongest party, gaining 82 seats, while the Social Democrats were reduced to 66 and the German Nationalists to 20. Mayr formed a cabinet composed of Christian Socialists; the Social Democrats went into opposition and never returned to the government during the First Republic.

This political division hardened, and no decisive change took place during the following years. The system of proportional representation combined with the ideological background of Austrian parties made oscillations of political allegiance unlikely. Of the two mass parties, the Social Democrats had an unshakable majority in Vienna (in which about a third of the republic's population lived), while the Christian Socialists had an equally secure majority among the Roman Catholic peasants and the conservative classes, the latter consisting largely of army officers, landowners, and big businesses. The urban middle classes, hostile to both workers and peasants, became German Nationalists. But German nationalism was not limited to the middle classes. Many workers and peasants felt themselves to be Germans and responded to the national appeal.

ECONOMIC RECONSTRUCTION AND POLITICAL STRIFE

The main task of the nonsocialist governments in power from the autumn of 1920 was to restore financial and economic stability. Between 1919 and 1921 Austria's urban population lived largely on relief from the United States and Great Britain, and, although production improved, distress was heightened by inflation that threatened financial collapse in 1922. In October 1922 the chancellor, Ignaz Seipel, secured a large loan through the League of Nations, enabling Austrian finances to be stabilized. In return, Austria had to undertake to remain independent for at least 20 years. The controller general appointed by the League of Nations reported in December 1925 that the Austrian budget had been balanced satisfactorily, and in March 1926 international financial supervision was withdrawn.

Seipel's success in October 1922 gave Austria some years of stability and made economic reconstruction and relative prosperity possible. In socialist-controlled Vienna, an ambitious program of working-class housing, health schemes, and adult education was carried out under the leadership of Karl Seitz, Hugo Breitner, and Julius Tandler. "Red Vienna" thus acquired a unique reputation in Europe.

In 1920 all three major parties spoke in democratic terms. Despite democratic rhetoric, however, preparations for civil war had never been abandoned. The Christian Socialists, led by Seipel, a believer in strong government, were convinced that they had to protect the existing social order against a Marxist revolution. In the provinces, reactionary forces known as the Heimwehr (Home Defense Force)—originally formed for defense against Slavs invading from the south or against marauding soldiers returning from service in World War I—gradually acquired fascist tendencies. The Social Democrats, who felt that their social-reform program was endangered, had their own armed force, the Schutzbund (Defense League), descended from the People's Guard of 1918.

The Schutzbund and the reactionary forces regularly demonstrated against each other. In 1927, in the course of a clash between members of the Schutzbund and reactionary forces at Schattendorf, an old man and a child were accidentally shot by reactionaries. When the latter were acquitted by a Vienna jury on July 14, the Social Democrats called for a mass demonstration, which got out of hand and ended in the burning down of the ministry of justice. In fighting between the police and the demonstrators, almost 100 people were killed and many more were

HEIMWEHR

Immediately after World War I, a number of local organizations known as Heimwehr ("Home Defense Force") formed in various parts of Austria to expel invading Yugoslavs or preserve order. Composed of conservative-minded country dwellers, the Heimwehr came to represent much of the Austrian right wing between World Wars I and II. Imbued with corporativism (an authoritarian view of the state as composed of interest groups rather than individuals), the Heimwehr also drew on strong monarchistic, patriotic, and religious feelings. Some members looked to Italy and Benito Mussolini for guidance, but historians disagree over whether the Heimwehr was outrightly Fascist.

Local Heimwehr sections were often quite distinct, some in eastern Austria being under Christian Social Party leadership, others in the west having Nazi sympathizers as directors. Though a "march on Vienna" by the Styrian Heimwehr in 1931 failed, Heimwehr forces assumed much power in the provinces after Parliament was suspended in 1933, and they played an important part in suppressing Socialists in February 1934. After the *Anschluss* (Union) with Germany of 1938, the Heimwehr was overshadowed by the Nazis; and some Heimwehr members found their reactionary views so much at odds with more "radical" right-wing tendencies that they turned against the Germans and actively helped opposition to the *Reich*.

wounded. The Social Democrats then launched a general strike, but it was called off after four days. Seipel had violently asserted the government's authority, and the balance between socialist and nonsocialist forces in Austria was never secure after this decisive date.

The Christian Socialists, pressed increasingly by the Heimwehr, began to take the offensive against the Social Democrats. Wilhelm Miklas, a leading Christian Socialist, was elected president in 1928, successor to the nonparty Michael Hainisch, who had been in office since December 1920. There were repeated attempts to revise the constitution, principally with the object of strengthening the power of the executive. After protracted negotiations, a compromise was reached late in 1929. On December 7 a series of constitutional amendments gave increased powers to the president. Of particular importance were the rights to appoint ministers and issue emergency decrees. But Vienna maintained its autonomy, and the democratic principle was preserved against the far-reaching authoritarian demands of the Heimwehr. In the elections of November 1930, the Social Democrats were returned as the largest single party, with 72 seats. The Christian Socialists held 66, the German Nationalists 19, and the Heimwehr, now posing as a fascist party on the Italian model, 8.

These political events were overshadowed by the great world economic crisis. Though the Social Democratic Party's leaders believed that the crisis should be met by the orthodox means of deflation and spending cuts, they were resolved not to be compromised by supporting these measures and refused to enter a coalition government. On the other hand, in October 1931 they acquiesced in suspending the election of the president by direct popular vote, as had been provided by the constitution of 1929, and agreed to the reelection of President Miklas by parliament. The government, meanwhile, led by Chancellors Johann Schober (1929–30) and Otto Ender (1930–31), was driven to desperate devices to stave off collapse. Schober, leader of the middle-class German Nationalists, launched a project for a customs union with Germany in March 1931; this provoked violent opposition from France and the alliance of the Little Entente (Czechoslovakia, Yugoslavia, and Romania) and was subsequently condemned by a majority of the Permanent Court of International Justice at The Hague. The bankruptcy in May 1931 of the Creditanstalt, the country's most influential banking house, brought Austria close to financial and economic disaster. This, together with the rise of the National Socialists in Germany, resulted in considerable support being given to the Nazis in Austria. Provincial elections in 1932 showed that the Nazis were draining off votes from the conservative parties. The Nationalists began to demand a general election, and this demand was taken up by the Social Democrats, who saw a chance of winning a majority in parliament.

AUTHORITARIANISM: DOLLFUSS AND SCHUSCHNIGG

After the election, when Engelbert Dollfuss came to form a Christian Socialist government on May 20, 1932, he could count on a majority of only one vote. Chancellor Dollfuss belonged to a new generation that had been educated in the conservative conviction that the Western form of parliamentary government had been forced upon the central Europeans as a result of military defeat and socialist revolution and that the political and social order could be restored only by the establishment of some kind of strong authority. The leaders of the Christian Socialist Party found themselves under attack from two ideological enemies, the Marxists and the Nazis, who apparently threatened the very basis of the conservative order. In reaction, Dollfuss determined to replace parliamentary government with an authoritarian system. The opportunity to do this came in March 1933, when, during a debate on a minor bill, an argument arose over alleged irregularities in the voting procedure. The president of the Nationalrat resigned, the two vice presidents followed his example, and Dollfuss declared that parliament had proved unworkable. It never met again in full, and Dollfuss governed thereafter by emergency decree.

By this time (spring of 1933), Adolf Hitler was in power in Germany, and Nazi propaganda for the incorporation of Austria was greatly increased. Dollfuss turned to fascist Italy and authoritarian Hungary for help, as he was convinced that British and French aid would be ineffective. This shift in foreign policy also can be attributed to the fact that Dollfuss had to rely ever more strongly on the help of the pro-fascist Heimwehr to stay in power.

The Social Democrats were subjected to increasing provocation and on February 12, 1934, took to arms. Civil war followed. After four days of fighting, Dollfuss and the Heimwehr were victorious. The Social Democratic Party was declared illegal and driven underground. In the course of the same year, all political parties were abolished except the Fatherland Front (Vaterländische Front), which Dollfuss had founded in 1933 to unite all conservative groups. In April 1934 the rump of the parliament was brought together and accepted an authoritarian constitution. The executive was given complete control over the legislative branch of government; the elected assemblies disappeared and were replaced by advisory bodies, appointed in a complicated and futile fashion. The rights of man guaranteed under the democratic constitution also were swept away. "Republic" was removed from the official name of the country, which became merely the Federal State of Austria.

On July 25, 1934, a group of Nazis seized the chancellery and attempted to proclaim a government. Dollfuss, whom they had taken prisoner, was murdered. The plan, however, miscarried: the Nazis in the chancellery were compelled to surrender, and their leaders were executed; a Nazi rising in Steiermark was suppressed; and Hitler, faced with the mobilization of an Italian army on the Brenner Pass, repudiated his Austrian followers. Franz von Papen was sent as German ambassador to reduce Austria by other means.

Kurt von Schuschnigg, who became chancellor on the death of Dollfuss, was a man of gentler personality and of less-violent political passions. His administration of the authoritarian constitution was in the easygoing Austrian fashion, less oppressive than in Italy and Germany. Schuschnigg had a mild preference for restoring the Habsburgs, but he shrank from the international complications this would involve. The regime drifted on without popular favour, weakened by the personal rivalries and ambitions of its leaders and sustained only by a guarantee from Italy. The temporary accord of Great Britain, France, and Italy in the Stresa Front (April 1935) seemed to promise new security, but the Italo-Ethiopian War soon destroyed the unity of the Western powers, and Austria's isolation was complete when Hitler and Italian leader Benito Mussolini allied themselves in 1936.

Schuschnigg had to negotiate a compromise with Germany, which was signed on July 11, 1936; Germany promised

Kurt von Schuschnigg. Encyclopædia Britannica, Inc.

to respect Austrian sovereignty, and in return Austria acknowledged itself "a German state." The agreement left Austria open to Nazi infiltration. In January 1938 the Austrian police discovered a new Nazi conspiracy. Schuschnigg hoped to defeat this by a meeting with Hitler, but at Berchtesgaden, Germany, where Hitler received him on February 12, 1938, Schuschnigg was faced with threats of military intervention in support of the Austrian Nazis. He had to agree to give them a general amnesty and to include some leading Nazis in his cabinet; the Ministry of the Interior had to be entrusted to Arthur Seyss-Inquart, the spokesman of Austrian Nazis. The open agitation of the Nazis threatened to destroy the government's authority, and confidential contacts in the European capitals brought Schuschnigg to realize that he could not count on the support of the western European powers. He therefore resolved to challenge Hitler alone. On March 9 he announced that a plebiscite would be held on March 13 to decide in favour of Austrian independence.

ANSCHLUSS AND WORLD WAR II

Though the Austrian crisis had taken him unaware, Hitler acted with energy and speed. Mussolini's neutrality was assured, there was a ministerial crisis in France, and the British government had made it known for some time that it would not oppose the union of Austria with Germany. On March 11, 1938, two peremptory demands were made for the postponement of the plebiscite and for the resignation of Schuschnigg. Schuschnigg gave way, and German troops, accompanied by Hitler himself, entered Austria on March 12. A Nazi government in Austria, headed by Seyss-Inquart, was established; it collaborated with Hitler in proclaiming the Anschluss on March 13.

France and Great Britain protested against the methods used by Hitler but accepted the fait accompli. The United States followed the British and French policy of appeasement, and the Soviet Union demanded only that the West should stop further German aggression and that the Anschluss should be handled by the League of Nations. The government of Mexico was the only one that did not accept the Anschluss. A questionable plebiscite on April 10, held throughout greater Germany, recorded a vote of more than 99 percent in favour of Hitler.

Austria was completely absorbed into Germany. Any official memory of Austrian existence was destroyed and suppressed. Austria was renamed Ostmark (Eastern March); Upper and Lower Austria became Upper and Lower Danube. Immediately after the invasion, the Nazis arrested many leaders of the anti-Nazi Austrian political parties and a great number of political opponents, particularly communists and socialists. Many Austrians, especially those of Jewish origin, were forced into exile.

The Viennese events during Kristallnacht—a short but devastating period of pogroms against Jewish people and property throughout Germany on November 9–10, 1938—proved that anti-Semitism was more virulent and violent in Austria than in most other German areas. A significant percentage of the Jews killed were in Vienna, where dozens of synagogues and hundreds of Jewish shops and apartments were destroyed and plundered. The degradation of the Austrian Jewish community—including the widespread threats against Jews' lives, the destruction or "Aryanization" (forcible confiscation) of Jewish property, and the exiling of Austrian, mostly Viennese, Jews—became known as the Viennese model (*Wiener Modell*), on which the Nazis based their later expulsion of Jews from all of Germany and German-occupied countries.

By the time World War II began in 1939, more than 100,000 Jews—roughly half of all Austrian Jews—had left Austria. When the fighting ceased, more than 65,000 Austrian Jews had perished, many of them in extermination camps. Jews were not the only victims of Nazi persecution. Thousands of Roma (Gypsies) also were deported or murdered, and tens

KRISTALLNACHT

On the night of November 9–10, 1938, mobs incited by German Nazis attacked Jewish persons and property throughout Germany, Austria, and the Sudetenland (German's recently annexed lands in Bohemia and Moravia). The name *Kristallnacht* refers ironically to the litter of broken glass left in the streets after these pogroms. The violence continued during the day of November 10, and in some places acts of violence continued for several more days. In Vienna, most of the synagogues were torched and destroyed.

The pretext for the pogroms was the shooting in Paris on November 7 of the German diplomat Ernst vom Rath by a Polish-Jewish student, Herschel Grynszpan. News of Rath's death on November 9 reached Adolf Hitler in Munich, Germany, where he was celebrating the anniversary of the abortive 1923 Beer Hall Putsch. There, Minister of Propaganda Joseph Goebbels, after conferring with Hitler, harangued a gathering of old storm troopers, urging violent reprisals staged to appear as "spontaneous demonstrations." Telephone orders from Munich triggered pogroms throughout Germany, which then included Austria.

Jewish women suffering public humiliation in Linz, Austria during the pogroms that followed Kristallnacht. The cardboard signs state, "I have been excluded from the national community." Galerie Bilderwelt/Hulton Archive/Getty Images

Just before midnight on November 9, Gestapo chief Heinrich Müller sent a telegram to all police units informing them that "in shortest order, actions against Jews and especially their synagogues will take place in all of Germany. These are not to be interfered with." Rather, the police were to arrest the victims. Fire companies stood by synagogues in flames with explicit instructions to let the buildings burn. They were to intervene only if a fire threatened adjacent "Aryan" properties.

In two days and nights, more than 1,000 synagogues were burned or otherwise damaged. Rioters ransacked and looted about 7,500 Jewish businesses, killed at least 91 Jews, and vandalized Jewish hospitals, homes, schools, and cemeteries. The attackers were often neighbours. Some 30,000 Jewish males aged 16 to 60 were arrested. To accommodate so many new prisoners, the concentration camps at Dachau, Buchenwald, and Sachsenhausen were expanded.

After the pogrom ended, it was given an oddly poetic name: Kristallnacht—meaning "crystal night" or "night of broken glass." This name symbolized the final shattering of Jewish existence in Germany. After Kristallnacht, the Nazi regime made Jewish survival in Germany impossible.

The cost of the broken window glass alone came to millions of Reichsmarks. The Reich confiscated any compensation claims that insurance companies paid to Jews. The rubble of ruined synagogues had to be cleared by the Jewish community. The Nazi government imposed a collective fine of one billion Reichsmarks (about $400 million in 1938) on the Jewish community. After assessing the fine, Hermann Göring remarked: "The swine won't commit another murder. Incidentally…I would not like to be a Jew in Germany."

The Nazi government barred Jews from schools on November 15 and authorized local authorities to impose curfews in late November. By December 1938, Jews were banned from most public places in Germany.

of thousands of Austrians with mental or physical disabilities were killed, most of them at Hartheim Castle, a so-called euthanasia centre near Linz.

Austrians were overrepresented not only in the system of terror against Jews but also on the battlefields. During the course of the war, hundreds of thousands of Austrians fought as German soldiers; a substantial number of Austrians served in the SS, the elite military corps of the Nazi Party. By the end of the war, approximately 250,000 Austrians had been killed or were missing in action. An even greater number of Austrians were held as prisoners of war, many of them for years in camps in the Soviet Union. In addition, more than 20,000 Austrians were killed in U.S. and British bombing raids.

As increasing numbers of Austrian men were enlisted in the German army, the resultant lack of workers, together with the tremendous buildup of the armament industries, brought compulsory labour on a massive scale to Austria. Foreign workers from many European countries were forced to work in industry as well as agriculture during the war, as were many thousands of concentration-camp inmates, most of them from the Mauthausen concentration camp, near Linz, or one of its satellite camps. (About half of the approximately 200,000 prisoners in these camps—many of them Russian soldiers—died.)

While the great majority of Austrians were not Nazis, popular support for Germany's wartime policies remained strong until the later phases of the war. The Austrian resistance was small, though it was by no means negligible. Left-wing resistance groups (mostly communists, with a smaller number of socialists) dominated, but conservative resisters (mainly Christian Socialists and monarchists) were active as well. During the war, tens of thousands of Austrians were arrested for political reasons; many of them died in concentration camps or prisons, and about 2,700 were executed. Additionally, a number of Austrians fought as Allied soldiers against the German army.

The resistance movement was hampered by the political antagonism that had weakened the First Republic of Austria between the two World Wars. This political divide was so deep and bitter that it blocked cooperation between Austrian émigrés and between the various resistance groups that had formed inside the country. Nevertheless, the possibility of reestablishing an independent Austria after the war was far from dead.

After the outbreak of the war, the Allied governments began to reconsider their attitude toward the Anschluss. In December 1941 Soviet premier Joseph Stalin informed the British that the U.S.S.R. would regard the restoration of an independent Austrian republic as an essential part of the postwar order in central Europe. In October 1943, at a meeting in Moscow of the foreign ministers of Great Britain, the U.S.S.R., and the United States, a declaration was published that declared the Anschluss null and void and pledged the Allies to restore Austrian independence; it also reminded the Austrians that they had to make an effort to rid themselves of the German yoke. Though the British prime minister, Winston Churchill, continued to make proposals for setting up a central European federation comprising the former Habsburg lands and even southern Germany, the European Advisory Commission in London assumed that Austria would return to sovereignty within the borders of 1937.

When Soviet troops liberated Vienna on April 13, 1945, representatives from the resistance movement and the former political parties were allowed to organize and to set up a free provisional government. Though Austria was once again an independent republic, the future looked more than bleak. Much of the infrastructure of Austrian cities had been damaged or destroyed, and the country emerged from the war as one of the poorest in Europe.

SECOND REPUBLIC

On April 27, 1945, former chancellor Karl Renner set up a provisional government composed of Social Democrats, Christian Socialists, and Communists and proclaimed the reestablishment of Austria as a democratic republic. The Western powers, afraid that the Renner government might be an instrument of communist expansion, withheld full recognition until the autumn of 1945. Because of similar suspicions, agreement on the division of Austrian zones of Allied occupation was delayed until July 1945.

ALLIED OCCUPATION

Shortly before the Potsdam Conference (which stipulated that Austria would not have to pay reparations but assigned the German foreign assets of eastern Austria to the U.S.S.R.), control machinery was set up for the administration of Austria, giving supreme political and administrative powers to the military commanders of the four occupying armies (U.S., British, French, and Soviet). In September 1945 a conference of representatives of all states extended the authority of the Renner government to all parts of Austria.

A general election held in November 1945, in which former Nazis were excluded from voting, returned 85 members of the Austrian People's Party (corresponding to the Christian Socialists of the prewar period), 76 Socialists (corresponding to the Social Democrats and Revolutionary Socialists), and 4 Communists. Renner was elected president of the republic; Leopold Figl, leader of the Austrian People's Party, became chancellor of a coalition cabinet. As the coalition government was formed in proportion to the parties' strength in parliament, the Austrian People's Party and the Socialists were the sole partners. This principle of proportional representation, originally introduced in 1919, was to be an important factor in Austrian political life after 1945.

The government decided not to draft a new constitution but to return to the constitution of 1920, as amended by the laws of 1929. In June 1946 the control agreement of July 1945 regulating the machinery of Allied political supervision was modified by restricting Allied interference essentially to constitutional matters. Denazification laws passed in 1946 and 1947 eliminated Nazi influence from the public life of Austria.

From 1945 to 1952 Austria had to struggle for survival. After liberation from Nazi rule, the country faced complete economic chaos. Aid provided by the United Nations Relief and Rehabilitation Administration and, from 1948, support given by the United States under the Marshall Plan made survival possible. Heavy industry and banking were nationalized in 1946, and, by a series of wage-price agreements, the government tried to control inflation. Interference by military commanders in political and economic affairs in the Soviet zone of occupation caused a considerable migration of capital and industry from Vienna and Niederösterreich to the formerly purely agricultural western states. This brought about a far-reaching transformation of the economic and social structure.

In 1949 former Nazis were allowed to participate in the general election. The Union of Independents (later renamed the Freedom Party), corresponding to the former German Nationalist group but free from ideological ties, won 16 seats in parliament. In subsequent elections (1953, 1956, 1959, 1962), the relationship of this party with the two main parties (the Austrian People's Party and the Socialists) remained stable. After Renner died (December 31, 1950), Theodor Körner, the Socialist mayor of Vienna, was elected president by direct popular vote. He was succeeded in 1957 by the leader of the Socialist Party, Adolf Schärf, who was followed in 1965 by Franz Jonas, former mayor of Vienna, and in 1974 by Rudolf Kirchschläger, former minister of foreign affairs.

The influence of the Socialists in the coalition government, which had been relatively strong under Figl's chancellorship, was reduced when the Austrian People's Party replaced Figl with Julius Raab in the spring of 1953 and had Reinhard Kamitz appointed minister of finance. The subsequent economic reconstruction and the advance to a prosperity unknown to Austrians since the years before World War I is generally identified with the so-called Raab-Kamitz course, which was based on a modified free-market economy. The nationalized steel industry, electric power plants, and oil fields, together with the privately owned lumber and textile industries and the tourist traffic, were the major economic assets. The Austrian economy came to be dominated to a disproportionate extent by a trend toward the service sector because of the importance of tourism, which transformed the economic and social character of the rural Alpine areas. In addition, a heavy burden had been removed from the economy in 1953, when the Soviet government declared that it would pay its own occupation costs (as the United States had done since 1947). Thereupon, the British and the French followed suit.

The Berlin conference of the foreign ministers of France, Great Britain, the U.S.S.R., and the United States in January 1954 raised Austrian hopes for the conclusion of a peace treaty. For the first time, Austria was admitted as an equal conference partner, but the failure of the foreign ministers to agree on the future of Germany again prejudiced Austria's chances. The Soviet government was not prepared to forgo the strategic advantages of maintaining forces in Austria as long as Germany was not "neutralized." In February 1955, however, the Soviet government suddenly extended an invitation to the Austrian government for bilateral negotiations. An Austrian delegation visited Moscow in April 1955, and an agreement was reached by which the Soviet government declared itself ready to restore full Austrian sovereignty and to evacuate its occupation troops in return for an Austrian promise to declare the country permanently neutral.

RESTORATION OF SOVEREIGNTY

The State Treaty—signed in Vienna on May 15, 1955, by representatives of the four occupying powers and Austria—formally reestablished the Austrian republic in its pre-1938 frontiers as a "sovereign, independent, and democratic state." It prohibited Anschluss between Austria and Germany as well as the restoration of the Habsburgs. It also guaranteed the rights of the Slovene and Croatian minorities in Kärnten, Steiermark, and Burgenland. Great Britain, the United States, and France relinquished to Austria all property, rights, and interests held or claimed by them as former German assets or war booty. The U.S.S.R., however, obtained tangible payment for the restoration of Austrian freedom. This included $150 million for the confiscated former German enterprises, which Austria bought back from the Administration of Soviet Property in Austria; $2 million for the confiscated German assets of the First Danube Steamshipping Company; and 10 million metric tons of crude oil as the price of Austrian oil fields and refineries that had been Soviet war booty.

The treaty came into force on July 27, 1955, and by October 25 all occupation forces were withdrawn. On October 26 a constitutional law of perpetual Austrian neutrality was promulgated. The Austrian government had never left any doubts that the pledge to neutrality could be interpreted only as a military one and never as an ideological one. Throughout the Soviet occupation, the Austrians had proved their anticommunist attitude, and the spontaneous reaction of the Austrian people during the Soviet suppression of the Hungarian Revolution in 1956 demonstrated their sympathy with Western democratic ideas. Austria preserved political stability; changes in the personal and ideological structure of the government and political parties were effected without major political crisis.

Austria became a member of the United Nations in 1955 and of the Council of Europe in 1956. Major problems in foreign relations were the conflict with Italy over Südtirol (southern Tirol; now part of the Italian Trentino–Alto Adige region) and the problem of association with the European Economic Community (EEC; later succeeded by the European Union). During the Paris Peace Conference of 1946, an agreement had been signed guaranteeing the rights of the German-speaking population of Südtirol, a region that Italy had obtained after World War I. The Austrian government, claiming that the Italians had not lived up to their obligations, initiated bilateral talks. In the early 1960s, acts of terrorism committed by German-speaking chauvinists interfered with the progress of the negotiations, but in 1969 agreement was finally reached on implementing the guarantees provided in the agreement of 1946. In 1958 Austria joined the European Free Trade Association, but a special arrangement with the EEC, accompanied by prudent dealings with the communist neighbours, maintained Austria's status as a neutral nation. In that capacity, Austria provided for large numbers of refugees from eastern Europe; it also functioned as a transit link for Jewish émigrés from the U.S.S.R.

From 1962, disagreement over economic problems generated friction between the coalition parties. The annual budget led to grave disunity in the coalition, and in the autumn of 1965 the government resigned and called new elections. The elections, held on March 6, 1966, brought a setback for the Socialist Party, and the Austrian People's Party was returned to parliament with an absolute majority. Negotiations for a new coalition government failed. The Socialists, led by a former foreign minister, Bruno Kreisky, went into opposition, and Josef Klaus formed the first one-party cabinet of the Second Republic. Contrary to widespread misgivings, the political stability of the country was not disturbed, and parliament was given new vigour and influence.

In ensuing provincial elections, the Socialist Party demonstrated recovery from the setback of 1966, and in the national elections of 1970 the Socialists managed to win a plurality of votes, becoming the strongest party in parliament, with 81 seats, though falling short of a majority. After negotiations for a new coalition cabinet failed, in May 1970 Kreisky was appointed chancellor, and he formed the country's first all-Socialist cabinet. Sensing increased support for the Socialists, he called for new elections in October 1971, which gave his party a clear majority of 93 seats. In the subsequent elections of 1975 and 1979, Austrian voters demonstrated their approval of Kreisky's policy of moderate social reform and economic stability by returning the Socialist Party to parliament in increasing strength: the elections of May 1979 gave the Socialists 95 seats, while the Austrian People's Party, continually weakened by regional animosities and leadership squabbles, received 77 seats and the Freedom Party 11.

The stability of Austrian politics in the 1970s was paralleled by an equally stable economy: besides having an elaborate system of social security and health insurance, Austrians enjoyed an unbroken prosperity with one of the lowest rates of unemployment in Europe. The Kreisky governments carried through a host of reform programs, among which the reorganization of the legal code under the minister of justice Christian Broda had truly historic dimensions.

In 1978 Kreisky suffered his first defeat when a majority voted against the opening of a nuclear power plant. The late 1970s also witnessed the first of a series of scandals, many of them related to the technocratic wing of the Socialist Party. This wing centred around Kreisky's minister of finance and political heir-apparent, Hannes Androsch. In particular, the dubious link between Androsch's tax-consulting firm and the contractors building Vienna's new general hospital began a series of setbacks for the Socialist Party; these were aggravated by the troubles of the nationalized industries.

The scandals that plagued Austria in the 1980s overshadowed the considerable reforms enacted by the Kreisky government. Voters grew increasingly dissatisfied with a stagnant sociopolitical system in which all important decisions were made behind closed doors by the interest groups represented in the "Social Partnership" (i.e., the chambers of industry, trade, and agriculture and the labour unions). A growing environmental awareness intensified voter frustration.

After the Socialist Party lost its absolute majority in 1983, Kreisky resigned, and the Socialists, under Chancellor Fred

KURT WALDHEIM

The Austrian diplomat and statesman Kurt Waldheim (born December 21, 1918, Sankt Andrä-Wördern, Austria—died June 14, 2007, Vienna) served two terms as the fourth secretary-general of the United Nations (UN), from 1972 to 1981. He was the elected president of Austria from 1986 to 1992.

Waldheim's father, a Czech by ethnic origin, changed his name from Waclawik to Waldheim. Kurt Waldheim served in the Austrian army as a volunteer (1936–37) before he began to study for a diplomatic career. He was soon conscripted into the German army, however, and served on the Russian front until 1941, when he was wounded. Waldheim's later claims that he spent the rest of World War II studying law at the University of Vienna were contradicted by the rediscovery in 1986 of documents suggesting that he had been a German army staff officer stationed in the Balkans from 1942 to 1945.

Waldheim entered the diplomatic service in 1945. He served in Paris (1948–51) and was head of the personnel department of the Ministry of Foreign Affairs in Vienna from 1951 to 1955. He led Austria's first delegation to the UN (1955) and subsequently represented the country in Canada (1956–60), first as minister plenipotentiary and then as ambassador. After a period as director general for political affairs in the Austrian Foreign Ministry, he became his country's ambassador to the UN (1964–68, 1970–71). During 1968–70 he served as Austrian foreign minister. After the electoral defeat of the Austrian People's Party, Waldheim was elected chairman of the Safeguards Committee of the International Atomic Energy Agency. In 1971 he ran for president on the People's Party ticket but lost.

Waldheim's UN secretaryship beginning in 1972 was characterized as efficient and ministerial. He oversaw effective and sometimes massive relief efforts in Bangladesh, Nicaragua, the Sudan-Sahel area of Africa, and Guatemala, as well as peacekeeping operations in Cyprus, the two Yemens, Angola, Guinea, and, especially, the Middle East. Waldheim also took a special interest in the future of Namibia and South Africa. He was reelected in 1976 despite some opposition from less-developed countries, but a third term was vetoed by the Chinese government in 1981.

In 1986 Waldheim ran once again as the People's Party candidate for president of Austria. His candidacy became controversial, however, with the dissemination of wartime and postwar documents that pointed to his having been an interpreter and intelligence officer for a German army unit that engaged in brutal reprisals against Yugoslav Partisans and civilians and deported most of the Jewish population of Salonika (Thessaloníki), Greece, to Nazi death camps in 1943. Waldheim admitted that he had not been candid about his past but disclaimed all knowledge of or participation in wartime atrocities. He won election to the Austrian presidency in June 1986 for a six-year term. An international investigation by a committee of historians cleared Waldheim of complicity in war crimes, but as president he was a rather isolated figure on the international scene. Consequently, he chose not to run for a second term in 1992. The "Waldheim affair" triggered a fundamental debate in Austria about the country's past during World War II.

Sinowatz, entered into a coalition with the Freedom Party. The coalition stumbled from one scandal to another until it was finally brought down by the election of Kurt Waldheim, who was alleged to have been a Nazi war criminal, as president in 1986. Although an international historians' commission found no evidence that Waldheim had personally committed war crimes, it proved his indirect complicity. With Waldheim's insistence that he had only done his duty, the domestic political intrigue, the not-altogether-hidden anti-Semitism of some of his supporters, and the U.S. government's decision to place Waldheim on its watch list of undesirable aliens, the incident undermined Austria's domestic consensus more than any other event since 1945.

After the Waldheim debacle, Sinowatz resigned as chancellor, and the Socialist Party under Franz Vranitzky called for new elections, which resulted in a grand coalition of the Socialist and Austrian People's parties. This government introduced partially successful budgetary and tax reforms and a privatization scheme for the nationalized industries. These reforms promoted the economic growth and social stability of the late 1980s. However, more scandals (notably the Noricum affair, involving the illegal sale of arms to Iran by a state-owned company), division within the Austrian People's Party, and the public's continued dissatisfaction with backroom deals weakened support for the coalition, while the environmentalist Greens (in parliament since 1986) and the Freedom Party enjoyed growing appeal.

In the 1990 elections the Socialists avoided disaster only through a combination of Vranitzky's popularity and the weakness of the Austrian People's Party. The reshaped coalition of the Socialist Party (renamed the Social Democratic Party in 1991) and the Austrian People's Party faced new problems that were largely due to the dramatically changed international situation: Austria's application for membership in the EEC (which, renamed the European Community, was embedded in the European Union [EU] in 1993) renewed heated debates over domestic repercussions and over membership's compatibility with neutrality. The latter issue was raised again in connection with the breakdown of the Warsaw Pact and the turmoil in Yugoslavia. In 1990 the Austrian government unilaterally revoked some of the provisions of the 1955 State Treaty governing Austria's neutrality. During the Persian Gulf War in 1991, in a controversial decision the government permitted air-transit rights to Allied planes and the transportation of U.S. salvage tanks through Austrian territory.

With the end of the Cold War and the opening of Austria's eastern borders, the country was faced with an explosive increase of refugees (particularly from the Balkans) and immigrants (especially from Turkey). Many Austrians blamed the now-suffering Austrian economy on the influx of newcomers. In the early 1990s, heavy industry struggled, national debt rose, and unemployment reached a 40-year high. Popular discontent was reflected at the polls, as the right-wing Freedom Party and smaller opposition parties made gains against the ruling coalition.

AUSTRIA IN THE EUROPEAN UNION

In a historic referendum in June 1994, Austrian voters indicated their desire to join the EU, and in January 1995 Austria became a member. The following year, Austrians commemorated 1,000 years of common history. The festivities highlighted Austria's stature in Europe historically, while the country's increased regional cooperation underscored its current role in newly restructured Europe.

The Austrian economy, however, was not yet ready to meet EU criteria for financial stability. Further austerity measures were launched as Austria prepared to adopt the single European currency, the euro. In 1999 the majority of EU members began to replace their national currency with the euro, and by 2002 Austria, with its economy once again among the strongest in Europe, retired the schilling.

Meanwhile, the ongoing concern about immigration paralleled fears of foreign (particularly German) ownership of Austrian businesses, especially as Austria began privatizing more state-owned operations. Reflective of these fears was the ascendancy of Freedom Party leader Jörg Haider, whose extreme brand of conservatism regularly drew international censure but whose party narrowly eclipsed the Austrian People's Party in the parliamentary elections of 1999. By 2000 the People's Party had deserted the weakened Social Democratic Party to form a right-of-centre coalition government with the Freedom Party. The

JÖRG HAIDER

Austrian politician Jörg Haider (born January 26, 1950, Bad Goisern, Austria—died October 11, 2008, near Klagenfurt, Austria) was the controversial leader of the far-right Freedom Party of Austria (1986–2000) and Alliance for the Future of Austria (2005–08). He also served as governor of the *Bundesland* (federal state) of Kärnten (1989–91; 1999–2008).

Haider studied at the University of Vienna, where he received a law degree in 1973 and subsequently taught law. As a student, he became chairman of the youth organization of the Freedom Party of Austria (Freiheitliche Partei Österreichs; FPÖ). He later was elected secretary of the party in Kärnten (Carinthia). In 1979, at age 29, he was elected to the national parliament. In 1983 Haider was chosen to be chairman of the FPÖ in Kärnten; in 1986 he became chairman of the federal party. The charismatic Haider transformed the party, increasing its popular appeal. Prior to his leadership, it had performed poorly, while the country's two main parties, the Social Democratic Party of Austria (Sozialdemokratische Partei Österreichs; SPÖ) and the conservative Austrian People's Party (Österreichische Volkspartei; ÖVP), had dominated at both state and federal levels. Following state elections in 1989, however, the FPÖ finished second to the SPÖ and formed a coalition with the ÖVP, enabling Haider's election as governor of Kärnten. But in 1991, partly as a result of Haider's praise for the employment policies of Adolf Hitler, the coalition dissolved, and he was forced to resign.

Nevertheless, under Haider's leadership, the FPÖ had a virtually unbroken string of successes in increasing its strength at all levels, as well as in elections for the European Parliament. Some observers attributed a measure of his support to the Austrian people's disgust with their government, which had become an entrenched bureaucracy known for mismanagement and for a succession of scandals. Haider virulently denounced immigration and opposed the expansion of the European Union (EU) to the east—positions that were applauded by a wide spectrum of Austrians. Moreover, he was charismatic and a skillful orator. Yet many observers expressed alarm that the sentiments to which he gave voice could find such a large audience in Austria. Particularly controversial were the number of statements he made about Hitler and the Nazis. In a speech in 1995, for example, he defended and praised members of the Waffen-SS, calling them "decent people of good character." He also described Nazi concentration camps as "punishment camps." Still, he maintained that he was not anti-Semitic and that he deplored the Holocaust.

Haider was reelected governor of Kärnten in March 1999, when the FPÖ won the state elections with 42 percent of the vote. In the national parliamentary elections held that October, the FPÖ registered its strongest showing to date; garnering 27 percent of the national vote, it overtook the ÖVP for second place. Its success threatened the national coalition of the ÖVP and the SPÖ. After months of unsuccessful negotiations with the SPÖ, the ÖVP unexpectedly formed a coalition government with the FPÖ. This development sparked protests throughout Vienna and in the international community; it prompted the Israeli government to recall its ambassador, and the EU imposed political sanctions against the country. Haider was forced to resign as leader of the FPÖ, though he remained active in the party and continued as governor of Kärnten. Despite the FPÖ's poor showing in the 2002 national elections, Haider was reelected governor in 2004. His final split with the FPÖ occurred when he announced he was forming a new party, the Alliance for the Future of Austria (Bündnis Zukunft Österreich; BZÖ), in 2005.

In the 2006 national elections the BZÖ won 4 percent of the vote, capturing seven seats. Two years later the party showed strong gains, garnering 11 percent, and Haider seemed poised for a comeback on the national stage. On October 11, 2008, however, he died from injuries sustained in a car accident.

participation of the Freedom Party in the government brought condemnation from both the Austrian left and the international community, and the EU imposed sanctions on Austria. This move backfired within the country, where the governing parties mobilized patriotic support by portraying Austria as the victim of an international conspiracy. By the end of 2000 the EU had withdrawn its sanctions.

The government was buoyed by a surging economy, but the Freedom Party, inexperienced in matters of state and beset by internal turmoil, stumbled in the 2002 elections. Its losses were primarily the gains of the Austrian People's Party, which became the largest party for the first time in 36 years. But rather than renewing its traditional partnership with the Social Democrats, it again formed a coalition with the Freedom Party in 2003.

The Freedom Party splintered in 2005 as Haider and other leaders left to form a new party, the Alliance for the Future of Austria. The split followed a period of especially acrimonious fighting between moderate members and hard-liners over the party's direction. The Alliance for the Future of Austria replaced the Freedom Party as the junior partner in the coalition government.

In 2006 the Social Democrats won an unexpected victory in the parliamentary elections, narrowly defeating the Austrian People's Party. In January 2007 those two parties formed a coalition government, with Alfred Gusenbauer of the Social Democrats as chancellor. However, the unpopularity of Gusenbauer, who was perceived as an ineffective leader, as well as disputes over social policy, soon weakened the coalition. It collapsed in July 2008 following the withdrawal of the People's Party. Parliamentary elections held that September—the first in which 16- and 17-year-olds were allowed to vote—resulted in a narrow win for the Social Democrats over the People's Party. However, the Freedom Party and the Alliance for the Future of Austria enjoyed a resurgence: combined votes for the two right-wing parties exceeded those for the People's Party. Nevertheless, the Social Democrats and the People's Party agreed to form a new coalition government, excluding the far right, in November 2008.

CHAPTER 9

CROATIA: THE LAND AND ITS PEOPLE

Croatia, located in the northwestern part of the Balkan Peninsula, is a small yet highly geographically diverse crescent-shaped country. Its capital is Zagreb, located in the north. The present-day republic is composed of the historically Croatian regions of Croatia-Slavonia (located in the upper arm of the country), Istria (centred on the Istrian Peninsula on the northern Adriatic coast), and Dalmatia (corresponding to the coastal strip). Although these regions were ruled for centuries by various foreign powers, they remained firmly Western-oriented in culture, acquiring a legacy of Roman law, the Latin alphabet, and western European political and economic traditions and institutions.

The upper arm of the Croatian crescent is bordered on the east by the Vojvodina region of Serbia and on the north by Hungary and Slovenia. The body of the crescent forms a long coastal strip along the Adriatic Sea, and the southern tip touches on Montenegro. Within the hollow of the crescent, Croatia shares a long border with Bosnia and Herzegovina, which actually severs a part of southern Croatia from the rest of the country by penetrating to the Adriatic in a narrow corridor.

RELIEF

Croatia is composed of three major geographic regions. In the north and northeast, running the full length of the upper arm of the Croatian crescent, are the Pannonian and para-Pannonian plains. To the north of Zagreb, the Zagorje Hills,

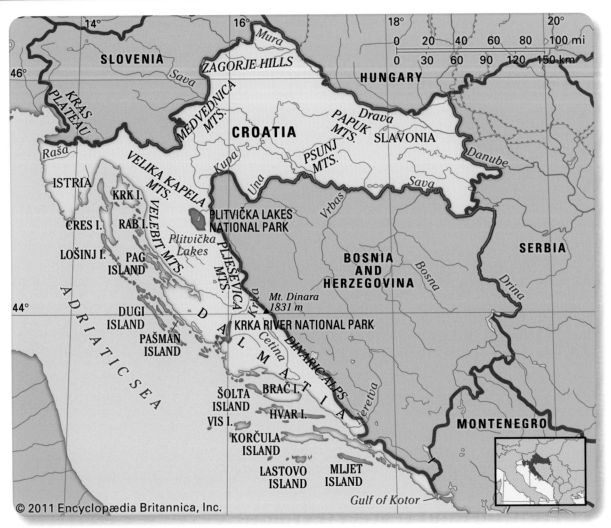

Physical features of Croatia.

fragments of the Julian Alps now covered with vines and orchards, separate the Sava and Drava river valleys.

To the west and south of the Pannonian region, linking it with the Adriatic coast, is the central mountain belt, itself part of the Dinaric Alps. The karst plateaus of this region, consisting mostly of limestone, are barren at the highest elevations; lower down, they are heavily forested. The highest mountain in Croatia, Dinara (6,007 feet [1,831 metres]), is located in the central mountain belt.

The third geographic region, the Croatian littoral, is composed of the Istrian Peninsula in the north and the

The Dinaric Alps rising from the Dalmatian coast at Makarska, a resort town south of Split, Croatia. Leo de Wys Inc./Van Phillips

Dalmatian coast extending south to the Gulf of Kotor. Wedged between the Dinaric Alps to the east and the Adriatic Sea to the west, its 1,100 miles (1,800 km) of coastline are fringed by more than 1,100 islands and islets.

DRAINAGE

Of the 26 rivers that flow for more than 30 miles (50 km) in Croatia, the Sava and the Drava, coursing through the Pannonian and para-Pannonian plains, are of particular importance—both because of their length and because, along with the Kupa River, they are in large part navigable. The Sava originates in Slovenia, passes Croatia's capital city of Zagreb, and then forms most of the border between Croatia and Bosnia and Herzegovina along the inside of the Croatian crescent. The Drava enters Croatia from Slovenia and forms all but a small section of the border with Hungary before joining the Danube, which in turn forms most of the border between Croatia and the Vojvodina province of Serbia. The Kupa, which forms part of the frontier between Slovenia and

Croatia, and the Una River, which meanders along part of the border between Croatia and Bosnia and Herzegovina, both flow into the Sava. In Dalmatia the Krka and Cetina rivers are of particular importance because of their hydroelectric potential and because they flow into the Adriatic Sea.

In addition, a great deal of water circulates in underground rivers and pools in the karstic regions of the central mountain belt and the littoral. These waters account for many of the unique geologic formations and the picturesque landscape of central and western Croatia.

SOILS

The Pannonian and para-Pannonian plains are enriched with alluvial soil deposited by the Sava and Drava rivers. These plains are the most fertile agricultural regions of Croatia and form the country's breadbasket. The soil of the central mountainous belt is rather poor but offers some cultivable land in the fields and meadows and some grazing land in the plateaus. The Croatian littoral is mostly mountainous and barren, with rocky soil and poor agricultural land.

CLIMATE

Two main climatic zones dominate Croatia. The Pannonian and para-Pannonian plains and the mountain regions are characterized by a continental climate of warm summers and cold winters. In the plains, temperatures average in the low 70s F (low 20s C) in June and in the low 30s F (around 0 °C) in January—although they can range from a low of -5 °F (-20 °C) in the winter to a high of 105 °F (40 °C) in the summer. The central mountain regions of Lika and Krbava have slightly cooler summers and cold winters, with a milder climate in the valleys. The average temperature range is between about 65 °F (about 18 °C) in June and the upper 20s F (about -2 °C) in January. Considerable rainfall, turning to snow in winter, is characteristic of the region.

The Dalmatian coast, Istria, and the islands have a mild Mediterranean climate. In southern Dalmatia, where the sirocco winds (known there as the *jugo*) bring a moderating influence from Africa, summers are sunny, warm, and dry, and winters are rainy. In the north the winters are drier and colder as a result of the cold northeast wind known as the bora (*bura*). In the summer the mistral wind has a cooling effect on the coast and the islands. The average temperature ranges from the low 40s F (about 5 °C) in January to the low 70s F (low 20s C) in June. Rainfall is moderate and occurs mainly in the winter.

PLANT AND ANIMAL LIFE

Reflecting the country's diverse geography, the flora and fauna of Croatia are highly varied. On the Dalmatian coast, grapes and olives are grown to produce wine and oil, while Istria is dominated by firs, and Slavonia has many oak forests.

The harbour of Pula, Croatia, on the Istria Peninsula . Orlovic

In terms of animal life, lizards are found on the coast, while wolves and even bears can be found in the inland forests. Hares, foxes, boars, wildcats, and mouflons (wild sheep) also inhabit Croatia. Sea life in the Adriatic is rich as well, with many coral reefs and underwater caves serving as habitats.

ETHNIC GROUPS AND RELIGIONS

A variety of ethnic groups coexist within the republic. Croats constitute about nine-tenths of the population. Serbs make up the largest minority group; however, their proportion fell dramatically as a result of the 1990s war of independence—from more than one-tenth of the population before the war to less than half that figure in 2001. In addition to the Croats and the Serbs, there are small groups of Bosnian Muslims (Bosniaks), Hungarians, Italians, and Slovenes, as well as a few thousand Albanians, Austrians, Bulgarians, Czechs, Germans, and other nationalities.

It has been estimated that the number of Croats living outside the borders of Croatia is comparable to the number living inside the country. Many ethnic Croats reside in Bosnia and Herzegovina, where Croats have lived since the Slavs first migrated to the western Balkan Peninsula in the 6th and 7th centuries CE. Although there has traditionally been a yearning for unification with Croatia among the Croats of Herzegovina (a region contiguous to Dalmatia), this sentiment has not generally been shared by Croats within Croatia or even by Croats in Bosnia. Many of the Serbs in Croatia are descendants of people who migrated to the border areas of the Holy Roman Empire between the 16th and 18th centuries, following the Ottoman conquest of Serbia and Bosnia.

There is traditionally a close correlation between ethnic identity and religious affiliation. The Croats are overwhelmingly Roman Catholic and more Western-influenced than the Serbs, who are overwhelmingly Eastern Orthodox. A small minority of people are nonreligious or atheist. Bosniaks constitute most of the Muslim population.

LANGUAGES

Croats speak Croatian, a South Slavic language of the Indo-European family. Croatian is quite similar to Serbian and Bosnian, but political developments since the collapse of Yugoslavia have encouraged the three ethnic groups to emphasize the differences between their languages. The clearest distinction between the Croatian and Serbian variants of what was previously called the Serbo-Croatian language is the script, with Croatian written in the Latin alphabet and Serbian in the Cyrillic. Distinctions of grammar and pronunciation also occur, as do more striking differences in vocabulary, which result partly from differential historical patterns of foreign domination. For Croats, this has resulted in a sprinkling of German, Hungarian, and (in Dalmatia and Istria) Italian vocabulary, while the Serbs' speech shows Turkish and Russian influences. In addition, there have been various movements to "purify" the Croatian language, which have led to further differences.

Another linguistic distinction, reflecting the legacies of history as well as the effects of geography, can be heard in the colourful medley of regional dialects and subdialects that survive to this day. The standard Croatian literary language, based on the Shtokavian dialect, emerged in the second half of the 19th century as a result of an effort to unite all South Slavs. Although all three major branches of Serbo-Croatian (Shtokavian, Chakavian, and Kajkavian) were spoken by Croats (as they still are today), the Shtokavian dialect was the most widely heard in Croatian regions of eastern Slavonia, the Adriatic littoral from Makarska to Dubrovnik, and Herzegovina, as well as Montenegro and Serbia. It was therefore adopted by leading Croatian national intellectuals of the 19th century.

SERBO-CROATIAN LANGUAGE

The name "Serbo-Croatian language" is a term of convenience used to refer to the forms of speech employed by Serbs, Croats, and other South Slavic groups (such as Montenegrins and Bosniaks, as Muslim Bosnians are known). The term Serbo-Croatian was coined in 1824 by German dictionary maker and folklorist Jacob Grimm. These forms of speech have often been termed "a language," but they are also seen as separate languages. Neither view is completely right or wrong; the concept "language" has multiple definitions, and the status of Serbo-Croatian depends on the definition one adopts.

The earliest writing in the region was done in a Slavic language called Old Church Slavonic. This had been standardized about 860 CE by the earliest Christian missionaries to the Slavs, who created an alphabet for it, Glagolitic. A second alphabet, Cyrillic, whose letters strongly resemble Greek letters, dates to the 900s. Orthodox churches among the Slavs utilized Cyrillic in Church Slavonic books, whereas some early Croat Catholics continued using Glagolitic for centuries both for Church Slavonic and for local Croatian.

Among the Serbs, one man, Vuk Stefanović Karadić , worked from 1814 to 1864 to replace the previous Serbian/Church Slavonic mixed writing style with straight Serbian and to simplify the Cyrillic alphabet. Croats had for some centuries been writing primarily in Latin letters. In the 1830s Ljudevit Gaj, a journal editor in Zagreb, urged all Croats to adopt Shtokavian in writing, the geographically most widespread dialect. After discussions lasting most of the century, Croats did accept that suggestion, though they went on using some traditional vocabulary and, notably, the Latin alphabet associated with Catholicism and western Europe. Throughout the 19th century, Serbs spoke of "the Serbian language" and Croats of "the Croatian language," though they ended the century with standard forms much more similar and mutually intelligible than they had had previously.

During the 19th century, Serbia gradually freed itself from Ottoman Turkey, while most of Croatia remained in the Austro-Hungarian Empire until World War I. At the war's end in 1918, Serbia, Croatia, Bosnia, and Montenegro were put together to form a single country, named first the Kingdom of Serbs, Croats, and Slovenes and later Yugoslavia. Government policy was to downplay Serb-Croatian language differences.

After World War II the government of Yugoslavia at first treated Croatian and Serbian as separate languages but soon began pressing for a unified Serbo-Croatian (or Croato-Serbian). In practice Croats went on using the Latin alphabet and some—but not all—of their specifically Croatian words, while Serbs used both Latin and Cyrillic and were tolerant of words of foreign origin.

After the breakup of Yugoslavia in the early 1990s, each of the new countries began setting its own standards of language usage, and the term "Serbo-Croatian" dropped out of official use. In language studies, it is sometimes still used by authors outside the region, but BCS (meaning "Bosnian-Croatian-Serbian") has also become popular.

SETTLEMENT PATTERNS

Nearly three-fifths of the population resides in urban areas, particularly in the upper arm of the country and along the Adriatic coast. Settlement is relatively sparse in the central mountainous area. While most of Croatia's Serbs live in urban centres, a significant number are scattered in villages and towns, mostly in lightly populated parts of the central mountain belt, in the regions of Lika and Banija, and in northern Dalmatia. There is also a smaller concentration of Serbs in Slavonia, although this area was particularly hard-hit by anti-Serb ethnic cleansing during the 1991–95 war.

ZAGREB

The capital and chief city of Croatia is Zagreb. It is situated on the slopes of Medvednica Hill (Zagrebačka Gora) to the north and the floodplain of the Sava River to the south.

Zagreb's old town consists of two medieval settlements on the hill: Grič, the civil settlement, which was renamed Gradec ("Fortress") when it was encircled by walls that were built to defend against the Mongols in the 13th century; and Kaptol, the ecclesiastical settlement, which was fortified in the 16th century. These two towns continued as rival entities until the 19th century, when a spate of new building joined them together and expanded south onto the Sava floodplain, with a rectilinear

Aerial view of Zagreb, Croatia. © Dario Bajurin/Fotolia

new town of squares and public buildings. The city experienced rapid growth from 1860 to 1914. Its expansion in the 20th century proceeded eastward and westward, and after 1945 new residential construction went up on the south (right) bank of the Sava River. North of Medvednica Hill is the Zagorje region of woodlands, vineyards, picturesque villages, and ancient châteaus.

Croatian National Theatre, Zagreb, Croatia. © ataly/Fotolia

Gradec numbers among its notable old buildings the Gothic-style Church of St. Marcus, the Baroque Church of St. Catherine, the palaces of Zrinski and Oršić, a former Jesuit monastery, and the Neoclassical Drasković Palace. Kaptol has the Gothic Cathedral of St. Stephen (13th–15th century), whose sacristy contains a 13th-century fresco; the cathedral was restored at the end of the 19th century. Near the cathedral is the Baroque palace of the archbishops of Zagreb, with a chapel of St. Stephen (mid-13th century).

The city has many open squares and parks. As the cultural centre of Croatia, Zagreb is the seat of the Academy of Sciences and Arts and of the University of Zagreb (1669). Several art galleries have both old and modern collections, and there are various museums and academies of art, theatre, and music. The Croatian National Theatre is housed in a neo-Baroque building in the city.

The site of modern Zagreb was first mentioned in 1093, when a Roman Catholic bishopric was established there. After the Mongol invasion of 1241–42, Gradec became a royal free town and was fortified; several towers that were part of these fortifications still stand. As a political centre, Zagreb played an important role in the history of Croatia, which struggled first against Turkey and later against attempted Germanization by Austria. At the time of the Croatian national revival in the 19th century, the city was the centre of both a pan-Yugoslav movement and a Croatian independence movement.

Zagreb is the principal industrial centre of Croatia. Its manufactures include heavy machinery, rolling stock, electrical and metal consumer products, cement, textiles, footwear, chemicals, pharmaceuticals, paper and newsprint, and foods. The city's extensive chemical industry is based on exploitation of local reserves of petroleum and natural gas. Zagreb also serves as host to an annual International Trade Fair. The city is now an important junction of roads and rail lines from west and central Europe to the Adriatic Sea and the Balkans; Zagreb (Pleso) Airport has services to most of Europe.

DEMOGRAPHIC TRENDS

The major demographic trend of the post-World War II period was rapid urbanization and a consequent migration from rural areas—especially from the less-prosperous karstic regions of Lika and Gorski Kotar in the central mountain belt, from Dalmatia, and from islands in the Adriatic but also from the Pannonian regions of Banija and Baranja. As a result, in the second half of the 20th century, the portion of the population employed in agriculture dropped from about two-thirds to less than one-fifth, and larger cities grew significantly; Zagreb, for example, more than doubled its metropolitan population. Parallel to this rapid urbanization was a sharp decrease in the birth rate. A much larger drop in infant mortality meant that Croatia's population continued to increase—although at a very low rate—until the 1990s, when wartime displacement, emigration, and deaths caused the population to plummet by several hundred thousand. After hitting a plateau in the second half of the '90s, the population remained at roughly the same level into the 21st century. The many emigrants who left Croatia during the 20th century have created significant diasporas in Canada, the United States, Australia, and other countries. Croatian expatriates have sometimes played an important role in political developments in their homeland.

CHAPTER 10

THE CROATIAN ECONOMY

Croatia has a diversified economy. The primary contributors to the country's gross domestic product (GDP) are finance, the service sector, and mining, quarrying, and manufacturing. There is also a small agricultural sector.

AGRICULTURE, FORESTRY, AND FISHING

Agriculture (grazing and tilling) occupies less than one-fourth of Croatia's land and contributes less than one-tenth of the country's GDP. Most agricultural land is privately held, but many landholdings are too small for profitable production. Croatian agricultural produce is exported mainly to nearby countries, particularly Bosnia and Herzegovina, Italy, Slovenia, and Serbia.

Slavonia, the granary of Croatia, is the most fertile agricultural region. Farming there is characterized by capital-intensive, market-oriented production and larger landholdings. Most of the land previously under social ownership has been nationalized by the Croatian government and is leased to farmers. Major crops of the region are sugar beets, corn (maize), wheat, potatoes, barley, soybeans, sunflowers, and tobacco. Oats, rye, millet, rice, beans, peas, and chicory are also grown. Pigs, cattle, and poultry are important to the economy of the region, while there is also some beekeeping and silkworm cultivation.

The hills of the western part of the para-Pannonian region are characterized by smallholdings, mixed farming, and generally low yields. Fruit growing, viticulture, and cattle and pig breeding are typical agricultural occupations.

The central mountain belt contains some of the poorest land and climate for agriculture. The large areas of meadow and pasture, however, are suitable for raising sheep and cattle, and there is also some cultivation of barley, oats, rye, and potatoes. Fruits grown include plums, apples, pears, sour cherries, sweet cherries, peaches, and apricots.

The Adriatic littoral of Istria and Dalmatia is characterized by rocky soil and long periods of drought, with small parcels of arable land and poor pasture. Sheep and goats are raised, while grapes, olives, almonds, figs, tangerines, and other Mediterranean fruits and vegetables round out the agriculture of this region. Beekeeping is also of some commercial importance, especially on the islands.

Croatia's large forests, covering about two-fifths of the country's area, form the basis of a wood and pulp industry. Fish and shellfish are harvested commercially in the waters off the Adriatic coast, although fish stocks in the sea declined in the late 20th and early 21st centuries. Around nine-tenths of the fish catch comprises small oily fish (e.g., anchovies and pilchards), much of which is consumed locally, but there is also an increasing demand for nonoily fish, or whitefish (e.g., sea bass). Aquaculture, or fish farming, is of growing importance, with sea bass, tuna, and mussels all popular. Almost all commercially sold freshwater fish is raised in ponds as well, though freshwater fishing has some significance for tourism. Farmed fish are exported to countries such as Spain and Japan, while canned fish is sold mainly to surrounding countries.

RESOURCES AND POWER

Deposits of oil and natural gas are found in the Pannonian valleys of eastern Slavonia, but Croatia consumes more oil and gas than it produces and thus is dependent on imports. Bauxite and coal mining had ceased by the early 21st century. Clay, stone, and gravel are still quarried, however, and gypsum and quartz are mined. There are small deposits of other minerals, including salt, throughout the country. Although Croatia's numerous rivers offer hydroelectric potential, the country imports a significant portion of its electricity.

MANUFACTURING

Already more industrialized than most of its neighbours when the communists assumed power over Yugoslavia in 1945, Croatia continued its rapid industrialization under socialist policies of economic and social development. One unfortunate result was the squandering of a great deal of money through inefficiency and the misallocation of resources through the building of so-called political factories, which served more to enhance the prestige of politicians than to use most rationally the endowments of a specific region. Nevertheless, large investments in industry (as well as transportation and education) ensured the continued growth of that sector and allowed the absorption into an industrial workforce of Croatia's rapidly urbanizing population. On the eve of Yugoslavia's disintegration into war in 1991, industry and mining accounted for more than one-third of Croatia's GDP.

Today manufacturing and other secondary industries account for a smaller but still important portion of GDP. Significant industries include food processing and wine making, as well as the production and refining of petroleum. Also important are chemical products, building materials, metallurgy (particularly aluminum and iron and steel), the wood and paper industries, machine engineering, electronics, textiles, and shipbuilding. The future of the shipbuilding industry in Croatia, once one of the largest in the world, was in question in the early 21st century. The restructuring and privatization of the industry, which had historically been dependent on state subsidies, was one of the European Commission's key requirements for Croatia's ascension to the EU. Most enterprises are concentrated around such urban centres as Zagreb, Rijeka, Split, Osijek, Karlovac, Zadar, Slavonski Brod, Sisak, and Varaždin.

FINANCE, TRADE, AND SERVICES

The banking sector has consolidated considerably since the late 1990s, through mergers, takeovers, and bankruptcies.

The sector is also now overwhelmingly privately and foreign-owned, with Italian, Austrian, and German banks dominating. Banks in Croatia have invested heavily in technology; hence, Internet, telephone, and drive-in banking are widely offered. Card transactions are the norm in cities. There has been a major expansion in credit since the late 1990s, with consumers eager to borrow money in order to satisfy pent-up demand. The sector is overseen by the Croatian National Bank, the country's central bank, which earned a good record of achieving price stability in the period after the independence war.

The Croatian economy is very open to international trade. About two-thirds of trade is conducted with European Union (EU) countries, while trade with Croatia's neighbours in southeastern Europe is also significant. Italy, Bosnia and Herzegovina, Germany, Slovenia, and Austria are top buyers of Croatian exports, while Croatia imports primarily from Italy, Germany, Russia, China, and Slovenia. Important exports include fuels, ships, chemical products, food, machinery, and textiles. Fuels, chemical products, and transport equipment are also among the main imports.

The service sector employs well over half the workforce and accounts for the majority of GDP. A substantial portion of service workers are employed in retailing. Although the retail market has long been dominated by small shops, newly constructed shopping malls have proliferated since 2000. Croatia's beautiful coastline and numerous islands form the basis of another major component of the service sector—tourism. A historically important source of revenue, tourism was negatively affected by the war in the 1990s. The conflict deterred potential tourists from traveling to the country, and many empty hotels were used to house refugees and displaced persons. Significant investment has been necessary to revive the tourist industry.

LABOUR AND TAXATION

The service and manufacturing sectors employ the bulk of the workforce, which, in general, is well educated and has excellent foreign-language skills, reflecting and facilitating the tourist trade. However, employing people in Croatia is expensive, owing to a combination of relatively high wages, burdensome social security contributions, and the high cost of dismissing workers. The Union of Autonomous Trade Unions of Croatia, founded in 1990, affiliates a number of unions in the country.

The tax burden on businesses in Croatia is moderate. Under a number of incentive programs, a business may reduce the tax on its profits. Profit tax is reduced, for example, on investments in areas with significant war damage or high unemployment. Income tax is levied on individuals at varying rates. A large part of revenue is raised through a value-added tax, although this tax is reduced for many tourist services and is eliminated for some products, such as books, basic foodstuffs, and certain medical goods.

TRANSPORTATION AND TELECOMMUNICATIONS

Croatia has excellent access to shipping routes because of its long coastline

SPLIT

The seaport of Split, Croatia (ancient: Spalatum), is situated on a peninsula in the Adriatic Sea with a deep, sheltered harbour on the south side. The Romans established the colony of Salonae nearby in 78 BCE, and the emperor Diocletian lived at Split until his death in 313 CE. After the Avars sacked the town in 615, the inhabitants built a new town within Diocletian's 7-acre (3-hectare) palace compound; this "old town" has been continuously inhabited since that time. Split came under Byzantine rule in the 9th century, shifted to Venetian control in 1420, and was held by Austria in the 18th and 19th centuries. It came under Yugoslavian rule in 1918, finally becoming part of independent Croatia in 1992. The port facilities were destroyed in World War II, but the old city sustained little damage, and repairs were subsequently made. Split is a commercial, educational, and tourist centre. Collectively with the historic royal residences, fortifications, and churches in the city, the palace was designated a UNESCO World Heritage site in 1979.

on the Adriatic. The major seaports of Rijeka, Zadar, Šibenik, Split, Ploče, and Dubrovnik link Europe, via the Suez Canal, with Asia and Australia. There are also several international airports in Croatia, with a number of them used largely for tourism.

There has been significant investment in highways and railways within the country since the 1990s war. Highways run between Zagreb and Split—a route also well served by rail connections—and between Zagreb and the Serbian border. In addition to the direct eastward routes to Serbia and Romania, road access to central Europe is good. However, connections to the south, to Albania and Greece, are cumbersome.

Croatia possesses a good telecommunications infrastructure. By the second decade of the 21st century, Croatian businesses had near-universal access to the Internet, and nearly three-fifths of households had access. About half the population regularly uses the Internet. Mobile phone usage has outpaced that of landlines; there is more than one cellular subscription for every member of the population. The telecommunications market is fully liberalized, with numerous landline, cellular, and Internet service providers in operation.

CHAPTER 11

CROATIAN GOVERNMENT AND SOCIETY

On December 22, 1990, the constitution of the Republic of Croatia was promulgated. In addition to such classic civil rights as freedom of speech, religion, information, and association, the equality of nationalities is guaranteed in a number of constitutional articles. Cultural autonomy, along with the right to use one's own language and script (the latter specifically intended for the Serb minority), is also guaranteed.

The 1990 constitution changed the structure of the Sabor (parliament) from a tricameral body under the Yugoslav system to a bicameral body consisting of the House of Representatives (lower house) and the House of Districts (upper house). Constitutional amendments in 2001 abolished the upper house, thereby rendering the Sabor a unicameral body. Members are elected from party lists every four years. In addition, a small percentage of seats are reserved for national minorities and for representatives of Croats living outside the country.

The president of the republic is elected directly by popular vote for a period of five years and is limited to two terms. The 1990 constitution originally granted the president very broad powers; this "superpresident" appointed and could dismiss the prime minister, who was nominally responsible to both the parliament and the president but was actually directly dependent on the president. Constitutional amendments in 2000 reduced the importance of the president, who thenceforth served solely as head of state, and increased the

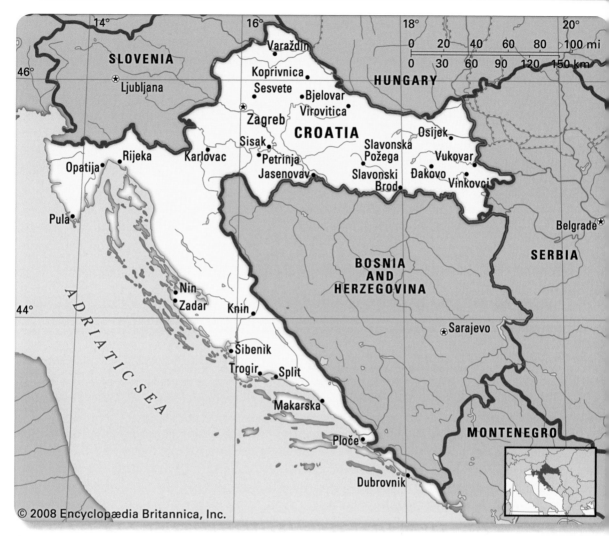

Croatia.

power of the parliament and of the prime minister, who assumed the role of head of government. The president continues to nominate the prime minister, but the Sabor must confirm the appointment. In addition, the prime minister is typically the head of the leading party in the Sabor.

LOCAL GOVERNMENT

Below the national level, Croatia is divided into 20 administrative districts called *županije* (counties). One city, Zagreb, has an administrative status equivalent to that of the counties.

Within the *županije* are hundreds of *općine* (municipalities).

JUSTICE

The Supreme Court, county courts, and municipal courts constitute the three-tiered judicial system. The Supreme Court is the highest legal authority in all matters but constitutional questions, which are decided by the Constitutional Court. Justices on the Supreme Court are appointed by a judicial council, which is elected by the Sabor. The independence of the judiciary has been questioned, largely because many of the judges who were politically appointed in the 1990s remained in office well into the 21st century. However, there have been significant reforms to the judiciary, largely under EU pressure.

POLITICAL PROCESS

Suffrage is universal from age 18, although employed individuals may vote

FRANJO TUDJMAN

The Croat politician Franjo Tudjman (born May 14, 1922, Veliko Trgovisce, Kingdom of Serbs, Croats, and Slovenes [now Croatia]—died December 10, 1999, Zagreb, Croatia) led the country to independence from Yugoslavia in 1991 and was president until his death. Having joined the Partisans in 1941, Tudjman launched a military career in the Yugoslav army, rose quickly in rank, and in 1960 became one of its youngest generals. The following year he left military service and became the director of the Institute for the History of the Workers' Movement. He received a doctorate in history from the University of Zagreb's faculty of arts in Zadar (now the University of Zadar) in 1965.

Tudjman was outspoken on nationalist issues, including the charge that Yugoslav authorities had inflated the crimes committed by Croatian Nazis (Ustaša) during World War II. His criticism of the government led to his expulsion from the Communist Party in 1967 and dismissal from his job, and twice, in 1972 and in 1981, he was sentenced to prison terms for antigovernment activities.

In 1989 Tudjman founded the Croatian Democratic Union (HDZ), which won Croatia's first free parliamentary elections in 1990. Named president, he pressed for the creation of a homogenous Croat state. When Serb areas of Eastern and Western Slavonia and the Krajina revolted, they were occupied by the Yugoslav army. Beginning in 1995, Tudjman reasserted control over these areas and established virtual control over portions of Bosnia and Herzegovina with majority Croat populations. Although he signed the 1995 Dayton Peace Agreement on Bosnia, his authoritarian style, along with his refusal to cooperate with the International Criminal Tribunal for the Former Yugoslavia, led to the international isolation of Croatia.

beginning at age 16. Multiparty elections have been held in Croatia since independence. The Croatian Democratic Union (Hrvatska Demokratska Zajednica; HDZ) and the Social Democratic Party (Socijaldemokratska partija Hrvatske; SDP) are the predominant political parties. The HDZ dominated politics in the first years of the post-Yugoslav era, having come to power in the parliamentary elections of 1990. The party leader, Franjo Tudjman, served as the first president of independent Croatia. The HDZ initially based its ideology on Croatian nationalism and the struggle for independence, but it began to lose favour after the war ended in 1995 and the population felt the pain of economic collapse. In 2000, the year after Tudjman died, the HDZ was resoundingly defeated in parliamentary and presidential elections. A multiparty centre-left coalition, led by the SDP, then governed until 2003, when the HDZ, having repositioned itself as a typical centre-right party, returned to power. The HDZ and the SDP continued to be the main contenders in subsequent elections. Both parties favoured Croatian accession to the EU.

SECURITY

Croatia's armed forces—comprising an army, a navy, and an air force—were created in the early 1990s with significant support from the international community, particularly the United States. Although Croatia had no army to speak of when it declared independence in 1991, within a few years an army had been trained and equipped sufficiently to be able to conduct two major operations to reclaim territory from Serb paramilitaries in 1995. However, Croatia is not a militaristic country, and it relies on the security of the North Atlantic Treaty Organization (NATO), which it joined in 2009.

The Croatian police force, under the authority of the central government, has been reformed since independence. Reform efforts have focused on improving service and stamping out corruption.

HEALTH, WELFARE, AND HOUSING

The health of Croatians is good compared with that of the populations of neighbouring countries. Life expectancy at birth is higher than the eastern European average, and the infant mortality rate is significantly lower. The rate of HIV infection is low, reflecting competent prevention efforts. However, the health care system is in need of investment and far-reaching reform because, being almost entirely state-provided, it imposes a substantial burden on the budget. The social welfare system is also burdensome, partly because Croatia has a large number of retirees and unemployed individuals. In urban areas, large portions of the population live in concrete tower blocks built during the Yugoslav era, which are in dire need of investment.

EDUCATION

During its 45 years in power, the communist Yugoslav regime reduced illiteracy in Croatia from 16 percent of the population over 10 years of age to less than 4 percent. By the early 21st century, the literacy rate for Croatians over age 14 was nearly 99 percent. In addition to thousands of elementary schools, secondary schools, commercial and technical institutions, and vocational schools, the Yugoslav emphasis on education led to the founding of universities in Rijeka in 1973, in Split in 1974, and in Osijek in 1975. The oldest university in Croatia is the University of Zagreb (1669), which traces its beginnings to a Jesuit school of moral theology founded in 1632.

CHAPTER 12

CROATIAN CULTURAL LIFE

The Yugoslav version of communism—which evolved following Yugoslavia's 1948 break with the Soviet Union and the agency of international communism known as Cominform—allowed far greater autonomy and self-expression in cultural and other spheres of life than did the communist societies of most of Yugoslavia's neighbours. As a result, Croatian culture was able to develop in continuity with the Western heritage of which it has long been a part and to which it has contributed for the last thousand years.

DAILY LIFE AND SOCIAL CUSTOMS

With a predominantly Roman Catholic population, Croatia observes Catholic religious holidays. Other important national holidays commemorate historical events. Anti-Fascist Resistance Day, June 22, marks the formation of the first Partisan unit in Croatia in 1941. Statehood Day, June 25, celebrates Croatia's declaration of independence from Yugoslavia in 1991. Independence Day, marking the day in 1991 on which Croatia formally broke with Yugoslavia, is October 8.

Croatian cuisine is heavily influenced by Turkish, central European, and Italian cuisine. Typical dishes are cabbage leaves stuffed with minced meat, *ćevapčići* (rolls of seasoned grilled meat), dumplings, and pickles. Along the coast, fish is served with *blitva*, a dish of Swiss chard mixed with potatoes and crushed garlic in olive oil. There are also local delicacies, such as cheese from the island of Pag and wine from any number of good-quality small producers, particularly in Dalmatia.

THE ARTS

Croatians take pride in their literary tradition, which dates to about 1100, with the dedication of the Baška Tablet (Bašćanska Ploča), a stone monument inscribed with Glagolitic script that was found in the 19th century on the island of Krk. The first printed book in the Croatian language was *Hrvoje's Missal*, a liturgical text printed in 1483. Among the 20th-century giants in Croatian literature are the much-translated novelist, poet, essayist, dramatist, polemicist, and critic Miroslav Krleža

MIROSLAV KRLEŽA

The writer Miroslav Krleža (born July 7, 1893, Zagreb, Croatia-Slavonia, Austria-Hungary [now in Croatia]—died December 29, 1981, Zagreb, Yugoslavia [now in Croatia]) was a dominant figure in modern Croatian literature. Krleža trained in the Austro-Hungarian military academy at Budapest. He tried unsuccessfully to join Serbian forces twice, in 1912 and against the Turks in the Second Balkan War of 1913. For this latter action, he was expelled from the academy and subsequently sent to the Galician front as a common soldier during World War I. This firsthand experience of the "Great War" profoundly marked Krleža's work. Owing to his leftist politics, his works were banned in the interwar period, but his opinions influenced greatly the cultural and political arenas of post-World War II Yugoslavia. His critical stance on Socialist Realism—with its emphasis on the didactic flattening of literature in the service of socialist tenets—proved decisive in extinguishing that mode of writing from postwar Yugoslav letters. Krleža directed the Croatian Institute of Lexicography and became president of the Yugoslav Writers' Union.

A man of vigorous, powerful intellect and wide learning, Krleža wrote with great intensity, fearlessly criticizing political and social injustices. The strength and importance of his work should be judged from his entire opus—some 40 volumes of stories (e.g., *The Cricket Beneath the Waterfall and Other Stories*, 1972), essays, political commentaries, plays, poetry, as well as several novels—rather than from any one text in particular. The vast scope of his themes spread out across his texts, which often function as interdependent parts of one organic unity. His novels, such as *Povratak Filipa Latinovicza* (1932; *The Return of Philip Latinovicz*) and *Na rubu pameti* (1938; *On the Edge of Reason*), have as central characters intellectuals who have lost their power to act in a world characterized by the willingness to enslave one's mind for material gains or for a sense of belonging. With its first volume published in 1938, his three-volume novel of ideas, *Banket u Blitvi*, 3 vol. in 1 (1961; *The Banquet in Blitva*), deals with characters and events in an imaginary eastern European country; it portrays in an allegorical and satirical manner both eastern European backwardness and western European decadence and opportunism in response to rising fascism in the interwar period. Krleža's dramatic trilogy *Glembajevi* (1932; "The Glembaj Family") is an indictment of the decadence of the Croatian bourgeoisie under the rule of Austria-Hungary. He also wrote works concerned with the past exploitation and sufferings of the Croatian peasants—for example, the stories in the collection *Hrvatski bog Mars* (1922; "The Croatian God Mars") and the *Balade Petrice Kerempuha* (1936; "Ballads of Petrica Kerempuh"), which is considered by most to be his single best work.

Krleža's works are characterized by his relentless commitment to humanism and the freedom of the individual mind against the social and mental confines of either a developed bourgeois society or a dogmatic socialist one. He was arguably the greatest writer of 20th-century Croatian literature.

(1893–1981) and the lyric poet, essayist, and translator Tin Ujević (1891–1955), both of whom treated psychological and sociopolitical struggles at individual and universal levels.

The monumental sculptures of the Croatian-born American artist Ivan Meštrović (1883–1962), whom the French sculptor Auguste Rodin once called "the biggest phenomenon among sculptors," synthesize a particularly Croatian national romanticism with the entire European tradition. His works include many religious reliefs and figures carved in walnut. Meštrović designed his own house in Split, now used as a museum for his works.

Croatian visual artists also have been active in several other genres. Hundreds of painters and photographers are represented in galleries throughout the country, and traditional Croatian arts, including fine textile and lacework, can still be seen. Croatian naive painting, through a simple depiction of the timeless concerns of men and women, struck a universal chord in the mid- to late 20th century and brought worldwide fame to its main exponents, Ivan Generalić, Ivan Rabuzin, and Ivan Lacković-Croata.

Film enjoys a particularly important place in contemporary Croatian culture. The Zagreb school of film animation has acquired world renown and recognition, including an Academy Award in 1961 for Dušan Vukotić's animated film *The Substitute*. Since 1972, Zagreb has periodically hosted an international animated film festival. Acclaimed Croatian filmmakers of the late 20th and early 21st centuries include Dejan Šorak, Krsto Papić, and Zrinko Ogresta.

Croatians enjoy music of many varieties, ranging from folk to opera, jazz,

Dancers in Turopolje, Croatia, in 1987 performing a kolo in a cross-hand hold. © Elsie Ivancich Dunin

and rock. In Croatia and among the Croatian diaspora, traditional music featuring the *tamburitza*, a stringed instrument similar to a mandolin, has a fervid following. In addition, the traditional kolo dance is still performed at weddings and festivals. Zagreb, Split, and Dubrovnik teem with nightclubs that showcase local musical talent. Tereza Kesovija, arguably Croatia's most famous singer, first received acclaim in the 1960s as a singer of French chansons. In the late 20th and early 21st centuries Sandra Nasić sang and wrote lyrics for Guano Apes, one of Germany's most popular rock groups.

CULTURAL INSTITUTIONS

UNESCO has inscribed several sites in Croatia on its World Heritage List. These include the old city of Dubrovnik and the historical area of Split that contains ruins of the palace of the Roman emperor Diocletian. Zagreb hosts the National Theatre, the National and University Library, and a concert hall named after the 19th-century Croatian composer Vatroslav Lisinski.

DUBROVNIK

The port city of Dubrovnik, Croatia, is situated on the southern Adriatic coast southwest of Sarajevo. Founded in the 7th century by Roman refugees, it came under Byzantine rule after the fall of Rome. It acknowledged Venetian suzerainty (1205–1358) but remained largely independent and became a mercantile power. It was known as a centre of Slavic literature and art in the 15th–17th centuries. Subjugated by Napoleon I in 1808, it was passed to Austria in 1815 and to Yugoslavia in 1918. It was bombed by the Serbs (1991–92) during Croatia's struggle for independence. The old city, enclosed by medieval city walls, contains 14th-century convents and the 15th-century Rector's Palace.

SPORTS AND RECREATION

Like most Europeans, Croatians are passionate about football (soccer). Since independence, Croatia's national team, made up largely of players from Zagreb and Split, has performed with great distinction. Basketball is also widely popular, with Croatian club teams winning several European championships. The well-known basketball players Dražen Petrović and Toni Kukoč played for Croatia's Olympic team in 1992 as well as in the National Basketball Association. Croatian tennis players have performed well in international competitions; in particular, Goran Ivanišević won the men's Wimbledon championship in 2001.

Croatian athletes participated on Yugoslavia's Olympic team from 1948. The independent Republic of Croatia formed a national Olympic committee in 1991, and its athletes competed at the 1992 Summer Olympics in Barcelona, where its basketball squad earned the silver medal.

The country's greatest Summer Olympics strengths are handball (for which it won gold medals in 1996 and 2004) and weight

Plitvička Lakes, Croatia. Donar Reiskoffer

lifting (one gold in 2000), as well as rowing, water polo, sailing, swimming, and gymnastics. Croatia also has performed well in the Winter Olympics, with Alpine skier Janica Kostelić winning a total of four gold medals in 2002 and 2006 and her brother, Ivica Kostelić, winning silver medals in 2006 and 2010.

Croatia has a number of national parks and reserves that are popular with hikers and other nature enthusiasts. Plitvička Lakes National Park features an extensive waterfall system. The stunning natural beauty of many of Croatia's islands is preserved in the national parks of Brijuni, Kornati, and Mljet. The North Velebit, Paklenica, and Risnjak national parks encompass mountainous terrain, while the Krka National Park is centred on the river of the same name.

MEDIA AND PUBLISHING

During the 1990s, the Croatian media appeared to be easily influenced by the political agenda of the government. Although media freedom and independence have progressed significantly since that time, market pressures now may pose a greater threat to media freedom. Several newspapers, based in various cities, focus on politics or business, but a number of the daily papers are tabloids. Croatia's well-respected independent weekly newspaper, *Feral Tribune*, closed down in 2008 because of financial problems. The departure of *Feral* left *Nacional*, another weekly, as the main source of independent commentary. However, the assassination of its editor in 2008 revived concerns about freedom of the press.

Television is dominated by the state provider, Croatian Radio-Television (Hrvatska Radiotelevizija; HRT), which derives a good portion of its revenue from a compulsory subscription fee. It has some respected current affairs programs but largely focuses on sports and entertainment. Two significant privately owned channels are Nova TV and RTL; both tend toward sensationalism. In addition to the HRT-run radio networks, there are a few private radio operations.

CHAPTER 13

CROATIA: PAST AND PRESENT

The territory of Croatia bridges the central European and Mediterranean worlds, and its history has been marked by this position as a borderland. It lay near the division between the two halves of the Roman Empire and between their Byzantine and Frankish successors. The Eastern and Western churches competed for influence there, and, as the frontier of Christendom, it confronted the limits of Muslim expansion into Europe. As a part of Yugoslavia after both World Wars, it struggled within the Serbian-dominated state of the interwar years and emerged from World War II as a separate republic in the communist federation that navigated between the Soviet and Western blocs. All these competing interests have had an influence on Croatia's development.

CROATIA TO THE OTTOMAN CONQUESTS

The lands where the Croats would settle and establish their state lay just within the borders of the Western Roman Empire. In the 6th and 7th centuries CE, Slavs arrived in the western Balkans, settling on Byzantine territory along the Adriatic and in the hinterland and gradually merging with the indigenous Latinized population. Eventually they accepted the Roman Catholic Church, though preserving a Slavonic liturgy. In the 9th century an independent Croatian state developed with its centre in northern Dalmatia, later incorporating Croatia proper and Slavonia as well. This state grew into a powerful military force under King Tomislav (reigned

c. 910–928). Croatia retained its independence under native kings until 1102, when the crown passed into the hands of the Hungarian dynasty. The precise terms of this relationship later became a matter of dispute. Nonetheless, even under dynastic union with Hungary, institutions of separate Croatian statehood were maintained through the Sabor (an assembly of Croatian nobles) and the ban (viceroy). In addition, the Croatian nobles retained their lands and titles.

Over the following centuries, the area associated with the name Croatia shifted gradually north and west as its territory was eroded, first with the loss of Dalmatia to Venice by 1420 and then as a result of Ottoman conquests in the 16th century. The Croatian nobility maintained their claims to lands occupied by the Ottomans, hoping to repossess them once liberated. A Croatian national tradition also survived within these territories, as well as in lands under Venetian rule. A broader Croatian ethnic identity would be further consolidated among the Catholics of Dalmatia and of Bosnia and Herzegovina during the nationalist movements of the 19th century.

The Austrian Habsburgs, elected to the throne of Croatia in 1527 after the death of King Louis II of Hungary at the Battle of Mohács, defended the "remnant of the remnants" of Croatia by establishing the Military Frontier (German: Militärgrenze; Serbo-Croatian: Vojna Krajina), a defensive zone along the border with the Ottoman-controlled lands. Because it was ruled directly by the Habsburg war council, the Military Frontier further reduced the amount of land under the control of Croatian nobles, the Sabor, and the ban. Furthermore, its military units and their land rights attracted not only some Croatian peasants but also a larger Orthodox inflow from the Ottoman-conquered territories. Such was the origin of Croatia's minority Serb population.

Under the pressures caused by the Ottoman invasions and increased obligations to landlords, the position of the Croatian peasantry deteriorated, leading to a number of rebellions—most notably in 1573. The nobility, too, was under pressure from Habsburg absolutism. An anti-Habsburg conspiracy of Croatian and Hungarian nobles was unsuccessful, and its leaders, including Petar Zrinski, ban of Croatia, were executed in 1671. Their extensive properties in Croatia were confiscated by the Habsburg crown.

RAGUSA AND THE CROAT RENAISSANCE IN DALMATIA

The Adriatic port of Ragusa had been founded by Latinized colonists, but by the 14th century it had been largely Slavicized and had acquired its alternate name of Dubrovnik. The largely Croat republic of Ragusa maintained a precarious autonomy under the suzerainty of Venice, Hungary, and (after 1397) the Ottoman Empire. Its wealth as a trading power was based on its role as an intermediary between East and West, and it nurtured a flourishing cultural life. In the 16th and 17th centuries, Ragusa and other Dalmatian cities under the rule of Venice became the centre of the Croat Renaissance, which produced, in addition to works of art and science, an extensive and powerful literature that had a lasting influence on the development of the Croatian literary language. As a mercantile power, however, Ragusa eventually entered a decline parallel to that of Venice, so that by the 18th century it had become little more than an economic backwater. Ragusa retained its autonomy as a city-state until 1806, when it was occupied by Napoleon I's armies. During the French occupation of all of Dalmatia, which lasted until 1813, the region was designated as part of the Illyrian Provinces, where education and publications in South Slav languages were allowed.

CROATIAN NATIONAL REVIVAL

From the end of the 17th century, the Habsburgs began to regain Croatian crown lands, first from the Ottomans (with the treaties of Carlowitz in 1699 and Passarowitz in 1718) and then from Venice after the Napoleonic Wars (confirmed by the Congress of Vienna in 1815). For the most part these territories were not rejoined to Croatia but were either incorporated into the Military Frontier or organized as separate provinces—as in the case of Austrian Habsburg Dalmatia.

Much of the land was distributed to German or Hungarian magnates and military dignitaries.

The Croat nobility was impoverished, often culturally assimilated, and too weak to withstand the Habsburg centralization and Germanization that began in the 18th century under the Austrian archduchess and Holy Roman empress Maria Theresa and continued under her son, the Holy Roman emperor Joseph II. As the best defense of their rights and privileges, the Croats turned to cooperation with the Hungarians, but this choice would later expose them to the rising force of Hungarian nationalism. When Hungarian, rather than Latin, was imposed as the official language in Hungary and Croatia, Croatian resistance took shape in the Illyrian movement of the 1830s and '40s. The Illyrianists—primarily intellectuals, professionals, clergymen, and gentry led by the linguistic reformer Ljudevit Gaj—strove to defend Croatian interests by calling for the unification of all the South Slavs, to be facilitated through the adoption of a single literary language. Though the Illyrianists failed to win over the other South Slavs, they did succeed in integrating the linguistically and administratively divided Croats within one national movement.

Threatened by Hungarian nationalism in the Revolution of 1848 and hoping for national unification and autonomy within the Austrian Empire, the Croats, under Ban Josip Jelačić, an Illyrianist, sided with the Austrian dynasty against the Hungarians. Yet, instead of a reward, the Croats received the same central control and Germanization that were dealt out to the Hungarians as punishment. Reaction against these disappointments encouraged the development of the Party of Right, led by Ante Starčević, which emphasized the idea of Croatian "state rights" and aspired to the creation of an independent Great Croatia. The necessity of relying on the other South Slavs in opposition to the Habsburgs and Hungarians also kept alive the Illyrian idea, revived in the 1860s under the name Yugoslavism. The Yugoslavists, under the patronage of Bishop Josip Juraj Štrossmajer (Joseph George Strossmayer), advocated South Slav unity within a federated Habsburg state as the basis for an independent Balkan state. Croatian separatism and South Slav cooperation (Yugoslavism) thus became the two alternatives that would shape much of Croatian political thought in the future.

CROATIA IN AUSTRIA–HUNGARY

The Habsburg monarchy was reconstituted in 1867 as Austria-Hungary, with Croatia-Slavonia placed under the rule of Hungary and with Dalmatia, Istria, and the Military Frontier remaining under Vienna. Under an 1868 agreement between Croatia and Hungary, known as the Nagodba, Croatian statehood was formally recognized, but Croatia was in fact stripped of all real control over its affairs. The Sabor requested that Bosnia and Herzegovina, under Habsburg occupation from 1878, be incorporated into Croatia on the grounds that those lands had been part of the medieval kingdom. The request was rejected, but the Military Frontier was rejoined to Croatia in 1881. In the following decades, Hungarian domination of Croatian politics was maintained by Ban Károly Khuen-Héderváry, a Hungarian magnate, and supported by those in Croatia who favoured cooperation with Budapest. The government also gained support through concessions to the Serbs, who, with the incorporation of the Military Frontier, had become a larger proportion of Croatia's population. These changes increased Croat-Serb antagonism in Croatia, as did the Croatian opposition's demands for greater Croatian autonomy.

However, the crisis of Austro-Hungarian dualism and the accession of the Russophilic Karadjordjević dynasty in Serbia in 1903 created a more favourable climate for cooperation, embodied in the Croat-Serb Coalition of political parties. Launched by the Rijeka Resolution of 1905, the coalition emphasized the links between Croats and Serbs, and in the following years it attracted wide support. Discontent with the existing order contributed to the growing belief that the problems of Croatia could best be solved in a South Slav state, either within Austria-Hungary or outside it—although there was disagreement about what shape such a state would take and about the status of its constituent nationalities.

NAGODBA

When the Ausgleich, or Compromise, of 1867 created the Austro-Hungarian Dual Monarchy, Croatia (which was part of the Habsburg empire), was merged with Slavonia and placed under Hungarian jurisdiction. Although many Croats who sought full autonomy for the South Slavs of the empire objected to that arrangement, a Croatian Sabor (assembly), elected in a questionable manner, confirmed the subordination of Croatia to Hungary by accepting a pact known as the Nagodba (Serbo-Croatian: "Agreement") in September 1868.

While explicitly stating that Croatia was a component part of the kingdom of Hungary, the Nagodba recognized the region as a distinct political unit with its own territory. It permitted the Croats to elect their own legislative Sabor and have their own executive authorities. In addition, Serbo-Croatian became the official language of the land.

Despite the large degree of internal autonomy granted by the Nagodba, it designated that the governor (*ban*) of Croatia was to be nominated by the Hungarian prime minister and appointed by the king; it also restricted Croatia's representation in Hungary's parliament as well as its access to the central government institutions of the Dual Monarchy. As a result, Croatia's control over some matters vital to its interests—e.g., taxation and budgetary matters and foreign and military policies—was minimal.

Consequently, opposition to the Nagodba remained strong, and in 1871 the dissidents elected a Sabor that declared the compromise invalid and stimulated a revolt. The compromise, however, was reaffirmed after the suppression of the insurrection and remained in effect until the end of World War I, when Croatia seceded from Hungary and joined the new Kingdom of Serbs, Croats, and Slovenes (later called Yugoslavia).

FROM WORLD WAR I TO THE ESTABLISHMENT OF THE KINGDOM OF SERBS, CROATS, AND SLOVENES

New solutions to Croatia's problems became possible with the dissolution of Austria-Hungary during World War I. However, Croatia's postwar future was threatened by the 1915 Treaty of London, which promised Italy extensive Habsburg territories on the Adriatic in return for entering the war on the Allied side. Representatives of the Habsburg South Slavs in exile, led by the former Croat-Serb Coalition politicians Ante Trumbić and Frano Supilo, set up the Yugoslav Committee to promote the cause of a new Yugoslav state that was to be based on the national unity of the South Slavs and on the principle of self-determination. In July 1917 the leaders of the Yugoslav Committee and representatives of the Serbian government-in-exile signed the Corfu Declaration, announcing the intention of founding at the end of the war a unified South Slav state, conceived of as a democratic, constitutional, and parliamentary monarchy under the Karadjordjević dynasty. The agreement with Serbia would save Croatia from being partitioned by the Allies as part of vanquished Austria-Hungary, but the declaration did not specify whether the new state would be a federation of equal partners or would merely represent an extension of the Serbian administrative system.

At the same time, a movement for unification developed among South Slav politicians still living under Habsburg authority in Croatia. With the Habsburg monarchy collapsing, the peasantry in revolt, and the Serbian and Italian armies advancing toward Croatian territory, the Croatian Sabor voted in October 1918 to break relations with Austria-Hungary and declared the unification of the lands of Croatia, Dalmatia, and Slavonia in an independent Croatian state. Soon, however, the Sabor announced the incorporation of Croatia into a South Slav state and transferred its power to the newly created National Council of Slovenes, Croats, and Serbs in Zagreb. One dissenting voice was that of Stjepan Radić, leader of the Croatian Peasant Party, who opposed unconditional unification with no reference to the will of the people of Croatia and with no guarantees of national equality in the future state. Notwithstanding the Peasant Party's objections, in November 1918 representatives of the National Council, the Yugoslav Committee, and the Serbian government signed the Geneva declaration calling for the establishment of a South Slav state with a form of government to be decided by a national Constituent Assembly. On December 1, 1918, delegates of the National Council

CROATIAN PEASANT PARTY

The dominant political party in Croatia during the first half of the 20th century was the Croatian Peasant Party. Founded in 1904 by Stjepan Radić and his brother Ante Radić it advocated home rule for a Croatia dominated by peasants on homesteads increased by redistribution of land. The party formed the almost constant opposition to the Serbian-dominated government of Yugoslavia after the foundation of the kingdom in 1918. The assassination of Radić in 1928 precipitated the assumption of state power by King Alexander I in 1929. Led thenceforth by Vladimir Maček, the party opposed the royal dictatorship and the succeeding regency (1935–41) until 1939, when it accepted control of an autonomous Croatia and participated in the new central government of Yugoslavia. In 1935 the party created the peasant cooperative Gospodarska Sloga. Elements of the party joined the World War II Partisan movement in resisting the Nazi occupation. The party was submerged in the communization of Yugoslavia, beginning in 1945.

met Serbia's regent, Alexander I, to affiliate themselves to the Kingdom of Serbs, Croats, and Slovenes.

CROATIA IN YUGOSLAVIA, 1918–41

In many respects, the Kingdom of Serbs, Croats, and Slovenes represented an expansion of Serbian hegemony over new territories, particularly in Kosovo and Macedonia. In Croatia, discontent with the new state was demonstrated by the massive electoral success of Radić's Croatian Peasant Party. Refusing to accept the unification act, Radić called instead for an independent Croatian peasant republic. In elections to the Constituent Assembly in 1920, his party received the fourth largest bloc of votes, but Radić boycotted the assembly, thus making possible the adoption of a constitution in 1921 that imposed a highly centralized administration on the new state. In the following decade the kingdom's multiparty parliament came to be controlled by Serbian centralists, while Croatia's elected representatives, led by Radić and the Peasant Party, continued to demand a federal system that would allow Croatia autonomy. The parliament made some progress in agrarian reform, with peasants receiving land expropriated from large estates. However, by 1928, when Radić and four other Croatian deputies were assassinated on the floor of the parliament by a Montenegrin deputy, national conflict had brought the political system to a standstill.

Under the dictatorship established in 1929, King Alexander attempted to override ethnic divisions by introducing a supranational patriotism symbolized by the new name of Yugoslavia. The internal borders of the country were redrawn, so that historical Croatia was subdivided into several new *banovine* (provinces) named after rivers and natural features. However, Croatian nationalism and opposition to the state system were not eradicated by this policy of unitarism—and neither was Serbian hegemony, which simply continued under the name of Yugoslavism. Political repression bred extremism among some opponents of the regime. In 1934 Alexander was assassinated as the result of a plot hatched by the Croatian Ustaša ("Insurgence"), a separatist association founded in 1929 by Ante Pavelić and enjoying the support of Italy's fascist leader, Benito Mussolini. Unlike the majority of Croats, who still believed in a federal solution, members of the Ustaša insisted that only the destruction of Yugoslavia could liberate Croatia.

The new Yugoslav regent, Prince Paul Karadjordjević, permitted some relaxation in political life, though he prevented the restoration of full democratic rights. The desire for political change led to the formation of a united Yugoslav opposition, which argued for the reinstatement of democracy and for constitutional reform. In Croatia this opposition included the Peasant Party, now led by Vladko Maček. In the elections of 1938, the Peasant Party received 80 percent of the vote in Croatia and Dalmatia.

Faced with such evidence of popular support for the opposition program, Prince Paul encouraged negotiations between the government and Maček. These culminated in the Sporazum ("Agreement") of August 26, 1939, which created an autonomous Croatian *banovina* (administrative district) that was largely self-governing except in defense and foreign affairs. The agreement provoked resentment among the Serbs, even in the opposition.

WORLD WAR II

War broke out soon after the Sporazum was signed, and Yugoslavia declared its neutrality. Invasion, occupation, and partition followed in 1941. In their campaign against Yugoslavia, the Germans exploited Croatian discontent, presenting themselves as liberators and inciting Croats in the armed forces to mutiny. In April 1941 Germans and Italians set up the Independent State of Croatia, which also embraced Bosnia and Herzegovina and those parts of Dalmatia that had not been ceded to Italy. Though in fact this state was under occupation by the German and Italian armies, Pavelić's Ustaša was put into power—a takeover facilitated by the refusal of Maček to take part in a puppet government and by the passivity of the Roman Catholic archbishop of Zagreb, Alojzije Stepinac. Initially there was enthusiasm for the independent state, but once in power the Ustaša ruthlessly persecuted Serbs, Jews, Roma (Gypsies), and antifascist Croats. The Ustaša planned to eliminate Croatia's Serb minority partly by conversion from Orthodoxy to Catholicism, partly by expulsion, and partly by extermination. As many as 350,000 to 450,000 victims were killed in Ustaša massacres and in the notorious concentration camp at Jasenovac.

Sporadic resistance, particularly by Croatia's Serbs, began almost immediately, but it was the communist Partisans, under Josip Broz Tito (himself a Croat), who provided the resistance with leadership and a program. Croatian Serbs joined the Partisans in flight from Ustaša terror. Antifascist Croats subsequently were attracted by the Partisans' broad popular front and by their emphasis on national self-determination, particularly the proposed reordering of postwar Yugoslavia along federal lines. Mass enlistment in their ranks made the Partisans more successful in Croatia and in Bosnia and Herzegovina than anywhere else outside their mountain strongholds. By 1944 most of Croatia—apart from the main cities—was liberated territory, and Croats were joining the Partisans' ranks in large numbers. As the war neared its end, however, many Croats, especially those compromised by involvement with the Ustaša regime and those who opposed the communists, fled north along with other refugees toward the Allied armies. British commanders refused to accept their surrender and handed them over to the Partisans, who took a merciless revenge. Tens of thousands, including some civilians, were subsequently slaughtered on forced marches and in death camps.

CROATIA IN YUGOSLAVIA, 1945–91

After 1945 Croatia was a republic within the Socialist Federal Republic of Yugoslavia. This new federation was intended to satisfy the national aspirations of all its peoples, but a centrally controlled Communist Party and a supranational push for Yugoslav unity undermined this structure. The effects were felt in Croatia in such matters as the purge in 1948 of the Croatian communist Andrija Hebrang and others who had supported first Croatian national interests and then the Soviet side in Tito's split with Joseph Stalin. A later issue was the Partisan-based Serb predominance in

JOSIP BROZ TITO

Josip Broz Tito. Keystone-France/ Gamma Keystone/Getty Images

Josip Broz Tito (originally Josip Broz; born May 7, 1892, Kumrovec, near Zagreb, Croatia, Austria-Hungary —died May 4, 1980, Ljubljana, Yugoslavia [now in Slovenia]) served as Yugoslavia's premier (1945–53) and president (1953–80). Born to a peasant family, he fought in the Austro-Hungarian army in World War I and was captured by the Russians in 1915. While in Russia, he took part in the July Days demonstrations (1917) and joined the Bolsheviks. In 1920 he returned to Croatia, where he became a local leader of the Communist Party of Yugoslavia. He rose in the party hierarchy, interrupted by a prison term (1928–34), to become its secretary-general in 1939. In World War II, Tito (a pseudonym he adopted about 1935) proved an effective leader of Yugoslav Partisans. As marshal from 1943, he strengthened communist control of Yugoslavia. As premier and president, he developed an independent form of socialist rule in defiance of the Soviet Union, pursued a policy of nonalignment, built ties with other nonaligned states, and improved relations with the Western powers. Within Yugoslavia, he established a system of "symmetrical federalism" (1974) that created equality among the six republics and Serbia's autonomous provinces (including Kosovo), while maintaining tight control to prevent separatist movements. After his death, resentment of Serbian domination led gradually to a dissolution of the federal system.

the Yugoslav army and the local Croatian police. By the 1960s Croats had grown increasingly critical of the economic centralization that appropriated part of the republic's income for investment in other parts of the federation.

Beginning in the early 1960s, the Yugoslav government instituted a number of economic reforms and attempts at political liberalization and decentralization. Encouraged in Croatia by a reformist party leadership under Miko Tripalo and Savka Dabčević-Kučar, these reforms contributed to the flowering of a "Croatian Spring" in 1969–71. The movement took the shape of a cultural and national revival, expressed in large part through the activities of the cultural organization Matica Hrvatska, but it soon culminated in calls for greater Croatian autonomy. Warning of the danger of civil war, Tito intervened and reimposed "democratic centralism" through a series of purges and trials that decimated the ranks of Croatian politicians and intellectuals. The political restrictions were not alleviated by the 1974 Yugoslav constitution: although the republics gained greater autonomy within the federation, they were still controlled by their single-party regimes.

This centralized control began to break down in the late 1980s, however. In 1989, as communist hegemony was challenged throughout eastern Europe, the Slovene and Croatian communists agreed to free multiparty elections. The right-wing, nationalist Croatian Democratic Union (Hrvatska Demokratska Zajednica;

HDZ), led by Franjo Tudjman (a former party member who had been jailed during the suppression of the Croatian Spring), was victorious in the Croatian elections of 1990. The Serb minority was deeply alarmed by Croatia's new constitution (promulgated in December 1990), which omitted Serbs as a "constituent people," and by the actions of the new government, which purged Serbs from public administration, especially the police. Serbs' fears also were aroused by accusations, especially from Belgrade, that Croatian nationalism meant a return to fascism and the anti-Serb violence of World War II.

When independence was declared on June 25, 1991, armed clashes spread in protest throughout Serb enclaves in Croatia. This violence coincided with the hasty withdrawal of the Yugoslav People's Army from a newly independent Slovenia. Turning to oppose Croatia's independence, a larger contingent of army forces attacked the new regime. In the ensuing war, the city of Vukovar in Slavonia was leveled by bombardment, Dubrovnik and other Dalmatian cities were shelled, and about one-third of Croatian territory was occupied by Yugoslav forces. Warfare was halted by an agreement whereby European troops, sponsored by the United Nations (UN), were installed in the disputed areas in order to stabilize and demilitarize them. Although Croatia was granted international recognition in 1992, the government's control over its own territories remained incomplete.

Slobodan Milošević (third from left), Alija Izetbegović (fourth from left), and Franjo Tudjman (sixth from left) initialing the Dayton Accords at Wright-Patterson Air Force Base, outside Dayton, Ohio, November 21, 1995. Staff Sgt. Brian Schlumbohm/U.S. Air Force

INDEPENDENT CROATIA

In May and August 1995 two Croatian military offensives regained control of western Slavonia and central Croatia from rebel Serbs. Croatia was disappointed, however, when in November the U.S.-brokered Dayton Accords failed to provide a clear timetable for the return of eastern Slavonia to Zagreb's control. In 1996 Slobodan Milošević, Serbia's president and the effective leader of the rump Yugoslavia, agreed to give up claims to eastern Slavonia. Yugoslav troops then withdrew from the region under a UN mandate, and Yugoslavia established full diplomatic relations with Croatia. Croatia recovered full sovereignty over eastern Slavonia in 1998, and, with the withdrawal of UN troops from the Prelavka Peninsula in 2002, Croatia finally had full control of its territory.

Tudjman died in December 1999, and Stipe Mesić, who had broken with the HDZ over Tudjman's autocratic rule, was elected president in February 2000. Mesić quickly moved to cut down corruption and to improve Croatia's relations with its neighbours, but he failed to deliver on promises of early entry to the North Atlantic Treaty Organization (NATO) or the European Union (EU). Croatia continued to suffer deep economic and political divisions, particularly over cooperation with the International Criminal Tribunal for the Former Yugoslavia (ICTY), which indicted several Croatian generals who, according to many Croats, had heroic wartime reputations.

With the success of the HDZ in the 2003 parliamentary elections, Croatia's broad-based coalition government fell, and HDZ leader Ivo Sanader became prime minister of a new centre-right government. In 2004 Croatia became an official EU candidate, but negotiations were postponed in 2005 after the ICTY raised concerns about the country's commitment to bringing war criminals to justice. EU officials also questioned Croatia's dedication to eliminating corruption. By the following year, however, several key suspects had been arrested or tried for war crimes, and the government had adopted a strong anticorruption strategy. These developments bolstered hopes that Croatia could join the EU by the end of the decade. Meanwhile, the country's economy, helped by the spectacular growth of tourism, began to

improve. The status of the much-reduced Serb minority also was boosted by the inclusion of an ethnic Serb in the cabinet of the HDZ-led coalition government that came to power in 2008. On April 1, 2009, NATO officially welcomed Croatia as a member of the alliance.

By mid-2009 the outlook was not as promising. Although neighbouring Slovenia—a member of both NATO and the EU—had agreed to Croatia's NATO membership, it continued to block Croatian accession negotiations with the EU, claiming that the countries' ongoing border dispute needed to be resolved first. (The dispute, focused on the maritime border in the Bay of Piran, had originated in 1991 when both countries seceded from Yugoslavia.) Adding to Croatia's problems, the growing global financial crisis caused the economy to contract sharply during the first half of 2009, and by the end of the year it had suffered a decline of 6 percent of gross domestic product. Croatia faced yet another hurdle when Prime Minister Sanader resigned on July 1, 2009. Fellow HDZ member Jadranka Kosor, who had been serving as deputy prime minister, succeeded Sanader. She was the first woman to hold the Croatian prime ministership.

In January 2010 Ivo Josipović, a member of the opposition Social Democratic Party of Croatia (SDP), was elected president. Despite his political differences with the ruling HDZ, he promised to support Prime Minister Kosor's goals of expediting

STIPE MESIĆ

The Croatian politician Stipe (originally, Stjepan) Mesić (born December 24, 1934, Orahovica, Croatia, Kingdom of Yugoslavia) served as president of Croatia (2000–10). Mesić earned a degree in law from the University of Zagreb (1961), after which he returned to his hometown of Orahovica in eastern Croatia, which was then part of the Kingdom of Yugoslavia, and served as mayor. In 1971, however, the Yugoslav communist authorities jailed him as a counterrevolutionary for supporting the "Croatian Spring," a liberal nationalist awakening. He spent a year in the harsh Croatian Stara Gradiska political prison camp. Afterward, as a political outcast, Mesić focused his energies on serving as general manager of a small architectural firm in Zagreb.

In 1989 Mesić again became active in opposition politics, joining Franjo Tudjman and other antiregime dissidents, and became secretary of the new pro-independence and nationalist Croatian Democratic Union (Hrvatska Demokratska Zajednica; HDZ), which won power the following year. Mesić was appointed president of the new government and represented Croatia at the federal Yugoslav level, having the distinction of serving as the last president of the large Yugoslav Federation. He resigned on December 5, 1991, following attacks on Croatia by the Serb-dominated Yugoslav armed forces. Upon the creation of an independent Croatian state, Mesić became president of the parliament; Tudjman was elected president of Croatia.

By 1994 Mesić had broken with the HDZ over Tudjman's autocratic rule. Thus, he began another period of political wandering. He failed in an attempt to forge a new party among HDZ dissidents, and in 1997 he joined the small Croatian National Party (Hrvatska Narodna Stranka; HNS) and soon became its vice president. In 1999 the HNS joined other opposition parties to contest parliamentary elections that resulted in the HDZ's defeat. In late 1999 Tudjman died, and in the presidential elections of 2000 Mesić's folksy and populist campaign, as well as his well-honed political instincts, struck a chord with an electorate tired of government corruption and abuse of authority. Mesić won in a runoff, and he was sworn in as president on February 18, 2000.

Facing a fractious six-party coalition government, Mesić promised to reduce the powers of the presidency, scale back the intelligence services, reform a corrupt privatization process, restore friendly ties with Croatia's neighbours, and integrate Croatia into NATO and European institutions. In 2003 he visited Serbia and Montenegro, which marked the first presidential visit between the former warring countries. Mesić was easily reelected president in 2005. Government corruption slowed Croatia's attempt to join the European Union, and in 2006 Mesić led renewed efforts to combat malfeasance. In 2009 he oversaw Croatia's entrance into the North Atlantic Treaty Organization (NATO). At the end of his second term in February 2010, Mesić was succeeded as president by Ivo Josipovic, a member of the opposition Social Democratic Party of Croatia (Socijaldemokratska partija Hrvatske; SDP).

EU membership talks and fighting corruption. Nevertheless, the relative inexperience of the two new leaders and the jockeying of their parties for advantage in the 2011 parliamentary elections kept their differences in play. The HDZ's continued emphasis on an exclusively Croatian national identity and history still separated its adherents from many younger urban voters and the remaining Serb minority. Some HDZ supporters, for instance, objected to the public apology that President Josipović made in April 2010 to Bosnia and Herzegovina for Croatia's role in the warfare there in the early 1990s. Meanwhile, the SDP was drawn into the public's continued concerns about EU membership when one of the party's major supporters, a large public employees' union, objected to labour-related conditions imposed by the EU on prospective members. The objections slowed the full-scale labour reform that would be needed for EU accession. Larger concerns for EU accession, however, remained judicial reform in general and the conclusion of several corruption trials in particular. Still, the fact that both major parties and the respected Croatian National Bank supported membership in the EU was a major advantage in the accession process, which had gained momentum after November 2009, when Slovenia and Croatia agreed to have their border dispute settled by international arbitration.

After more than a decade of effort and six years of formal talks, the accession process reached a final milestone in June 2011, when Croatia closed negotiations with the EU. This accomplishment did little to bolster public approval of the HDZ, however, as corruption scandals—the most notable involving former prime minister Sanader—bogged down the party throughout the year. Croatia also struggled with the economic malaise that had afflicted the rest of Europe, and, like ruling parties across the continent throughout 2011, the HDZ suffered for it at the polls. In the general election on December 4, 2011, the opposition Kukuriku coalition, headed by Zoran Milanović, swept the HDZ from power and claimed an overall majority in parliament, winning 80 of 151 seats. Just days after the election, as Milanović began the work of constructing his government, Croatia signed the accession treaty that would enable it to join the EU in 2013. In a referendum held in January 2012, accession received approval from two-thirds of Croatian voters, but voter turnout, at 43.6 percent, marked the lowest level of participation for any poll on EU entry.

CHAPTER 14

SLOVENIA: THE LAND AND ITS PEOPLE

Slovenia, in central Europe, was part of Yugoslavia for most of the 20th century. It is a small but topographically diverse country made up of portions of four major European geographic landscapes—the European Alps, the karstic Dinaric Alps, the Pannonian and Danubian lowlands and hills, and the Mediterranean coast. Easily accessible mountain passes (now superseded by tunnels) through Slovenia's present-day territory have long served as routes for those crossing the Mediterranean and transalpine regions of Europe.

Slovenia is bordered by Austria to the north and Hungary to the far northeast. To the east, southeast, and south, Slovenia shares a 416-mile- (670-km-) long border with Croatia. To the southwest Slovenia is adjacent to the Italian port city of Trieste and occupies a portion of the Istrian Peninsula, where it has an important coastline along the Gulf of Venice. Italy's Friuli-Venezia Giulia region is situated to the west.

Slovenia is mostly elevated. Outside the coastal area, its terrain consists largely of karstic plateaus and ridges, magnificently precipitous Alpine peaks, and (between the elevated areas) valleys, basins, and arable or pastorally useful karstic poljes. The only major flat area is in the northeast. Tectonic fault lines cross the country, and Ljubljana suffered a devastating earthquake in 1895.

RELIEF

In Slovenia four main physiographic regions can be distinguished. The first is the Alpine region, which takes up about

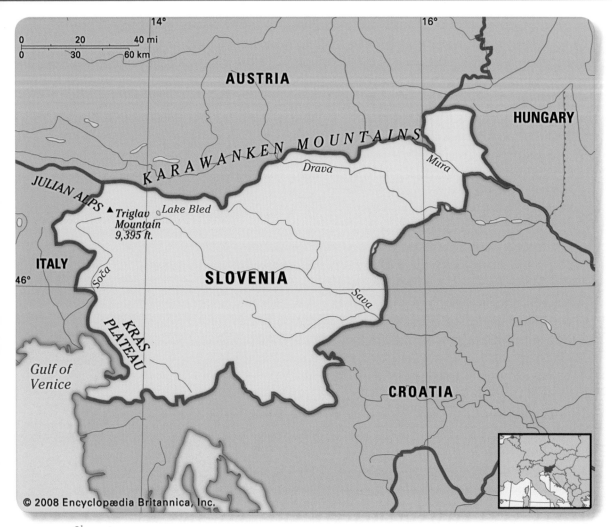

Slovenia.

two-fifths of Slovenia's surface area. In the north and northwest, along the borders with Italy and Austria, are the High Alps, comprising the Kamnik and Savinja, the Karavanke (Karawanken), and the Julian Alps; the latter includes Slovenia's highest peak, Mount Triglav, at 9,396 feet (2,864 metres). In a vale beneath Triglav lie idyllic Lake Bohinj and Lake Bled. Slightly lower than the High Alps is the subalpine "ridge-and-valley" terrain. The main subalpine range is the Pohorje, located south of the Drava River. The historical name for the central Alpine lands is Gorenjska (Upper Carniola), a name that Slovenes still use. Slovenes refer to the Mea and Mislinja river valleys as Koroška (Carinthia). On Gorenjska's southern edge is the spacious Ljubljana basin, which contains the capital as well as the industrial city of Kranj.

Slovenia's second major physiographic region, the Kras (Karst), a spur of the lengthy Dinaric Alps in the southwestern part of the country, is dotted with caves and underground rivers, the characteristic features of karst topography (whose term is derived from the name of the region). Although it constitutes one-fourth of Slovenia's area, the Kras region has only a fraction of the country's population, which is concentrated between the wooded limestone ridges in dry and blind valleys, hollows, and poljes. Water is scarce in this region. The Suha Krajina is a karstified plateau; the Bela Krajina is a transitional belt that contains plains and points toward the Subpannonia (Pannonian Plain). Most of the region is known to Slovenes by its historical names: Dolenjska (Lower Carniola) and Notranjska (Inner Carniola). Scientific study of karst terrain is a Slovene specialty, research having begun during the 18th century in Habsburg Carniola.

The next largest physiographic region (occupying one-fifth of the country) is the fertile Subpannonia; it is located in eastern and northeastern Slovenia and includes the valleys of the Sava, Drava, and Mura rivers. Its basins contain the cities of Maribor (on the Drava) and Celje (on the Savinja River, a tributary of the Sava). Subpannonia corresponds in part to the lower part of the old Austrian duchy of Styria; Slovenes call their portion Štajerska and share some traits with their Austrian neighbours. Beyond a saddle of hills known as the Slovenske Gorice is Prekmurje, a wheat-growing region drained by the Mura River in the extreme northeast of the country. It was ruled by Hungary until 1918; its main town is Murska Sobota.

The fourth principal region (occupying barely one-twelfth of Slovenia's surface) is Primorska, or the Slovene Littoral. It overlaps what were the Habsburg regions of Trieste and Gorizia and is made up of Slovenia's portion of the Istrian Peninsula, the Adriatic hinterland, and the Soča and Vipava river valleys. The 29-mile (47-km) strip of coast makes up Slovenia's riviera. The city of Koper (just south of Trieste) is Slovenia's major port.

DRAINAGE

Most of Slovenia's intricate fluvial network is directed toward the Danube River. The Sava originates in the Julian Alps and flows past Ljubljana toward Croatia; its narrow valley serves as a rail conduit to Zagreb, Croatia's capital, and farther to Belgrade, Serbia's capital. The Drava enters Slovenia from the Austrian state of Kärnten, and the Mura emerges from the Austrian state of Steiermark; they meet in Croatia and, like the Sava, ultimately

SAVA RIVER

The Sava is a river in the western Balkans whose basin, 36,960 square miles (95,720 square km) in area, covers much of Slovenia, Croatia, Bosnia, and northern Serbia. It rises in the Triglav group of the Julian Alps as two rivers, the Sava Bohinjka and the Sava Dolinka, which join at Radovljica. It then flows mainly east-southeastward through Slovenia, just north of Ljubljana, through Croatia touching Zagreb, and then forms the border between Croatia and Bosnia before entering Serbia and joining the Danube River at Belgrade after a course of 584 miles (940 km). The Sava River is navigable upstream to Sisak, 362 miles (583 km) from the Danube, for small freight vessels. Its tributaries are the Soča, Savinja, Krka, Kupa, Lonja, Una, Vrbas, Bosna, Drina, and Kolubara rivers. Major towns along the river are Kranj, Zagreb, Sisak, Slavonski Brod, Bosanski Šamac, Sremska Mitrovica, and Šabac.

reach the Danube. In the west the Soča originates beneath Mount Triglav and, after a precipitous course, reaches the Gulf of Venice in Italian territory.

The relatively steep gradients of Slovenia's topography create fast run-off, which in turn ensures most of Slovenia copious water and hydroelectric resources. On the other hand, it also washes away valuable soil nutrients. Pollution of the rivers remains a problem.

SOILS

Slovenia's complex geology has created a pedological mosaic. The small, thick Pleistocene cover is acidic and viscid. Permeable thin brown podzols —cambisols and fluvisols—are productive if fertilized, but they cover only about one-tenth of its surface, chiefly to the northeast. The carbonate bedrock underlying much of the country produces thin lithosols suited to forest growth. There are many good alluvial soils (particularly in Subpannonia) as well as bog varieties. Karstic sinkholes and poljes are famous for having terra rossa, a red soil produced by the degradation of the underlying limestone.

CLIMATE

Slovenia may be divided into three climatic zones. Conditions in Istria indicate a transition from the Mediterranean climate of the Dalmatian coast to a moderate continental climate. In the moderate zone the highest monthly precipitation (up to 15 inches [381 mm]) occurs in spring and autumn, and the highest temperatures (often rising above 80 °F [27 °C]) occur in June and July. Winter temperatures rarely drop below 50 °F (10 °C), but this mildness is sometimes interrupted by the strong bora, a cold northerly wind.

Central and northern Slovenia have a continental "cool summer" climate; the eastern third of the country also falls into the continental category but has warm summers. Monthly summer rainfall in the cool belt is more than 3 inches (80 mm), and high temperatures average in the upper 60s F (about 20 °C), although there are uncomfortable hot spells. The east and northeast have much less overall precipitation, and midsummer highs reach well past 70 °F (21 °C). From November to February, temperature readings below freezing occur frequently, but snow cover has become less frequent and usually melts rapidly.

PLANT AND ANIMAL LIFE

Slovenia's flora reflects the country's physiographic diversity, especially its varying elevations. At the highest elevations below the tree line, junipers alternate with high meadowland. Lower is a central belt of coniferous and deciduous trees (birch and beech) mixed with pasturage and arable lands, and, still lower, deciduous growth including karstic heath and maquis (good for rough grazing) is found. At sea level along the Slovene Littoral is a typically Mediterranean cover of brushwood, including maquis. Fruit and vegetable areas are scattered about the country, and forests, which are noted for their mushrooms, cover about three-fifths of the terrain.

Several animal species have been given protected status. Along with others of direct economic importance, they include the reintroduced (though still rare) ibex, the chamois, the wild boar, and red, fallow, and roe deer as well as standard varieties of small game. Once endangered, the European brown bear has a stable population in Slovenia. The lynx has reappeared. The Subpannonian habitat suits migratory fowl and upland birds, and the trout and grayling found in the Soča River are renowned among sport anglers. The Adriatic waters off Slovenia's coast are not an especially favourable environment for fish.

ETHNIC GROUPS

About nine-tenths of Slovenia's people are ethnically Slovene. They are descendants of settlers who arrived in the 6th century CE. Historians differ on the exact origin of the settlers, but they do agree that most of them were Slavs who migrated westward from the vast Russian Plain, probably from a locale in between the Black Sea and the Carpathian Mountains. Italians and Hungarians are Slovenia's two main ethnic minority groups, though neither community is large. Italians live mainly in Primorska (southwestern Istria) and Hungarians principally in the northeastern Prekmurje region. Communities of Roma (Gypsies) are also autochthonous to Slovenia and are found mostly in northeastern Slovenia or scattered throughout southern Slovenia near the border with Croatia.

The disintegration of the Federal Republic of Yugoslavia in 1991 took many immigrants to Slovenia from other former Yugoslav republics (mainly from Bosnia and Herzegovina and Kosovo). Despite linguistic kinship with people from the Balkan Peninsula, the Slovenes are culturally an Alpine folk who have more in common with northern Italians, southern Germans, and the Swiss.

LANGUAGES

Slovene, the official language of Slovenia, is a South Slavic language, but it also has affinities to West Slavic Czech and to Slovak. Eastern Slovene dialects blend with Kajkavian forms of Serbo-Croatian, but literary Slovene is remote from its Croatian counterparts, and it borrows words from the German and Italian languages, which are still spoken by older generations of Slovenians. In addition, there are marked differences between the eastern Slovene dialects and the standard Slovene spoken in most of the country. Slovene is one of the few languages to have preserved the dual grammatical number (used to refer to exactly two persons or things in addition to singular and plural forms) of Proto-Indo-European. Italian and Hungarian are the other major languages spoken in Slovenia, mainly in the regions where these two ethnic communities reside.

RELIGION

Christianity was accepted by the Slavic tribes in the 8th century CE. The authority of a once-powerful Roman Catholic Church hierarchy was broken by the flight of conservative Catholics (including many clerics) in 1945, and religious practice was further vitiated by communism and the acceleration of industrialization and consumerism. In the early 21st century about

SLOVENE LANGUAGE

Slovene (also called Slovenian, or in the language itself, Slovenščina) is a South Slavic language written in the Roman (Latin) alphabet that is spoken in Slovenia and in adjacent parts of Austria and Italy. Grammatically, Slovene retains forms expressing the dual number (two persons or things) in nouns and verbs, in addition to singular and plural. Slovene has great dialectal variation; some scholars distinguish as many as 46 individual dialects.

Although the earliest written record in the Slovene language is found in the Freising manuscripts dating from about 1000 CE, the language was not generally written until the Reformation, when Protestants translated the Bible and wrote tracts in Slovene. A Roman Catholic translation of the Bible in Slovene appeared at the end of the 18th century and was followed by grammars of the language during the first few years of the 19th century; by the middle of the 19th century, a standard written language was in use. Slovene is closely related to its eastern neighbour, Serbo-Croatian, from which it separated between the 7th and 9th century CE; the transition from the eastern Slovene dialects to the Kajkavian Croatian is a gradual one.

Church of the Assumption, on an island in Lake Bled, northwestern Slovenia. © Kavita/Fotolia

three-fifths of Slovenes adhered to Roman Catholicism, down from four-fifths in the 1990s. An influx of Muslim and Orthodox Christian immigrants to Slovenia in the 1970s and, later, in the 1990s further altered the religious composition of the country. Many Orthodox churches are in Ljubljana and southeastern Slovenia. Most of Slovenia's Muslim population (the second largest religious group in the country at the beginning of the 21st century) live in the capital. After much prolonged pressure from the Muslim community, the Slovenian government in 2004 approved the construction of the country's first mosque, a decision that was met with much opposition. There are a few Protestant communities in northeastern Slovenia, and Buddhism and other faiths are practiced in some urban centres. About one-fourth of Slovenians did not specify their religion in the country's 2002 census; many considered religion to be a sensitive issue.

SETTLEMENT PATTERNS

Slovenia was incorporated into the Kingdom of Serbs, Croats, and Slovenes (called Yugoslavia beginning in 1929) after World War I, and it entered a period of agricultural decline and rapid industrialization that induced people to settle at lower elevations or simply to emigrate—a process that accelerated after World War II. The expulsion of ethnic Germans following World War II, and later the collectivization of land during communist rule, also affected settlement patterns in Slovenia. Several villages were abandoned and essentially

LJUBLJANA

Ljubljana is Slovenia's capital city and its economic, political, and cultural centre, located on the Ljubljanica River. The city lies in central Slovenia in a natural depression surrounded by high peaks of the Julian Alps.

A walled Roman encampment was built there in the mid-1st century BCE by Roman legionnaires and developed into the settlement of Emona (Iulia Aemona), though the area had been settled earlier by the Veneti, the Illyrians, and the Celts, beginning about 1000 BCE. Sitting on the route to Pannonia and commanding the Ljubljana Gap, the strategically located city was destroyed by Attila in the mid-5th century. The Slovene Slavic tribes, migrating westward, rebuilt it in the 12th century, when its name was recorded first as Laibach (1144) and then as Luvigana (1146). It gained city rights in 1220.

In the late 13th century, rule passed to the Habsburgs, and in 1335 Ljubljana became the capital of the Habsburg-Austrian province of Carniola. From 1461 Ljubljana was the seat of a bishop. Taken by the French in 1809, it became the government seat of the Illyrian Provinces. In 1821 the Congress of Laibach, a meeting of members of the Holy Alliance, was held in Ljubljana. The completion of the southern (Vienna-Trieste) railway line in 1849 stimulated the economic and cultural growth of Ljubljana, which became a centre of Slovene nationalism under Austrian rule. Ljubljana gained a sugar refinery, a brewery, a foundry, and a paper and textile mill (later converted into a tobacco factory).

Foreign rule ended in 1918, when Ljubljana and Slovenia became part of the Kingdom of Serbs, Croats, and Slovenes (later Yugoslavia). In 1941 Italian troops occupied the city. After World War II, Ljubljana underwent significant industrialization and modernization. An airport was constructed, and a road tunnel was built under the Castle Hill. In 1991, when Slovenia gained its independence, Ljubljana became the national capital.

Ljubljana is dominated by a medieval fortress, which dates from the 12th century. The old quarter of the city lies between the fortress and the river. Only a few old buildings of the Austrian Baroque style survived a violent earthquake in 1895. The subsequent rebuilding of the city, particularly those buildings designed by the Art Nouveau architect Josef Plečnik, gave Ljubljana

Sunset view of Ljubljana, Slovenia. © Sykwong/Fotolia

(apart from the old town on the right bank of the river) a modern appearance. The city also received a grid pattern. Fine stone bridges, such as the Tromostovje (Triple Bridge), were constructed across the river.

Ljubljana is an important centre of rail and road communications with Austria, Croatia, Hungary, and Italy. Its industries include pharmaceuticals, petrochemicals, food processing, and electronics. A popular attraction is the Tivoli Park, which was built in the 19th century and which underwent significant alterations in the 1920s and '30s. The city's leading educational institution is the University of Ljubljana (1919); the National and University Library, the Joef Stefan Institute (a public research institute), and the Slovene Academy of Sciences and Arts are also located in the city. A philharmonic, among the first outside Italy, was established in 1701. The city's many fine museums and galleries include the National Museum of Slovenia, the Slovenian Museum of Natural History, the National Gallery, and the Gallery of Modern Art; there are also smaller museums centred on architecture, contemporary history, and ethnography, an opera house, and several theatres. Other attractions include a botanical garden and a zoo.

became ghost towns. (Some of the vacant dwellings from these deserted farms and villages now serve as second homes for urbanites.)

A second major change in settlement patterns occurred in the 1960s when the communist government began establishing industry in urban centres and, beginning in the 1970s, in towns as well. In cities and larger towns this shift was evident in the proliferation of high-rise housing. But though more housing was constructed, cities continued to suffer from a shortage of apartments (most of which were offered to unskilled migrant labourers from the southern republics of the Yugoslav federation). Under communist rule, efficient rail and bus systems were developed, and the majority of Slovenes who worked in cities commuted daily from the suburbs and outlying rural areas. Throughout the 1980s, when industry became more decentralized, the bulk of Slovenes still commuted to work. In general, commuting was part of the daily routine for much of the population.

At the beginning of the 21st century, Slovenia's population remained overdispersed. Three-fourths of the country's population centres were hamlets with fewer than 200 residents, and only about half of the population lived in urban areas. Commuting to urban jobs remained common.

DEMOGRAPHIC TRENDS

A comparison of 20th-century census data with Slovenia's first official census (1857) reveals that the population of what is present-day Slovenia increased by only about 500,000 people from the mid-19th century to the mid-20th century. This was partly due to emigration, which was highest in the decades prior to World War I, when about one-third of the population left Slovenia for overseas countries. Italy occupied Slovenian territory at the conclusion of World War I, and the threat of fascism drove out more Slovenians, mainly to western Europe. Accelerated economic growth during the second and third decades of the 20th century helped to stanch emigration, however; but after World War II the communist regime, coupled with a depressed economy, caused another mass migration from Slovenia. About 100,000 Slovenes left for Argentina, Canada, the United States, and Australia from 1945 to 1970.

By the second half of the 20th century, Slovenia had undergone an intense transformation from a rural to a nonagrarian society. Population growth, however, was not as great as elsewhere in Europe, owing to emigration and, until the 1970s, the absence of immigration. However, a flow of migrants from the Balkan Peninsula to the highly industrialized regions of central and western Slovenia maintained the country's population levels. The disintegration of the Yugoslav federation in 1991 further increased the number of immigrants entering Slovenia. Moreover, the conflicts in Croatia, Bosnia and Herzegovina, and Kosovo brought an influx of about 70,000 refugees and asylum seekers to Slovenia. By the early 21st century, migration flows in and out of Slovenia had nearly balanced each other out, and the population of Slovenia was roughly the same as it had been in 1991. Also, about one-sixth of non-Slovenes had become Slovenian citizens.

Like much of central and eastern Europe, Slovenia has an aging population, and its birth rate is among the lowest in Europe. Life expectancy compares favourably with former communist countries in eastern and central Europe, standing at about 75 years for men and 80 for women.

At the beginning of the 21st century, the largest concentrations of Slovenes outside Slovenia resided in the Italian region of Friuli-Venezia Giulia, in the Austrian states of Kärnten and Steiermark, and in the Hungarian counties of Vas and Zala. There are also smaller groups in Croatian towns and other urban centres of the former Yugoslav federation.

CHAPTER 15

THE SLOVENIAN ECONOMY

Drawing upon a long tradition of crafts, Slovenes began the modernization and diversification of their economy in the early 20th century. Owing in part to this head start, Slovenia made great progress under Yugoslavia's market-oriented "self-management" form of socialism (communism). For most of the period of federation, Slovenes made up less than 10 percent of Yugoslavia's population, yet they produced 20 percent of the country's wealth and 30 percent of its exports. By the 1980s, however, the Yugoslav economic system had succumbed to debt and stagnation, and resentment over the Belgrade central government's policy of distributing subsidies from the more prosperous northern republics to the less-affluent and often corrupt southern republics was probably the principal catalyst of Slovene independence. Yugoslavia's breakup, however, deprived Slovenia of a secure market and caused economic dislocation as Slovene enterprises were forced to compete for business in a broader market at a time of worldwide recession. Intrinsic weaknesses of "socially owned" enterprises were exposed, including featherbedding, limited professional skills, poor competitiveness, undercapitalization, outmoded production methods, and resistance to innovation. Positive features included the modern infrastructure and Slovenia's traditionally strong social discipline.

In the early 21st century the Slovene economy was based primarily on services and trade. The shift to a market economy has improved the standard of living in rural localities despite only modest changes in the traditional smallholding pattern of landownership. It also produced a small group of newly wealthy individuals, *tajkuni* ("tycoons"). Most of the economy has been privatized, and a significant source of income comes from the manufacture of automotive parts, pharmaceuticals, and electrical appliances.

AGRICULTURE AND FORESTRY

Archaic Slovene farming methods began to change in the late 1700s with the introduction of modern crop rotation and new plants such as potatoes, corn (maize), beans, and alfalfa, which helped to end a cycle of famine. By the mid-20th century, dairy and meat products dominated agriculture, and cereals had been largely abandoned. Under communist rule, private plots were limited to 25 acres (10 hectares), and expropriated lands were turned over to collective and state farms.

The resulting 250 "social" enterprises (collectives and state farms) were linked to food processing. They proved efficient, especially in raising poultry and cattle, but operated at high cost.

By the early 21st century, agriculture was making a relatively small contribution to Slovenia's gross domestic product (GDP) and employing less than one-tenth of the country's workforce. Since Slovenia produces about four-fifths of its food requirements, it is not wholly self-sufficient; however, progress in the agrarian sector has been immense. Leading agricultural crops include wheat, corn (maize), sugar beets, barley, potatoes, apples, and pears. There is also some viticulture. Formerly state-owned farms have been privatized. The majority of Slovenia's farms are family owned. Livestock raising (especially pigs, cattle, and sheep) is an important agricultural activity.

LIPIZZANER

The famous breed of horse known as the Lipizzaner derives its name from the Slovenian town of Lipica (Lipizza), near Trieste, formerly a part of the Austro-Hungarian Empire. Lipica was the home of the Austrian imperial stud. The founding of the breed dates to 1580, and detailed breeding records date from 1700. The ancestry is Spanish, Arabian, and Berber. The six strains (Pluto, Conversano, Neapolitano, Favory, Maestoso, and Siglavy) are named from their foundation sires.

Lipizzaners are of comparatively small stature with a long back, a short, thick neck, and powerful conformation. They average 15 to 16.1 hands (about 60 to 64 inches, or 152 to 164 cm) high and weigh from 1,000 to 1,300 pounds (450 to 585 kg). The head, with a Roman nose, lacks the refinement of most light breeds, but they have attractive, expressive eyes. The colour is usually gray; bay and brown occur rarely. They are found to a limited extent in countries that were originally a part of the Austro-Hungarian Empire, and a few have been exported to the United States. The best known Lipizzaners are those trained at the Spanish Riding School in Vienna.

Horse breeding, particularly at Lipica—the original home of Vienna's celebrated Lipizzaner horses—also contributes to the economy.

Timber remains crucial to the Slovene industry, but wood is often imported. Slovenia is heavily forested, with more than three-fifths of its land covered with trees. However, forests have been damaged by factory and motor-vehicle emissions, and the bark beetle has reduced the quality of wood in older forests.

RESOURCES AND POWER

Although limestone, which is quarried and used in construction, is abundant, mining has declined in importance in Slovenia, as resources have been exhausted and environmental restrictions have been applied. In the process many Slovene mines, including mercury, uranium, lead, zinc, and brown coal mines, have been closed, though the Velenje lignite mine is still important.

Because Slovene coal reserves have become meagre and are of declining quality, natural gas (through a pipeline from Russia) and oil have grown in relative importance as sources of energy. Fossil fuel-fired thermoelectricity provides about one-third of Slovenia's power. A number of hydroelectric plants on the Drava, Soča, and Sava rivers generate about another one-third of the country's total power. Nuclear power, produced at a plant in Krško (near the Croatian border), is also important, contributing roughly the final one-third of Slovenia's power.

Slovenia shares the power generated at Krško with Croatia.

MANUFACTURING

Slovenia's modern industrial history began in the 19th century with the injection of capital from major cities (e.g., Vienna, Prague, and Graz) and areas under the rule of the Habsburg monarchy. By 1910 one-tenth of workers were employed in industry. The post-1918 Yugoslav market especially benefited from the Slovene manufacture of textiles and iron and other metals, the mining of coal, and the production of wood products. Small industries evolved because of good transportation, electrification, and a skilled, highly motivated labour force, so that by 1939 the number of industrial employees had doubled. Under communist rule, industry was virtually force-fed. The manufacture of metals and engines received top priority; textiles came second; and electrical machinery, a new branch, followed.

In the immediate aftermath of the collapse of communism, about half of Slovenia's workforce was employed in the manufacturing sector, while employment in agriculture shrank to less than one-fifth. Because production had been oriented toward Yugoslavia's needs, not all Slovene industry could compete in more-developed markets. Nevertheless, Slovenia had a well-balanced manufacturing base that included metal products, automotive parts, furniture, paper, shoes, sporting goods, electronic equipment, and textiles. By the early 21st century,

Slovenia had begun to manufacture pharmaceuticals for export and specialized electronics as well. Foreign investment in Slovenia increased, evidenced by a proliferation of internationally owned vehicle assembly plants. Manufacturing contributed between one-tenth and one-fifth of GDP and employed about one-fourth of the labour force.

FINANCE

The Bank of Slovenia is the country's central bank. It issues Slovenia's currency, the euro, which replaced the Slovene toler in 2007. Capital controls were fully lifted upon Slovenia's entry into the European Union (EU). Austria, Germany, France, Switzerland, and Italy are Slovenia's leading foreign investors. There is a stock exchange in Ljubljana.

TRADE

With the loss of the Yugoslav market, Slovenia's trade goal became integration with its new main partner, the EU, and the majority of the country's trade is with other EU members—particularly Germany, Italy, France, and Austria—as well as with Croatia. At the beginning of the 21st century, Slovenia's trade with other former Yugoslav republics also had increased. Chief imports

Koper, Slovenia. © trevorb/Fotolia

Kranjska Gora, a resort town at the head of the Sava Dolinka valley, in the Julian Alps, Slovenia. Adrian Baker/Leo de Wys Inc.

SERVICES

The service sector is the largest component of Slovenia's economy. Tourism has greatly increased in importance since the early 1990s. Foreign visitors —many of whom simply used to pass through Slovenia on their way to the eastern Mediterranean—now take advantage of recreational opportunities such as skiing, hiking, boating, fishing, and hunting, which are plentiful as a result of Slovenia's diverse topography. A particularly notable attraction is the system of limestone caves at Škocjan, which was designated a World Heritage site in 1986. Another draw for tourists is Triglav National Park, featuring Mount Triglav. Hot-springs and mineral-water resorts have gained popularity; one such spa, Rogaška Slatina, is housed in a Neoclassical building from the Habsburg era. Other prominent resorts include Portoro-Portorose on the Adriatic Sea and those in the Alpine towns of Bled, Bohinj, Bovec, and Kranjska Gora, which are favourite destinations for skiers, hikers, and mountain climbers. Dozens of surviving medieval structures are found in Slovenia; one of the most imposing is the Castle of Ljubljana (Ljubljanski Grad), built in 1144 on a hilltop overlooking Ljubljana. The capital city is also home

include machinery and transport equipment, chemical products, mineral fuels, and metals. Slovenia's exports include automobiles and vehicle parts, electric machinery, pharmaceuticals and other chemical products, and furniture. A significant amount of Slovenia's exports pass through the country's Adriatic port of Koper.

to many excellent examples of Baroque architecture, including an Ursuline church and a Franciscan monastery. Visitors to Slovenia are largely from Europe (notably Germany, Italy, Austria, Croatia, and the United Kingdom).

LABOUR AND TAXATION

Labour unions began to emerge in Slovenia only following the collapse of communism. About two-thirds of the labour force belongs to unions. The two largest labour unions are the Association of Independent Trade Unions of Slovenia and Independence, Confederation of New Trade Unions of Slovenia. Strikes are not common.

The central government receives a major portion of its income from a value-added tax and a progressive income tax, whereas local governments derive most of their revenue from a flat-rate income tax and property levies. On all products a unified value-added tax was introduced in the 1990s. In general, tax evasion has been considered a widespread problem in Slovenia.

TRANSPORTATION AND TELECOMMUNICATIONS

Slovenia's eastern Alpine location and easily accessible transit routes have been crucial since antiquity. Vestiges of the Roman road and settlement network are still visible. During the 1840s the Habsburg government in Vienna built the monumental Southern Railroad, which passed through Slovenia on its way from the Austrian capital to Trieste.

Two major highway-rail corridors cross present-day Slovenia, one running from Iran to northwestern Europe and the other from Spain to Russia. *Avtocestas* (expressways) are the nexus of road travel to Italy, Austria, and Hungary. Routes leading into Croatia have been improved. In 2000 a railway line was built to directly connect Slovenia and Hungary. The Karavanke Tunnel, nearly 5 miles (8 km) long, opened in 1991 and connects Slovenia with Austria. Despite efforts to improve its highways, Slovenia suffers traffic congestion, particularly near Ljubljana and Maribor. Many of Slovenia's rail cars have been modernized, and high-speed intercity service has been introduced, linking the cities of Maribor, Celje, and Ljubljana; however, much of the system's track remains outdated, limiting the performance of the equipment.

The country's principal international airport is located about 12 miles (20 km) north of Ljubljana at Brnik, and there are other airports at Maribor and Portorož. Adria Airways, the national airline, provides direct service to most major European cities.

Although Slovenia's telecommunications market had been fully privatized by 2001, only a few companies dominate the sector. The number of Internet users in Slovenia is among the highest in Europe. Virtually all households in Slovenia have access to fixed-line telephone service, and cellular phones are prevalent.

CHAPTER 16

SLOVENIAN GOVERNMENT AND SOCIETY

Slovenia's constitution, which was adopted in 1991, established a parliamentary form of government. A president, whose role is largely ceremonial, serves as head of state; presidents are popularly elected for a five-year term and can serve two consecutive terms. The head of government is the prime minister, who is normally the leader of the majority party in the National Assembly (lower house of the parliament), with which most legislative authority rests. Of its 90 members, 88 are elected by proportional representation to four-year terms, with the remaining two seats reserved for one representative each from the Italian- and Hungarian-speaking communities. The nonpartisan National Council, which represents economic and local interests, principally performs an advisory role, but it has the authority to propose new laws, to request the Constitutional Court to review legislative acts, and to initiate national referenda.

LOCAL GOVERNMENT

The *občina* (municipality) is Slovenia's local administrative unit. The country is divided into hundreds of municipalities, about a dozen of which have the status of urban municipality. A popularly elected mayor, municipal council, and supervisory committee govern each municipality. Local government in Slovenia is chiefly responsible for municipal services, primary education, and the administration of social and cultural programs.

JUSTICE

Slovenia's judiciary consists of a Supreme Court and a system of lower courts, the district and regional courts, which hear both civil and criminal cases. The High Labour and Social Court deals with individual and collective labour issues and social disputes. The Constitutional Court is the highest body of judicial authority and upholds the constitutionality and legality of the legislative acts.

Judges are elected by the National Assembly after nomination by the 11-member Judicial Council. Every six years the National Assembly also elects an ombudsman, who is charged with protecting the public's human rights and fundamental freedoms. The Constitutional Court is composed of nine judges who are elected for a term of nine years.

POLITICAL PROCESS

All Slovene citizens age 18 and older are eligible to vote. The first free and democratic elections in Slovenia were held in April 1990. Until that time the only authorized political party was the Communist Party. Following the introduction of a multiparty system, the centre-left Liberal Democratic Party dominated the parliament at the head of various coalitions until 2004, when the centre-right Slovenian Democratic Party gained a majority in the 2004 elections and formed a coalition with the New Slovenia–Christian People's Party, the Slovenian Democratic Party of Pensioners, and the Slovenian People's Party. In the 2008 parliamentary elections the centre-left Social Democrats narrowly edged out the Slovenian

JANEZ DRNOVSEK

The Slovenian politician Janez Drnovsek (born May 17, 1950, Celje, Yugoslavia [now in Slovenia]—died February 23, 2008, Zaplana, Slovenia) helped lead the country to a relatively peaceful independence from Yugoslavia and, as the new country's prime minister (May 14, 1992–May 3, 2000, and November 17, 2000–December 11, 2002) and president (2002–07), led it to membership in NATO and the European Union. In 1989 Slovenia for the first time held a regional plebiscite to choose its president; Drnovsek defeated the Communist Party's preferred candidate and became Slovenia's representative to the collective presidency just as the head position rotated to Slovenia. (From 1980 Yugoslavia was ruled by a collective presidency of regional representatives, with the top position rotating.) After Slovenia became independent in 1991, he was elected its second prime minister. He followed a program of gradual liberalization. During his presidency Drnovsek, who had recently been diagnosed with cancer, transformed himself into something of a New Age guru, pursuing quixotic peace initiatives and publishing several books on finding inner balance. These activities exasperated the country's government but endeared him to the people.

Democratic Party, which returned to power at the head of a coalition government in 2012.

SECURITY

The Slovenian Armed Forces (Slovenska Vojska; SV) consist of an army, a navy, and an air force. Slovenes become eligible to serve in the country's voluntary military forces at age 17. Conscription was abolished in 2003, the year before Slovenia became a member of the North Atlantic Treaty Organization (NATO). Slovenia's specialized capabilities within NATO include mountain warfare, demining, policing, special operations, and field medicine. Slovenian troops have taken part in many United Nations peacekeeping missions, including those in Bosnia and Kosovo in the 1990s and in Afghanistan and the Middle East in the early 2000s.

HEALTH AND WELFARE

The state provides most medical services, and Slovenia's public health system is one of the best developed in central and eastern Europe, though there is a lack of physicians in some remote areas of the country and in certain specialized fields of medicine. Social services provided by the government include unemployment, disability, and pension insurance, as well as family and dependant allowances. Both the pension system and social service programs have faced problems owing to the country's aging population and shrinking workforce. In 2000 Slovenia's pension system was reformed to raise the retirement age and to introduce special circumstances that would allow some people to qualify for an earlier retirement. Pensioners accounted for about one-fourth of the population in the middle of the first decade of the 21st century.

The Slovene state started several social housing programs in 1996. By the early 2000s, several thousand one- and two-bedroom apartments had been built for low-income families. In general, real-estate prices in Slovenia are comparable to those in most European countries. Property is generally more expensive in the capital and along the Adriatic coast.

EDUCATION

Virtually all Slovenes age 15 and older are literate. Primary schooling is compulsory and free for all children between ages 6 and 15. Secondary schools are either vocational or academic. A diploma from a secondary school is the main requirement for admission to one of Slovenia's three chief universities—those of Ljubljana, Maribor, and Koper (University of Primorska). The University of Ljubljana, founded in 1595 and reopened in 1919, has divisions that include the natural sciences, the social sciences, the humanities and arts, education, theology, law, medicine, and engineering. The University of Maribor, founded in 1975, is vocationally oriented. There are also several independent technical and vocational schools. In the ethnically mixed regions of Istria and Prekmurje, classes are taught in Italian and Hungarian along with Slovene.

The Slovene government finances research institutes, especially in the natural sciences and technology. A Slovene scholarly tradition dates back to the 17th-century, when the Carniolan polymath Johann Weichard Freiherr von Valvasor provided some of the first written and pictorial descriptions of the Slovene landscape, in his encyclopaedic volumes *Die Ehre des Herzogtums Krain* (1689; "Glory of the Duchy of Carniola"). The premier centres of research include the Slovenian Academy of Sciences and Arts (1938) and the Joef Stefan Institute (1949), the latter for scientific research.

CHAPTER 17

SLOVENIAN CULTURAL LIFE

Slovenes enjoy a wide-ranging cultural life, dominated by literature, art, and music. Little of the Slovene culture is known outside the country, however, for few Slovene artists have attained international recognition. Slovenes are proud of their country's artistic accomplishments. Many European performers and tourists go to Maribor and Ljubljana to participate in and attend many musical galas.

DAILY LIFE AND SOCIAL CUSTOMS

Easter and Christmas are major holidays in Slovenia. Easter is a weeklong observance and involves feasting, processions, and caroling. Kurentovanje, a pre-Lenten festival marking the beginning of spring and grounded in fertility rites, is celebrated in most towns. Its name is derived from the Kurent, a mythical figure who was believed to have the power to chase away winter and usher in spring. Groups of people dressed as Kurents (Kurenti) wear sheepskin, don masks and fur caps, and travel through town chasing away winter and "evil spirits."

Summer in general is a festive time in Slovenia; the Ljubljana Summer Festival in July and August draws large crowds to its music, theatre, and dance performances, and the Kravji Bal ("Cows' Ball") in September celebrates the return of the bovines to the valleys. Folkloric festivals are held in the towns of Kamnik and Škofja Loka.

Traditional Slovene dishes include different type of sausages, among them are *krvavice* (blood sausages). Other mainstays are *pršut* (cured ham), cheeses, and desserts such as the *gibanica*, a layered pastry made with various fillings. Mushroom dishes of all kinds are popular.

THE ARTS

Austrian archduchess Maria Theresa's educational reforms of the 18th century produced a highly literate public. Slovene literature flourished in the late 18th and early 19th century—particularly the work of Slovenia's national poet, France Prešeren (1800–49). The luminaries of the Modern school—novelist and playwright Ivan Cankar and the poet Oton Župančič—were the first of a long list of politically influential writers. Among the key figures between World Wars I and II were the realistic novelist Prežihov Voranc and the avant-gardist Srečko Kosovel. Poet Edvard Kocbek was prominent during and after World War II; an antifascist, he suffered at the hands of former comrades. More-recent prominent Slovene writers include Drago Jančar, Boris Novak, Boris Pahor, Vlado abot, Vitomil Zupan, and Andrej Blatnik.

Slovenes' great pride in their country's musical accomplishments rests partly on the fact that Ludwig van Beethoven conducted the first performance of his *Sixth (Pastoral) Symphony* for the Philharmonic Society (now the Slovene Philharmonic Orchestra) in Ljubljana. Jakob Petelin Gallus-Carniolus, more commonly known as Jacob Handl, was one of Slovenia's most renowned Renaissance composers. In the second half of the 20th century, the traditional music of Slovene brothers Slavko and Vilko Avsenik became popular worldwide. Their accordion-dominated folk music continues to be a model for other Slovene bands.

Slovene visual arts became internationally recognized through the works of 20th-century Impressionist painters such as Anton Ažbe (who established a private art school in Munich), Ivan Grohar, Matija Jama, Matej Sternen, and Rihard Jakopič. More-recent influential Slovene painters include Zoran Mušič and Metka Krašovec. Early visual art in Slovenia is represented through the dozens of frescoes, carvings, and sculptures in churches and monasteries throughout the country, many dating from as early as the 12th and 13th centuries. The International Biennial of Graphic Arts is held annually in Ljubljana.

Slovene theatre also became more recognized worldwide in the late 20th century, though its origins date from December 28, 1789, when dramatist Anton Tomaž Linhart translated and adapted Joseph Richter's German comedy *Die Feldmühle* ("The Country Mill") into Slovene as *upanova Micka* ("Micka, the Mayor's Daughter"). In 1867 the Slovene Dramatic Society was founded in Ljubljana. The capital remains the focus of Slovene theatre; however, there are a smattering of professional theatres throughout the country, including puppet theatres and youth theatres. A small but influential film industry emerged in Slovenia after World War II. In the early 21st century Slovene directors of note

FRANCE PREŠEREN

France Prešeren (born December 3, 1800, Vrba, Holy Roman Empire [now in Slovenia]—died February 8, 1849, Kranj, Austrian Empire [now in Slovenia]) is Slovenia's national poet and was its sole successful contributor to European Romanticism. Prešeren studied law in Vienna, where he acquired a familiarity with the mainstream of European thought and literary expression. Guided by his close friend and mentor Matija Čop, a literary scholar of unusual breadth and sensitivity who drowned tragically in 1835, Prešeren introduced to Slovene poetry several new genres, including the *ghazal*, the ballad, and the sonnet wreath, as well as pattern poetry. He also raised other genres, particularly the sonnet, to levels that many believe have never been surpassed in Slovene literature.

Prešeren first came to the notice of the Slovene reading public—a small, heavily Germanized group—in the early 1830s on the pages of *Kranjska čbelica* ("The Carniolan Bee"), a literary journal that Čop edited. There Prešeren published several important works, including the magisterial poem *Slovo od mladosti* (1830; "Farewell to Youth") and the sonnet cycles *Ljubeznjeni sonetje* (1831; "Love Sonnets") and *Sonetje nesreče* (1834; "Sonnets of Unhappiness"). In 1834 he published *Sonetni venec* ("A Wreath of Sonnets"), an artistic and technical tour de force that nonetheless scandalized the prudish readers of his day because he had dared to spell out in an acrostic the name of a well-to-do young woman whom he hoped, quite unrealistically, to marry.

In 1836 he published his longest work, *Krst pri Savici* ("The Baptism on the Savica"), commemorating Čop's death, which marked the high point of his poetic efforts and the beginning of the end of his literary career. He produced several fine pieces in the final decade and a half of his life—not the least of which is *Zdravljica* (1844; "The Toast"), which is today the Slovene national anthem—and he published *Poezije dr. Franceta Prešerna* (1847; "The Poetry of Dr. France Prešeren"), a collection of his best work in Slovene. (He also wrote in German.) But his career beyond literature was precarious: he was an attorney but was not permitted by the Austrian authorities to practice until almost the end of his life. That, combined with his deteriorating health and his unhappy marriage, undermined his poetic creativity after 1836. He died destitute and alone.

Prešeren was a Promethean Romantic spirit, trapped in a time and place that could not appreciate his talents. But today he is commemorated annually on the date of his death—it is in fact a national holiday that celebrates Slovene culture—and a central square in Ljubljana is named for him.

included Damjan Kozole, Metod Pevec, Janez Burger, Andrej Košak, and Mitja Okorn.

Architecture plays a special role in Slovenia's cultural heritage as well. Particularly renowned is architect Jože Plečnik, some of whose most impressive works are visible on the banks of the Ljubljanica River. One of the best known of these is the National and University

Tromostovje (Triple Bridge) over the Ljubljanica River, Ljubljana, Slovenia. © Xtravagan/Fotolia

Library, in Ljubljana. Also in the capital are his impressive Three Bridges and Central Market.

CULTURAL INSTITUTIONS

Ljubljana is the cultural capital of Slovenia. Most of the country's cultural institutions are located there, including the Slovenian Philharmonic Building (1891), the National Gallery of Slovenia (1918), the Slovene National Theatre for Opera and Ballet (1892), the Slovene National Theatre for Drama (1992; born from the Slovene Dramatic Society), and the National Museum of Slovenia (1921). The National and University Library (1941) holds the largest collection of reference materials in the country. Cankarjev Dom (1982), a cultural and exhibition centre, hosts major concerts and international congresses. Bled Castle, located near the capital on a cliff over Lake Bled, was awarded to the

The old town section of Ljubljana, Slovenia. © maljalen/Fotolia

bishops of Brixen in the 11th century; today it is part of the National Museum of Slovenia. The Slovenian Literary Society (1919) was established after World War I to support and foster the Slovene identity.

SPORTS AND RECREATION

Like most Europeans, Slovenes have a passion for football (soccer), and there are several leagues at all levels throughout the country. Despite its short tenure—a result of the country's relatively recent independence—the Slovene national team has had more than a little success in European and World Cup competition (it qualified for the European Cup in 2000 and its first World Cup in 2002). During the last decades of the 20th century, basketball and hockey also became popular. The national basketball and hockey teams participated in several world championships.

Slovenia has well-developed winter sports centres at Kranjska Gora and Planica, where World Cup skiing events for men are traditionally held, and at Maribor, where the women's competitions are hosted. Summer sports are also well represented, with numerous hiking trails, dozens of Olympic-quality swimming centres, and equestrian rings, which are centred on the village of Lipica.

The 1992 Winter Olympic Games in Albertville, France, were the first in which the country's team participated under the flag of an independent Slovenia. Previously, Slovene athletes had competed for the Kingdom of Serbs, Croats, and Slovenes and for Yugoslavia. One of Slovenia's most famous athletes, gymnast Leon Štukelj (1898–1999), won six Olympic medals, three of which were gold.

MEDIA AND PUBLISHING

Slovenia's independent daily newspapers include *Delo* ("Work"), *Slovenske Novice* ("Slovene News"), and *Dnevnik* ("Journal"), which are published in Ljubljana, and *Večer* ("Evening"), which is published in Maribor. The weekly journals *Mladina* and *Mag* are politically oriented. The monthly scholarly and literary journal *Nova revija* ("New Review") was influential in Slovenia's political transition. Perhaps its most famous issue was No. 57, released in 1987 with an article titled *Contributions to a Slovenian National Programme*, in which Slovenian intellectuals called for independence and a democratic republic. The Nova Revija publishing house was established in 1990 and produces works in the humanities and social sciences.

Following the abolition of a state radio and television monopoly in the early 1990s, dozens of privately owned radio and television stations were established. The Slovenian Radio-Television national broadcasting service (RTV Slovenija), established in the 1920s, offers programming in Slovene, Hungarian, and Italian.

CHAPTER 18

SLOVENIA: PAST AND PRESENT

During the 6th century CE, ancestors of the Slovenes, now referred to by historians as Alpine Slavs or proto-Slovenes, pushed up the Sava, Drava, and Mura river valleys into the Eastern Alps and the Karst. There they absorbed the existing Romano-Celtic-Illyrian cultures. At that time the Slavs owed allegiance to the Avar khans. After the defeat of the Avars by the Byzantine emperor Heraclius, a Slavic kingdom emerged under Samo (reigned 623–658) that extended from the Sava valley northward as far as Leipzig. It came under Frankish rule in 748.

THE SLOVENE LANDS THROUGH EARLY MODERN TIMES

Over the next two centuries, Alpine Slavs living in present-day Austria and western Hungary were absorbed by waves of Bavarian and Magyar invaders, so that the Slovene linguistic boundaries contracted southward. Nevertheless, a Slovene tribal duchy, centred in Austria's Klagenfurt basin, managed to survive for some 200 years. Though it is still imperfectly understood, ancient Carantania (or Carinthia) serves as a symbol of nationhood for contemporary Slovenes.

In the 10th century, after the partitioning of the Frankish empire, the lands in which Slovene speakers lived were assigned to the German kingdom. As part of the defense of that kingdom against Magyar invaders, they were divided among the marks, or border marches, of Carinthia, Carniola, and Styria. German lay and clerical lords arrived, along with dependent peasants, and enserfed the Slovenes, whom they called Wends or Winds. Over the next three centuries, the marches came under the tenuous authority of several territorial dynasts. In the 13th century they fell to Otakar II of Bohemia, who, like Samo, tried to establish a Slavic empire. Following the defeat of Otakar in 1278, Styria was acquired by the Habsburg family. Carinthia and Carniola fell into Habsburg hands in 1335, Istria in 1374, and the city of Trieste in 1382. Habsburg rule was based on a bureaucracy that shared power with local noble-run estates. One of these was run by the counts of Celje, who were powerful in the Middle Ages but whose lineage died out in 1456.

Modern Slovenes tend to view the coming of German rule as a national calamity, as it subjected the Alpine Slavs to steady pressure to Germanize. Nonetheless, it was from this time that they were included in the Western, or Roman Catholic, church. German episcopal and monastic foundations, along with local diocesan establishments, enriched and fructified the native Slavic culture with western European civilization. Indeed, the first missionaries to the area, arriving from Ireland in the 8th century, taught the Alpine Slavs to pray in their own tongue. The Freising Manuscripts, a collection of confessions and sermons dating from about 1000 CE, are the earliest known document in what eventually became the Slovene language.

A page from the Freising Manuscripts, written in the Slovene language. Bayerische Staatsbibliothek München, Clm 6426, f. 78r.

Along with the rest of the Habsburg empire, Slovene-inhabited lands experienced fully the Reformation and Counter-Reformation. The area was left firmly Roman Catholic, but in fact Slovene national development was assisted by such Protestant scholars as Primož Trubar and Jurij Dalmatin, who in the 16th century propagated the gospel in the vernacular and even printed a Slovene translation of the Bible.

The Slovenes never lived under Ottoman rule, although Turkish invaders were only partially deflected by the Habsburg's Military Frontier, established in Croatian lands to the south. Turkish raids occasionally penetrated even Carinthia. The failure of the Ottoman siege of Vienna in 1683 and Habsburg victories in Hungary ended the Turkish menace. Baroque civilization was free to permeate all of Austria, including Slovene-inhabited lands.

Economically, the Slovene lands had been incorporated fully into the system of German feudal tenure. The topography of the region militated against the development of large-scale agriculture, and the larger feudal estates typically contained substantial areas of forest. Cultivation was confined in the main to peasant holdings. Peasant rights were at times defended only with difficulty. There are records of several uprisings by both German and Slovene peasants against onerous seignorial exactions, including substantial Slovene participation in a Croatian revolt in 1573. Generally speaking, however, direct attachment to the crown meant that the Slovene lands escaped much of the economic and political upheaval that affected life among other South Slavs living under Habsburg rule. As a consequence of this and of their greater proximity to the major urban and economic centres of the Habsburg empire, the Slovenes reached relatively high levels of both literacy and technical development and achieved an early integration into a market economy.

The reforms decreed by Empress Maria Theresa and her son Joseph II in the 18th century particularly improved the lot of the peasantry.

THE LATER HABSBURG ERA

From 1809 to 1814 a large part of the Slovene lands was included in the Illyrian Provinces of Napoleon I's French Empire, along with Dalmatia, Trieste, and parts of Croatia. French occupation had a profound impact on the politics and culture of the area. The French encouraged local initiative and favoured the use of Slovene as an official language. Many of the changes did not survive the return to Habsburg rule, but the period contributed greatly to the national self-awareness of both the Croats and the Slovenes and aroused in some intellectuals an "Illyrian" ideal that stressed the common political and cultural interests of the South Slavs.

Moved by this ideal, the poet and philologist Jernej Kopitar published the first grammar of the Slovene language in 1808. In his position as imperial censor, Kopitar made the acquaintance of the great Serb linguistic reformer Vuk Karadžić, and he tried to apply Karadžić's ideas concerning the standardization of Slavonic orthography to Slovene by eliminating its many Germanic accretions and stressing its South Slav origins. Kopitar's ideas bore fruit in 1843 with the publication of the first Slovene-language newspaper in Ljubljana (or Laibach, as it was known to its German-speaking population).

ILLYRIAN PROVINCES

A stretch of territory along the Dalmatian coast constituted a part of Napoleon's French Empire known as the Illyrian Provinces. When the French victory of 1809 compelled Austria to cede a portion of its South Slav lands to France, Napoleon combined Carniola, western Carinthia, Görz (Gorica; modern Gorizia), Istria, and parts of Croatia, Dalmatia, and Ragusa (modern Dubrovnik) to form the Illyrian Provinces, which he incorporated into his empire. Napoleon's dominant interest in creating this political unit was to cut off Austria's access to Italy and the Mediterranean Sea. He also placed the capable marshal A.-F.-L. Viesse de Marmont in charge of the provinces.

Under Marmont's supervision, the provinces' government organization was revised, the Code Napoléon was introduced, and roads and schools were constructed. Local citizens were given administrative posts, and native languages were used to conduct official business. In addition, serfs were freed and given possession of the land they cultivated.

As a result of the French administration, which ended in 1814, when the French were forced to return the Illyrian Provinces to the Austrian Empire, the region not only made cultural and economic advances but also began to develop a sense of Slav unity and national awareness that matured and manifested itself in the 1830s and 1840s in the powerful literary and political Illyrian movement.

The revolutionary upheavals that swept many parts of Europe in 1848 had their counterpart in Slovenia, with the formulation of the first Slovene national program: this demanded a unified Slovene province within the Austrian Empire. Vienna stifled this program, as it did rebellion everywhere, but Slovenia, like Europe, had changed. As the relics of manorialism vanished and plowmen became freeholders, Austrian nobles such as the Auerspergs lost their ancient grip. German remained the normal language for merchants and the tiny educated elite, but a Slavic bourgeoisie was growing and gradually becoming enfranchised. Change was most evident in Carniola, where by 1900 Ljubljana became truly Slovene.

In the 1890s political parties were formed, including the Progressive (Liberal) Party, the Socialist Party, and the Slovene People's Party. The Slovene People's Party had close links to the Roman Catholic Church, which had also been instrumental in establishing large-scale cooperative movements earlier in the century. By providing credit, marketing, and other facilities to peasants and artisans, the cooperatives enabled both rural and urban Slovenes to break free from German institutions.

During World War I, Slovenes fighting in the Austrian army suffered huge losses against the Italians in incessant battles of attrition along the Soča (Italian: Isonzo) front. In May 1917, as the war turned against the Central Powers, the

Slovene Anton Korošec and other South Slav deputies in the Austrian Reichsrat put forward a declaration in favour of "the unification of all territories of the monarchy inhabited by South Slavs in one independent political body, under the sceptre of the Habsburg dynasty." Known as Trialism, this ideal of a partnership between South Slavs, Austrians, and Hungarians fell victim to the collapse of Austria-Hungary in October 1918. The next best choice seemed to be a federation of South Slav states, and Slovene political leaders collaborated in the hasty formation of the Kingdom of Serbs, Croats, and Slovenes.

SLOVENIA SINCE 1918

At the Paris Peace Conference after the war, the Allies awarded Italy all the coastal areas that had given Slovenes access to the sea—including Gorizia (Gorica), Trieste, and Istria. The Yugoslav kingdom was given the Prekmurje region and southern Styria but only a small part of southern Carinthia. Yugoslav troops occupied much of the Klagenfurt basin, but the Allies insisted that a plebiscite be held in two zones to decide the fate of the rest of southern Carinthia. In October 1920 the more southerly zone chose Austria, so that no plebiscite was held in the northern zone around Klagenfurt; both zones were left to Austria. Almost one-third of Europe's Slovene speakers were thus left outside the boundaries of Slovenia. Slovene speakers in Italy and Austria continued to be subject to discrimination and political pressure by the dominant majorities—as were Slovenia's Germans between 1918 and 1941.

Incorporation into the Yugoslav kingdom also proved disappointing. Anton Korošec reached high positions in the government, but Slovene politicians overall had minimal influence in Belgrade. Strong central control—in effect, Serbian hegemony—was imposed over the kingdom in an effort to discipline its hybrid citizenry. As a "province" of Yugoslavia, Slovenia found its autonomy restricted mainly to cultural affairs. Its economy, which had already industrialized more than the rest of the kingdom, benefited somewhat from greater commercial

YUGOSLAVIA

Between 1929 and 2003 three federations bore the name Yugoslavia ("Land of the South Slavs"). After the Balkan Wars of 1912–13 ended Turkish rule in the Balkan Peninsula and Austria-Hungary was defeated in World War I, a Kingdom of Serbs, Croats, and Slovenes was established, comprising the former kingdoms of Serbia and Montenegro (including Serbian-held Macedonia) as well as Croatia, Bosnia and Herzegovina, Austrian territory in Dalmatia and

Slovenia, and Hungarian land north of the Danube River. The Kingdom of Yugoslavia, officially proclaimed in 1929 by King Alexander I and lasting until World War II, covered 95,576 square miles (247,542 square km). The postwar Socialist Federal Republic of Yugoslavia covered 98,766 square miles (255,804 square km) and had a population of about 24 million by 1991; it consisted of six republics (Serbia, Croatia, Slovenia, Macedonia, Montenegro, and Bosnia and Herzegovina) as well as two autonomous provinces (Vojvodina and Kosovo). After the violent breakup of federal Yugoslavia and the declarations of independence of Slovenia, Croatia, Bosnia, and Macedonia, the "third Yugoslavia" was inaugurated on April 27, 1992. It had roughly 45 percent of the population and 40 percent of the area of its predecessor and consisted of the republics of Serbia and Montenegro. In 2003 the name Yugoslavia was abandoned, and the country was renamed Serbia and Montenegro. In 2006 Montenegro declared its independence, and the Republic of Serbia became a country in its own right. After serious violence, NATO intervention, and nine years of UN administration, Kosovo declared its independence in 2008.

Historical map of Yugoslavia showing the boundaries of the country from 1946 to 1992.

contact with Belgrade, but progress was limited by the detachment of Slovene producers from the economically vital Habsburg centres of Klagenfurt and Trieste. Also, as one of the kingdom's wealthiest areas, Slovenia was taxed more heavily than other regions. By the late 1930s Slovene politics was riven by political factions, including ardently Catholic conservatives, anticlerical liberals, and ever-more-militant leftists.

WORLD WAR II

After the German invasion of Yugoslavia in 1941, Slovenia was partitioned. Italy took the southwest, including Ljubljana; Germany annexed the north directly into the Reich; and Hungary recovered Prekmurje. Although the Slovenes had been deemed racially salvageable by the Nazis, the mainly Austrian rulers of the Carinthian and Styrian regions commenced a brutal campaign to destroy them as a nation. Resistance groups sprang up; after Germany invaded the Soviet Union, they came under the domination of the communist-led Slovene National Liberation Front. From its principal base in the forests near Kočevje, in the mountainous region of Kočevski Rog, the Front combined operations against the occupiers and their Slovene collaborators in the White Guard with a ruthless struggle against potential rivals, such as members of the Slovene People's Party. In November 1943 the Front joined Josip Broz Tito's Partisans in proclaiming a new Yugoslavia, and in May 1945 Ljubljana was liberated. After the armistice the British repatriated more than 10,000 Slovene collaborators who had attempted to retreat with the Germans, and Partisan forces massacred most of them at the infamous "Pits of Kočevje."

THE COMMUNIST ERA

Having occupied Trieste in May 1945, the Partisans hoped that its possession was assured, but the Allies forced the establishment of a Free Territory of Trieste, consisting of an Italian-administered zone in and around the city and a Yugoslav zone on the Istrian Peninsula. In 1954 Tito agreed to allow the return of Trieste to Italy. The Yugoslav zone was incorporated into Slovenia; this gave the Slovenes access to the sea and left fewer Slovene speakers outside Yugoslavia, but it also brought a small Italian minority into the republic.

As a constituent of the Federal People's Republic of Yugoslavia, Slovenia underwent a complete restructuring of its economy, politics, and society along Stalinist lines. Following the rupture between Tito and Stalin in 1948, however, conditions improved. Over the next two decades, Slovenia managed to achieve greater prosperity than the southern Yugoslav republics under the unique economic system known as "socialist self-management"—designed largely by Tito's chief ideologue, the Slovene Edvard Kardelj. By the 1970s, liberalization had spurred the development of a number of local autonomy movements, especially in Croatia and Slovenia, obliging the League of Communists of Yugoslavia to reassert party control throughout the federation. Through the 1980s, as the Yugoslav economy succumbed to inflation and debt, even Slovene communists steadily lost patience with what they perceived to be profound cultural differences between them and the southern Yugoslav peoples. In May 1990 Slovenia held free, multiparty elections in which Milan Kučan, a former communist official, was elected president, and in December a referendum calling for a sovereign,

EDVARD KARDELJ

The Yugoslav revolutionary and politician Edvard Kardelj (born January 27, 1910, Ljubljana, Austro-Hungarian Empire [now in Slovenia]—died February 10, 1979, Ljubljana, Socialist Republic of Slovenia, Yugoslavia) was a close colleague and the chosen successor of Josip Broz Tito. He was the chief ideological theoretician of Yugoslav Marxism, or Titoism.

The son of a railroad worker, Kardelj graduated from the Ljubljana Teachers' College. From the age of 16 he was a member of the outlawed Communist Party, initially in its youth league. He was imprisoned (1930–32) for his trade-union and party activities, and in 1934 he fled into exile, eventually making his way from Czechoslovakia to the Soviet Union, where he received indoctrination in underground methods. It was in 1934, prior to his leaving, that Kardelj first met Tito. Back in Yugoslavia from 1937 on, he was arrested several times and imprisoned.

After the German occupation of Yugoslavia (1941), Kardelj helped organize the resistance front in Slovenia and thereafter accompanied Tito in much of the Partisans' fighting. After the war he served as vice president (1945–53) under Tito, and he drew up (1946) the Soviet-inspired federal constitution of Yugoslavia. He became one of the country's major theoreticians and legalists, directing the creation of all the succeeding constitutions of 1953, 1963, and 1974. His ideas strongly influenced subsequent political developments, especially those concerning the nature of national identity and the constitutional position of national minorities, in Yugoslavia and the post-Yugoslav states.

Over the years Kardelj handled many foreign missions and tasks as well, though he officially held the post of foreign minister only from 1948 to 1953. Throughout, he was a key figure in the collective leadership of the Yugoslav Communist Party, known as the League of Communists. Kardelj was the main architect of a theory known as socialist self-management, which served as the basis of Yugoslavia's political and economic system and distinguished it from the Soviet system. In foreign affairs he pioneered the concept of nonalignment for Yugoslavia between the West and the Soviet Union.

independent Slovenia was endorsed by more than 90 percent of the voters. The Belgrade government—by then dominated by Serbia's nationalist strongman, Slobodan Milošević, and by the Serb-led Yugoslav People's Army (YPA)—began an economic blockade of Slovenia and expropriated Ljubljana's bank assets. Slovene and Croatian proposals for a looser Yugoslav confederation were rejected by Serbia, and on June 25, 1991, Slovenia seceded from Yugoslavia.

Two days later the YPA attacked border posts that had been taken over by Slovenia. In what became known to the Slovenes as the Ten-Day War, Slovene militiamen, adopting tactics originally intended to defend Yugoslavia against invading Soviet tanks, defeated the ineptly commanded, disintegrating YPA units with minimal loss of life. The last Yugoslav soldier left Slovenia on October 25, 1991.

THE POSTCOMMUNIST ERA

With independence secured, Slovenia adopted a democratic constitution on December 23, 1991. The following year Kučan became independent Slovenia's first democratically elected president. Slovenia reoriented its politics and economy toward western Europe and forged closer bonds with the countries of the European Union (EU). Over the next decade the economy grew quickly, and Slovenia enjoyed political stability. Kučan was reelected in 1997, and from 1992 to 2002 (except for a brief period) the government was headed by Prime Minister Janez Drnovšek, who succeeded Kučan as president in 2002. For part of the period Slovenia had tense relations with two of its neighbours—confronting Croatia over territorial rights in the Bay of Piran and sovereignty over certain inland villages and at odds with Italy regarding that country's pursuit of concessions for some 160,000 Italians who were expelled from Slovenia after 1945. There were also disputes with the Roman Catholic Church involving the church's role in Slovenia's educational system and the return of church properties that had been nationalized by the communist government.

Throughout the 1990s Slovenia, with the support of all major political parties, had pursued membership in both the North Atlantic Treaty Organization and the EU. In 2003, following invitations to join from both organizations, Slovenes overwhelmingly endorsed membership, and Slovenia became a full member of both organizations in 2004.

Slovenia adopted the euro in 2007 and during the first half of 2008 was the first postcommunist country to hold the EU presidency. In September 2008 the centre-left Social Democrats narrowly won parliamentary elections, thereby ending four years of government by the centre-right Slovenian Democratic Party. The government of Prime Minister Borut Pahor collapsed in September 2011, when members of his centre-left coalition withdrew in a disagreement over pension reform. The subsequent election, held in December 2011, was won by Positive Slovenia, a new centre-left party led by Ljubljana Mayor Zoran Janković. Having secured 28 of the 90 seats in Slovenia's parliament, Positive Slovenia lacked the numbers to form a government on its own, and Janković began coalition talks with various parties. After Janković failed to form a ruling coalition, Janez Jansa became prime minister in February 2012 at the head of a centre-right coalition government. That government introduced austerity measures in an attempt to cut the deficit and sought to right the economy, which had fallen into recession, largely as a consequence of the financial crisis that had arisen within the euro zone beginning in 2009.

CONCLUSION

The dissolution of Austria-Hungary in 1918 and the rise and fall of the various Yugoslav and Balkan federations throughout the 20th century had deep consequences for Austria, Croatia, and Slovenia. Austria had been the heart of the multinational empire of Austria-Hungary, and, after its fall, the small country experienced more than a quarter century of social and economic turbulence and a Nazi dictatorship. Yet the establishment of permanent neutrality in 1955, associated with the withdrawal of the Allied troops that had occupied the country since the end of World War II, enabled Austria to develop into a stable and socially progressive country with a flourishing cultural life reminiscent of its earlier days of international musical glory. Austria joined the European Union in 1995.

Croatia was a part of Yugoslavia for much of the 20th century and suffered considerably from the disintegration of that federation in the early 1990s. Its European trajectory—particularly its goal of joining the European Union, which was finally achieved in 2013—has only recently come to appear secure once more. Slovenia, for most of its history, was largely controlled by the Habsburgs of Austria, who ruled the Holy Roman Empire and its successor states, the Austrian Empire and Austria-Hungary. As part of Yugoslavia, Slovenia came under communist rule for the bulk of the post-World War II period. With the dissolution of the Yugoslav federation in 1991, a multiparty democratic political system emerged. Slovenia's economic prosperity in the late 20th century attracted hundreds of thousands of migrants from elsewhere in the Balkans. In the early 21st century, Slovenia integrated economically and politically with western Europe, joining the North Atlantic Treaty Organization as well as the European Union in 2004.

Glossary

ABSOLUTISM A political theory that absolute power should be vested in one or more rulers.

ACROSTIC A composition usually in verse in which sets of letters (as the initial or final letters of the lines) taken in order form a word or phrase or a regular sequence of letters of the alphabet.

ALLUVIAL Of or relating to sedimentary material consisting of silt, sand, clay, gravel, and organic matter deposited by rivers.

AUSTERITY Enforced or extreme economy.

AUTOBAHN A German, Swiss, or Austrian expressway.

BAILIWICK The office or jurisdiction of a bailiff ; a land agent.

BAROQUE A style of artistic expression prevalent especially in the 17th century that is marked generally by use of complex forms, bold ornamentation, and the juxtaposition of contrasting elements often conveying a sense of drama, movement, and tension.

BOLSHEVIK A member of the communist revolutionary group, led by Vladimir Ilich Lenin, that in 1917 seized control of the government of Russia

BURGRAVE A noble ruling a German castle or town and its adjacent lands.

CONCORDAT An agreement between a pope and a sovereign or government for the regulation of matters related to the church.

DECIDUOUS A type of tree or plant whose leaves fall off or shed seasonally or at a certain stage of development in the life cycle.

DEPUTATION A group of people appointed to represent others.

DIET A body of lawmakers; legislature.

FASCISM A political philosophy, movement, or regime that exalts nation and often race above the individual and that stands for a centralized autocratic government headed by a dictatorial leader, severe economic and social regimentation, and forcible suppression of opposition.

FILIBUSTER The use of extreme dilatory tactics in an attempt to delay or prevent action, especially in a legislative assembly.

ILLYRIAN MOVEMENT Movement begun in the 1830s, largely through the efforts of the poet and journalist Ljudevit Gaj. The movement involved the revival of Serbo-Croatian literary activity and sought the unification of all the South Slavs in the Habsburg Empire.

INFANTA A daughter of a Spanish or Portuguese monarch.

IRREDENTIST Of or relating to the recovery of irredentas, or territories historically or ethnically related to one political unit but under the political control of another.

KARST An irregular limestone region with sinkholes, underground streams, and caverns.

LITTORAL Of, relating to, or situated or growing on or near a shore, especially of the sea.

MARCH A border region or frontier; especially, a district originally set up to defend a boundary.

MARGRAVE The military governor especially of a German border province.

OPERETTA A usually romantic comic opera that includes songs and dancing.

ORTHOGRAPHY The art of writing words with the proper letters according to standard usage.

PLEBISCITE A vote by which the people of an entire country or district express an opinion for or against a proposal, especially on a choice of government or ruler.

POGROM An organized massacre of helpless people; specifically, such a massacre of Jews.

PRAGMATIC SANCTION A solemn decree of a sovereign on a matter of primary importance and with the force of fundamental law.

PREROGATIVE An exclusive or special right, power, or privilege.

SCION A descendant of a wealthy, aristocratic, or influential family.

SECUNDOGENITURE The right or system by which inheritance belongs to the second son.

SEIGNORIAL Of, relating to, or befitting a seignior, or the feudal lord of a manor; manorial.

SOCIALISM Any of various economic and political theories advocating collective or governmental ownership and administration of the means of production and distribution of goods.

STATUS QUO ANTE The state of affairs that existed previously.

WALTZ A concert composition in 3/4 time or music composed for a type of ballroom dance in 3/4 time with strong accent on the first beat and a basic pattern of step-step-close.

BIBLIOGRAPHY

AUSTRIA

GEOGRAPHY

Eugene K. Keefe et al., *Area Handbook for Austria* (1976), though old, is still valuable for its survey of physical features and its description of national traditions and culture. *Austria, Facts and Figures* (1990), published by the Federal Press Service, is an informative compendium of illustrations and statistics. Among the more comprehensive guidebooks are Ian Robertson, *Austria*, 2nd ed. (1987); and *Jonathan Bousfield, The Rough Guide to Austria* (2008). Katrin Kohl *and* Ritchie Robertson (eds.), *A History of Austrian Literature 1918–2000* (2010), places the work of Austria's many notable 20th-century writers within the context of the country's modern history.

Political developments are discussed in William T. Bluhm, *Building an Austrian Nation: The Political Integration of a Western State* (1973). John Fitzmaurice, *Austrian Politics and Society Today: In Defence of Austria* (1990), is a study of economic, social, and political characteristics against the traditional perception of Austrian neutrality. More-detailed analysis of the political forces in Austrian society is found in Max E. Riedlsperger, *The Lingering Shadow of Nazism: The Austrian Independent Party Movement Since 1945* (1978); Melanie A.

Sully, *Political Parties and Elections in Austria* (1981); and Anton Pelinka *and* Fritz Plasser (eds.), *The Austrian Party System* (1989).

HISTORY

Comprehensive chronological coverage is provided in Richard Rickett, *A Brief Survey of Austrian History*, 9th ed. (1988); and Lonnie Johnson, *Introducing Austria* (1987). Barbara Jelavich, *Modern Austria: Empire and Republic, 1815–1986* (1987), covers Austrian history from the end of the Napoleonic Wars to the end of the 20th century. Günter Bischof, et al. (eds.), *Global Austria: Austria's Place in Europe and the World* (2011), offers a number of essays on Austria's place in the world of the 21st century. *Austrian History Yearbook*, published by the University of Minnesota, is devoted to recent research. Paula Sutter Fichtner, *Historical Dictionary of Austria* (1999), provides easily accessible, reliable information.

Studies of particular historical periods include A.W. Leeper, *A History of Medieval Austria* (1941, reprinted 1978), focusing on the Middle Ages up to the middle of the 13th century; and Robert A. Kann, *A History of the Habsburg Empire, 1526–1918* (1974). A thorough overall interpretation of the period from the Thirty Years' War to the Congress of Vienna is given in Charles W. Ingrao, *The Habsburg Monarchy, 1618–1815*, 2nd ed. (2000).

Works on the monarchy include C.A. Macartney, *Maria Theresa and the House of Austria* (1969); and Paul P. Bernard, *Joseph II* (1968), a brief survey. Austria's great struggles against the French Revolution and Napoleon are covered in Gunther E. Rothenberg, *Napoleon's Great Adversaries: The Archduke Charles and the Austrian Army, 1792–1814* (1982).

Analyses of 19th-century politics and diplomacy include Harold Nicolson, *The Congress of Vienna: A Study in Allied Unity 1812–1822* (1946, reissued 1989); and Enno E. Kraehe, *Metternich's German Policy*, 2 vol. (1963–1983). *John W. Boyer, Culture and Political Crisis in Vienna: Christian Socialism in Power, 1897–1918* (1995), provides a bridge between the 19th and 20th centuries. Karl R. Stadler, *Austria* (1971); and *Elisabeth Barker, Austria, 1918–1972* (1973), cover 20th-century history in general. David F. Good, Margarete Grandner, *and* Mary Jo Maynes (eds.), *Austrian Women in the Nineteenth and Twentieth Centuries: Cross-disciplinary Perspectives* (1996), gives a good overview of women's history.

Surveys of the First Republic include Arthur J. May, *The Passing of the Hapsburg Monarchy, 1914–1918*, 2 vol. (1966); and Mary MacDonald, *The Republic of Austria, 1918–1934: A Study in the Failure of Democratic Government* (1946). Michael P. Steinberg, *The Meaning of the Salzburg Festival: Austria as Theater and Ideology, 1890–1938* (1990, reissued 2000), reviews the rejuvenation of the Austrian spirit after World War I.

Bruce F. Pauley, *Hitler and the Forgotten Nazis: A History of Austrian National Socialism* (1981), reviews early German national socialism in Austria. The development of anti-Semitism is chronicled in Ivar Oxaal, Michael Pollak, *and* Gerhard Botz (eds.), *Jews, Antisemitism, and Culture in Vienna* (1987), a history of Austrian Jews, from assimilation to forced emigration and extermination.

William B. Bader, *Austria Between East and West, 1945–1955* (1966); and *Alice Hills, Britain and the Occupation of Austria, 1943–45* (2000), study the various strategic plans, international problems, and political decisions surrounding the reestablishment of Austria during and after World War II. David F. Good *and* Ruth Wodak (eds.), *From World War to Waldheim: Culture and Politics in Austria and the United States* (1999), gives a good overview of the leverage of a small state in the shadow of a superpower.

Kurt Steiner (ed.), *Modern Austria* (1981); and Kurt Richard Luther *and* Peter Pulzer (eds.), *Austria, 1945–95: Fifty Years of the Second Republic* (1998), examine political, social, economic, and cultural developments under the Second Republic. Paul Lendvai, *Inside Austria: New Challenges, Old Demons* (2010), discusses Austrian political life from the perspective of a longtime Vienna-based journalist. Anton Pelinka, *Austria: Out of the Shadow of the Past* (1998); and Hella Pick, *Guilty Victim: Austria from the Holocaust to Haider* (2000), discuss the profound political changes in late 20th-century Austria.

CROATIA

GEOGRAPHY

Piers Letcher, *Croatia*, 3rd ed. (2007), is an introductory guide to the country. The first half of *Lexicographical Institute of Yugoslavia, Enciklopedija Jugoslavije*, 2nd ed., vol. 5 (1988), is a comprehensive Croatian-language study, covering physical and human geography as well as history. Various aspects of Croatia's physical and social geography also are presented in Francis H. Eterovich and Christopher Spalatin (eds.), *Croatia: Land, People, Culture*, 2 vol. (1964–70, reissued 1976). Tony Fabijančić, *Croatia: Travels in Undiscovered Country* (2003), provides interesting insights into the diversity of the people of Croatia, from the perspective of a son of Croatian immigrants to Canada. Marcus Tanner, *Croatia: A Nation Forged in War*, 3rd ed. (2010), contains chapters on the political and social conditions of newly independent Croatia. The main figures and features of Croatian literature and arts during the 19th and 20th centuries are surveyed concisely in Celia Hawkesworth, *Zagreb: A Cultural History* (2008).

HISTORY

Three comprehensive histories from earliest times to the present are Ivo Goldstein, *Croatia: A History* (1999); focusing on the long pre-Yugoslav period, *Branka Magaš, Croatia Through History: The Making of a European State* (2007); and, emphasizing the Yugoslav period, the work by Tanner cited in the section above, which draws on the author's presence as a journalist in the region at the time of Yugoslavia's dissolution.

On the emergence of the Croatian (and Serbian) national ideas in the 19th century and their conflicting roles in the creation of the first Yugoslavia, the seminal work remains Ivo Banac, *The National Question in Yugoslavia: Origins, History, Politics* (1984). The 19th-century Croatian origins of the Yugoslav idea also are discussed in Elinor Murray Despalatović, *Ljudevit Gaj and the Illyrian Movement* (1975). The pre-1914 Serb experience is examined in Nicholas J. Miller, *Between Nation and State: Serbian Politics in Croatia Before the First World War* (1997). Bridging the pre-1914 decade and the 1920s is Mark Biondich, *Stjepan Radić, the Croat Peasant Party, and the Politics of Mass Mobilization, 1904–1928* (2000); and connecting World War II to the founding of communist Yugoslavia is Jill A. Irvine, *The Croat Question: Partisan Politics in the Formation of the Yugoslav Socialist State* (1993). The controversial subject of Croatia in the Second World War is addressed in Jozo Tomasevich, *War and Revolution in Yugoslavia, 1941–1945: Occupation and Collaboration* (2001). Croatia since independence and the wars of Yugoslavia's dissolution are treated in William Bartlett, *Croatia: Between Europe and the Balkans* (2003); and Sabrina P. Ramet, Konrad Clewing, *and* Renéo Lukić (eds.), *Croatia Since Independence: War, Politics, Society, Foreign Relations* (2008).

SLOVENIA

GEOGRAPHY

J. Fridl et al. (eds.), *National Atlas of Slovenia* (2001), is a general atlas. James Stewart, *Slovenia* (2006), is a tourist guidebook. Anton Gosar *and* Matjaz Jeršič, *Slovenia—the Tourist Guide* (1999), provides a detailed description of the country. David Robertson *and* Sarah Stewart, *Landscapes of Slovenia*, 2nd ed. (2005), is a guidebook on Slovenian regions and towns.

Steve Fallon, *Slovenia*, 3rd ed. (2001), provides an excellent description of the country's landscape, people, and cultural heritage. James Gow *and* Cathie Carmichael, *Slovenia and the Slovenes: A Small State and the New Europe* (2000), examines the social, economic, and political aspects of the country and its people. Rado L. Lencek, *Slovenes, the Eastern Alpine Slavs, and Their Cultural Heritage* (1989), is a brief interdisciplinary synthesis. Simona Pavlič Možina (ed.), *Facts About Slovenia*, 8th ed. (2005), discusses the data retrieved from various state institutions of Slovenia.

HISTORY

Janko Prunk, *A Brief History of Slovenia*, 2nd rev. ed. (2000; originally published in Slovenian, 1998), treats the history of Slovenes and Slovenia as a nation-state. Leopoldina Plut-Pregelj *and* Carole Rogel, *Historical Dictionary of Slovenia*, 2nd ed. (2007), is a useful source. Thomas M. Barker, *The Slovene Minority of Carinthia*, 2nd ed. (1979, reissued 1984), provides general information about Slovene history from the early Middle Ages to the 20th century, and *Social Revolutionaries and Secret Agents: The Carinthian Slovene Partisans and Britain's Special Operations Executive* (1990), contains general data about Slovenia during World War II. Carole Rogel, *The Slovenes and Yugoslavism, 1890–1914* (1977), discusses this important period, and "Slovenia's Independence: A Reversal of History," *Problems of Communism*, 40(4):31–40 (July–August 1991), addresses more recent events. Danica Fink-Hafner *and* John R. Robbins (eds.), *Making a New Nation: The Formation of Slovenia* (1997), looks at the events that led to Slovenia's independence. This topic is also analyzed in Jill Benderly *and* Evan Kraft (eds.), *Independent Slovenia: Origins, Movements, Prospects* (1994, reissued 1996). *Slovene Studies* (semiannual) contains significant though often highly specialized studies.

Index